THE NEGOTIATION BOOK

THE NEGOTIATION BOOK

YOUR DEFINITIVE GUIDE TO SUCCESSFUL NEGOTIATING

Third Edition

Steve Gates

This edition first published 2011

Edition History
First edition published 2011, second edition published 2016, all by John Wiley & Sons, Ltd.

Registered Office(s)
John Wiley & Sons, Inc., 111 River Street, Hoboken, NJ 07030, USA

Editorial Office
The Atrium, Southern Gate, Chichester, West Sussex, PO19 8SQ, UK

For details of our global editorial offices, customer services, and more information about Wiley products visit us at www.wiley.com.

Wiley also publishes its books in a variety of electronic formats and by print-on-demand. Some content that appears in standard print versions of this book may not be available in other formats.

Library of Congress Cataloging-in-Publication Data:

Names: Gates, Steve (Business consultant), author. | John Wiley & Sons, publisher.
Title: The negotiation book : your definitive guide to successful negotiating / Steve Gates.
Description: Third edition. | Hoboken, NJ : Wiley, 2023. | Includes index.
Identifiers: LCCN 2022040098 (print) | LCCN 2022040099 (ebook) | ISBN 9780857089502 (paperback) | ISBN 9780857089519 (adobe pdf) | ISBN 9780857089526 (epub)
Subjects: LCSH: Negotiation in business. | Negotiation in business—Case studies.
Classification: LCC HD58.6 .G38 2023 (print) | LCC HD58.6 (ebook) | DDC 658.4/052—dc23/eng/20221003
LC record available at https://lccn.loc.gov/2022040098
LC ebook record available at https://lccn.loc.gov/2022040099

Cover Design: Wiley
Cover Image: © schab/Shutterstock

Set in 11.5/15pt Adobe Jenson Pro by Straive, Chennai, India

SKY10037594_110722

Contents

About the Author

Steve Gates is the founder and Chairman of The Gap Partnership, the world's leading negotiation consultancy. Since 1997, Steve has consulted with and supported global corporations from all business sectors facing the challenges of optimizing value from their many and varied negotiations. His interest in economics, capitalism, and business psychology continues to inspire his innovative flair and passion for greater insights into the art and science of negotiation. His home remains in the Hampshire, United Kingdom.

Acknowledgments

I would like to thank an exceptional team of negotiators from across The Gap Partnership with whom I have shared so many experiences and drawn so much inspiration. They have committed their lives to pushing negotiation capability and practice to a new level, which inspired me to write this account of the Complete Skilled Negotiator. *The Negotiation Book* is a philosophy based on the human challenges of negotiating today, which they have all helped to build. Every day this serves to inspire our clients around the world.

Preface — Context and relevance

I thought I would find you here. But why here? Why now? Well, if you want to save the world, you are going to have to negotiate with someone. If you want to be a millionaire or even a billionaire, you are going to have to negotiate with a lot of people. If you want to stay in a relationship, there will be times when you will need to concede or even capitulate so negotiation will definitely come into play. Do you want a pay rise? Do you want to start a business? Do you want to optimize an enterprise? Do you want to stay married, even get married?! Guess what?

Yes, negotiation is fundamental to your life and those around you. The way you distribute, create, protect, resolve, and manage anything of value and every minute you invest in you, becoming a better negotiator will pay back, throughout your life. It's an activity that many avoid at all costs. The prospect of perceived conflict of positions or interests and the discomfort that come from it is hardly appealing as a "fun pass time." My passion for this skill remains because it is central to the viability of every business, your business. Negotiated agreements go beyond viability or profitability. The way you identify and engage with the opportunities to negotiate can set the culture for how your business does business, contracts with others, and defines the types of client or supplier relationships you have. It has delivered peace in war, resolved bedtime tantrums with our children, helped avoid millions of court cases, and has probably helped save a few marriages along the way too. It can deliver immeasurable benefits, although we always like to measure them, for you or those you represent, your family, your business, your charity, and yourself. So yes, it's worth the effort. In the end, the outcomes determine viability or insolvency, profit-making or loss, growth or decline, certainty or ambiguity, fear or confidence.

If you buy or sell services, products, ingredients, components, platforms, solutions, licenses, accommodations, consumables, or raw materials you can and should negotiate your agreements.

Great negotiators often go unnoticed. So if you want recognition or gratification, it is not the place for you. Negotiators are not interested in winning or glory, which can be rather challenging when you, as I, have an ego that from time to time needs satisfying. It requires a state of mind, a patience, a tenacity that is motivated by curiosity rather than competitiveness, that simply wants to optimize value and opportunity.

As a great negotiator you recognize that the return on time invested is dramatic, perhaps in relationships, time saved, risk reduced, profit made, or even dilemmas resolved. No other skill offers so much value in return for competent performance. But it can take time in planning, preparation, and alignment with others. It takes patience in that nothing is agreed until everything is agreed and there may be lots to agree or negotiate around. In other words, it may not be quick, is rarely easy, and is often stressful. Are you still in?

The most valuable resource on this earth is your mind. My aim here is to help you make the most of life through the agreements you reach. For this to happen we need to open your mind to what really goes on in negotiation and how you can navigate the array of opportunities you will face.

So, why a third edition and what could have possibly changed when not much has changed about negotiation in the past 5000 years or so? The answer is: A lot. The acceleration of change and disruption on a global scale has meant that if this account of negotiation is to provide you with a way of negotiating, it should be relevant and provided with context. I dedicate this version of *The Negotiation Book* to the concept of CHANGE. Wherever there is change, there is a need to negotiate or re-negotiate, and in your life, where you finish up with your agreements will either move you on or hold you back.

The desire for convenience and instant gratification driven by 24/7 media and apps that will deliver you just about any service, are conditioning us to expect events to be quick and convenient. The world is moving faster fueled by technology and innovations. Time in negotiation has always been important but given the prevalence of change and the implication of time, I have dedicated a whole new chapter to Time and its central psychological influence on all negotiations.

Working practices have changed involving more remote, virtual negotiations being conducted. The 2020s is an environment presenting new dynamics to relationships, trust, accessibility, opportunity, and vulnerabilities. Therefore, I have dedicated Chapter 2, "Virtual Negotiations" as the attributes of The Complete Skilled Negotiator are not restricted to the meeting room.

So, why this third edition? Think back only six or seven years. In that time, social media has accelerated to become the primary marketing platform used from multi-national corporations to one-person start-up businesses. We now live in a world in which a small group of influencers can make or break your brand. A world where big tech is as influential in supporting or restricting social attitudes as are governments. Social pressure groups have literally changed political priorities and social values in the west resulting in equality, diversity, mental health issues, and well-being agendas, which have accelerated in certain parts of the world. So, the media has changed, communication has changed, as a result, personal relationships have become weaker, and trust as a glue for negotiation is challenged. Yet in many areas, dependencies have grown stronger as the world of "subscription-based relationships" serves to fuel the multiple value placed on many businesses.

There is massive momentum from globalization to nationalization or at least the deceleration of globalization affecting workforces, logistics, and supply chains leading to inflationary pressures and ultimately, the increase in the cost of money.

A global pandemic, which has challenged working practices; virtual communication involving Zoom, Teams, Google; and dozens of others. Zoom had over 300 million meeting participants per day in 2020 (Source: Business of apps). Google Meet had over 100 million daily meeting participants in 2020 (Source: The Verge). Microsoft Teams had 75 million active daily users in 2020 (Source: Windows Central Flexible).

We have enjoyed over the past 10 years in the west ultra-low interest rates, cheap money, trillions of dollars, euros, and pounds being printed as part of government quantitative easing programs resulting in a surge in stock values followed by inflation, lower growth, and a different backdrop against which to conduct business.

The emergence of Crypto currencies adds a further challenge to governments and banks around how to protect the integrity of the global banking system.

We have witnessed the acceleration of sustainability as a corporate priority. Global warming has now grown into a priority for how people lead their lives to how organizations deliver on their carbon neutral commitments to the growth in recycling, energy generation, and electric EV motors.

We have started to witness the material implications of efficiency through robotics and AI technology. So much change in the world and at such a pace further highlights a one-size-fits-all-way of negotiating that cannot work. We have even experienced war in Europe that has had a direct impact on economies, politics, and food and energy prices, which in turn has resulted in the need for even more negotiations with new partners.

None of these challenges, priorities, or innovations can be delivered without the alignment of interests of those who can make them happen. In other words, none will happen without building agreements to change, commitments, and action. The things which we thought were important before may have changed, the way you negotiate and with whom you negotiate may have changed at a pace never before experienced. So, it's time to reassess what it will mean for you and how I can help you become the Complete Skilled Negotiator in "today's world."

Of course, we still need homes, schools, cars, roads, planes, airports, ships, TVs, computers, and millions of other physical objects. Every industry continues to make the things we need to keep our communities operating. It is the working practices, the flexibility, the risks, the software, the financing, and the partnerships which are changing and are bringing with them the need to incorporate more complex ways of managing relationships and negotiations.

I've taken a fresh look at some of these agreements and how you can gain commitments to better deals. Technology is changing what is possible, what is expected, and what is traded, which is providing a new mix of variables featured in all types of agreements. Following the pandemic, even more negotiations are being conducted through multiple forms of communication. Virtual negotiations are becoming more common than face-to-face. With it, there are implications around time, trust, and the ability to negotiate collaboratively.

In this edition I have set out to challenge you with an insight into negotiation from a practitioner's perspective. It cannot be prescriptive because negotiations are by nature dynamic. I will help you to acquire better deals by being aware of what negotiating different deals involves and what it will do to you. Yes, do to you, and if you are not aware of this, you cannot begin to be prepared for your next negotiation. It is you who are responsible for making decisions based on your own judgment.

Any value you may take from reading this book will come from your motivation to change. For change to happen, you have to be open to your own awareness. Self-awareness into your own make up, preferences, discriminations, past experience. The percentage of time you spend actually negotiating is minimal within the context of your whole life, and yet the consequences of your performance during negotiations will often distinguish how successful you are in life and in business.

The art and science of negotiation is an interactivity that is influenced by culture, ever-changing circumstances, expectation, relativity, capability, and personal chemistry. The Complete Skilled Negotiator is an individual who has both the skills and mindset to do that which is appropriate to their circumstances and the ability to maximize opportunity during each and every negotiation.

The abilities of a Complete Skilled Negotiator, however, remain the same. Balanced in thinking, ego in check, and a focus on understanding the interests and priorities of the other party. In your chaotic world with multiple priorities, how can you possibly have the capacity to behave in a chameleon-like approach? How can I even start to suggest that you need to be what you need to be depending on your circumstances, and that you should not be burdened by personal values that wear away at your consciousness?

You can't just advocate reading situations better, taking more time to prepare, and developing the capacity to think around issues, as well as dealing with the relationship dynamics all at the same time. And then focus on the potential of the deal rather than trying to win, understanding that being competitive will only serve to attract friction, which is generally counterproductive (unless used for a specific purpose). That's six different things I have to work at and do all at once, and I haven't even got past the preface yet!

In this 3rd edition, I seek to simplify. If you can improve just one thing from each chapter of this book about the way you negotiate, it will improve your outcomes.

It can be the most rewarding of skills to exercise and the most nerve-wracking. Is it any wonder that to provide a common way of negotiating that helps everyone to negotiate more effectively has in the past proved such a challenge to so many? Yet simple disciplines, proactive planning, and a clear, conscious state of mind can provide a significant uplift in what you can achieve. I am going to help you to get better deals by first keeping it simple and realistic. One step at a time, and you will see the difference.

The Negotiation Book covers the traits and behaviors associated with the Complete Skilled Negotiator. I use the word complete rather than successful because who are we to judge if your performances are as successful as they might be? We will never know. In our time of rapidly-changing circumstances and measurement of success by *relativity*, it can prove hard to objectively measure if your negotiation has been ultimately successful.

I am going to refer to a clock face model that provides a way of differentiating the range of ways we negotiate in a dynamic, capitalist market. The model is there to help differentiate how power, process, and behavior have much to do with the way a negotiation take place and why and how you can move the climate, process, and scope for optimizing value. The clockface is not here to restrict but to empower you as a Complete Skilled Negotiator to negotiate that which is possible . . . given those opportunities you are presented with or those you create.

The experience I have gained from practical hands-on involvement in having negotiated with some of the largest corporations on the planet, including P&G, Walmart, Morgan Stanley, Nestle, Unilever, and Vodafone, has helped me to provide this account of what it takes to negotiate effectively. I have also been privileged to work with dozens of highly skilled negotiation practitioners at The Gap Partnership who have negotiated with, advised, and developed hundreds of such organizations globally. It is this experience that has helped us to crystallize what it takes to be a Complete Skilled Negotiator.

I am about to share with you a way of thinking, behaving, and performing. Adopting this approach is ultimately down to you. If you want to be comfortable, that's fine. Negotiation is not. If you want to improve your life, sometimes you have to endure the stress that comes with trying something different and finding yourself in less familiar and less certain circumstances. There is no magic formula or magic wand, but there are principles that you may or may not choose to adopt. The choice will be yours, as will the results.

Sometimes you will need to secure agreements with others who may not always see the world the way you do. This book is about you concluding more agreements and gaining more value from each agreement you're involved in. Understanding what to do, working out when to do it and, most importantly, providing you with the inspiration to do it if you want to . . . enough! Let's start.

CHAPTER 1

So You Think You Can Negotiate?

"It is what we know already that often prevents us from learning."
— Claude Bernard

SO WHAT IS NEGOTIATION?

So, you think you can negotiate? Most people do, to a point. Negotiation is a necessity, a process, and an art. It's necessary because life is not fair, and you have to engage in agreements throughout life that take care of your interests even when it requires you to look after their interests. We are living with a backdrop of social media that has promoted transparency, everyone's right to a view, pressure groups, comparison groups, often in the name of fairness.

Negotiation evokes complex feelings that many seek to avoid and yet it is fundamental to how agreements are accomplished and take place millions of times a day around the world. The perception in western culture that negotiation involves conflict means that many will seek to avoid or simply capitulate rather than engage in the process. If you can take control of yourself, your values, prejudices, your need for fairness, and your ego, you may begin to realize better outcomes in your negotiations. The biggest challenge here is not in educating you in how to be a better negotiator but motivating you to change the way you think about negotiations and yourself. Of the many thousands of negotiation workshops I have provided at The Gap Partnership, the greatest change I see clients make is that of self-awareness. Learning about how to negotiate is an exercise in self-awareness because understanding yourself and what effect a negotiation will have on you, enables you to accommodate the pressures, dilemmas, and stresses that go with it. Self-awareness helps us to recognize why we do the things we do and the effects they have on our results. It will also helps you to adapt your approach and your behavior to suit each negotiation rather than trying to make one approach fit every situation, simply because it suits your personal style.

Why bother negotiating?

Just because everything is negotiable doesn't mean that everything has to be negotiated. The value of your time versus the potential benefit that can be achieved by negotiating is always a consideration. Why spend ten minutes negotiating over the price of a $10 notebook when you normally make $100 an hour? So you may save $2 – that's 20 cents a minute! However, if it is your next car and a 5 percent saving could equate to $1,500, the time is probably worth investing.

There will be situations involving more important decisions where you are mutually dependent and yet hold different views. When an agreement needs working through, effective negotiation can help provide not only a solution but potentially a solution that both of you are motivated to carry through.

Volume threshold
This relates to a minimum order required for other benefits to be realized. The order may need to exceed a volume threshold of 1,000 before discount levels become applicable.

There is no other skill set that can have such an immediate and measurable level of impact on your bottom line and your life than negotiation. A small adjustment to the payment terms, the specification, the **volume threshold**, or even the delivery date, will all impact the value or profitability of the agreement. Understanding the effects of these moves, and the values they represent to you from the outset, is why planning is fundamental to effective negotiation. The skill in building enhanced agreements through trading off against different interests, values, and priorities is negotiation. In the business context, it is known as the skill of profit maximization.

So, effective negotiation provides the opportunity to build or dissolve value – but what does value *really* mean? It can be too easy and is too often a focus on price or money. The question of "how much?" is one, transparent, measurable issue and because of this, is also the most contentious issue in the majority of negotiations.

Yet price is but *one* **variable** you can negotiate over. It *is* possible to get a great price and feel as though you have won and yet get a poor deal at the same time. For example, because the item did not arrive on time, or it fell apart after being used twice, or you could not return it, and so on. (Ever heard the saying "you get what you pay for"?)

In negotiation, your ego and your competitiveness might fuel the need to "win," especially where you allow a sense of competition to become involved or become agitated by their irrational demands. However, negotiating agreements is not about competing or winning; it is about securing the best value, the best deal for you. This means understanding:

Variable
This can be a price or any term or condition that needs to be agreed upon.

- what the other person or party wants, needs or believes,
- their circumstances, options and timings,
- how that affects the possibilities.

As a Complete Skilled Negotiator your focus needs to be on what is important to the other party: *their* interests, priorities, options, if any, their deadlines, and their **perception of what is important** — all of which may change over time. Try to see the deal as they see it. If you set out, and by that, I mean plan to understand them and their motivations, you can use your understanding to your

Pressure points
Pressure points are things, time or circumstances, which influence the other party's position of power.

advantage and, ultimately, work out how to increase the value of the deal for yourself. Being driven to beat the other party will distract you from your main objective, which is usually to maximize value from the agreement.

Proactivity and control

Your first task is to be proactive – to be able to take control of the way you negotiate. The primary reason for suboptimal agreements is when your ego will tell you that you can "wing it" and it will be OK. So, map out each of the issues that will most likely feature in your negotiation or at least those that you are aware of to start with. It sounds obvious but try to be honest with yourself when deciding or agreeing on what these are. Remember, *price is only one element of the* deal, and winning on price may not result in you attracting the best deal. The single thing that matters is the **total value** over the lifetime of your agreement.

Becoming comfortable with being uncomfortable

The person on the other side of the negotiating table, phone, or screen may well take a tough position, which could make you feel challenged or even competitive. Human beings are often irrational, so you need to get used to ridiculous opening positions being tabled. Becoming *more* comfortable with being uncomfortable in situations like this, where you are also likely to experience pressure and tension is one of the most important prerequisites of a skilled negotiator. Without this, our ability to think and perform will become compromised. So you need to recognize that by negotiating, you are involved in a process, and the people you negotiate will need time to adjust as part of engaging in this process. Typically this is when:

- any new risks, obligations, conditions, or consequences are presented; and
- you make any new proposals that materially change the shape or perceived value of the agreement.

UNDERSTANDING WHAT IS IMPORTANT TO THEM

Drieser, a French manufacturer of electric motors designed specifically for opening and closing entry gates was owned and managed by Jean Luke who had built up a reputation for reliability and longevity (10-year guarantee) both in the domestic and industrial markets across Europe. Although his business was well diversified, his top three clients made up 40 percent of his orders equating to 2,800 motors a year. Carefully packaged and guaranteed next day delivery on any order ensured Drieser remained competitive. High quality and quick was what Drieser traded on and had done so successfully for 15 years.

Jean Luke managed to secure a meeting with AGP, a major installer of factory gates that offered the prospect of an order of 1,000 units a year. It appeared that they were keen to sign a new supplier, and he was one of three potential partners that they might choose to work with. He forwarded a link to his website, which presented in 3D images of each of the six electric motors in his range. Later that week, he travelled to Lyon and proudly presented his range of motors to a team of three buyers. The questions asked by AGP were "What is your sustainability strategy? How do you plan to reduce your packaging? Have you considered partnering with your customers' logistics to reduce transport?" These appeared to be the most important considerations of the buyers! Fifteen years of selling quality and speed appeared to no longer "tick the boxes" certainly of this buying group. Jean Luke did not have the answers other than "anything is possible" so retreated to his factory and set about revisiting his logistics and packaging arrangements. AGP had publicly set out to its investors that becoming a carbon net zero company was a primary objective. This was part of the reason they were in the process of reviewing their supplier base. Had Jean Luke identified this, he may

(Continued)

(Continued)
well have pitched his proposition differently and in reflecting on his assumptions adapted his own working practices proactively for his other customers. It was a lost opportunity. More research and preparation into what was important to AGP may have helped his pitch or even provided a basis for negotiation. The world was changing and Jean Luke had to get his head around this fact quickly.

In business meetings, people can become frustrated, emotional, and upset if they feel that you are not listening to their needs or are being irrational or unfair with your proposals. Some will even walk away before considering the consequences. So, understanding their interests and having an agenda, which reflects both parties' needs helps to promote collaboration.

The more experienced the negotiator you are working with, the less chance you will have of a deadlocked conversation. They are more likely to understand that they are engaged in a process and that nothing is agreed until everything is agreed. In fact, their experience can result in you attracting a better deal than when you negotiate with an untrained negotiator. Many of my clients insist that their suppliers attend the same training in negotiation as they do as part of ensuring that both parties work towards maximizing total value rather than becoming distracted by short-term gains or trying to "win".

THE NEED FOR SATISFACTION

Everyone likes to secure a bargain; the law of relativity: to buy something at a better price than was available before. You only have to visit department stores on December 27th to witness the effect that securing a bargain can have on people's behavior. Such can be the frenzy that it is not unknown for violence to be used where one person feels another has pushed ahead of them in the queue. Many people just can't help themselves when there's a good bargain to be had. In extreme cases, people will buy things they don't want or even need if the price is right.

In business, though, what is the right price? The answer depends on a whole range of other issues, which of course, need to be negotiated. So how do you manage the other party's need for satisfaction? That is, their natural need to feel as though they got a better deal than was originally available.

- Do you start out with an extreme opening on price?
- Do you introduce conditions that you are ready to concede on?
- Do you build in red herrings (issues that are not real, that you can easily, and expect to, concede)?

The psychological challenge here is to provide the other party with the satisfaction of having achieved, through hard work, a great deal for *themselves*. In other words letting them "win," or letting them have *your* way.

Negotiating versus selling

It is a commonly held view that a good "sale" will close itself and that negotiation follows only when outstanding differences remain. However, negotiation as a skill and as a process is fundamentally different from selling. To sell is to promote the positives, the match, to align the solution to the need. It requires explanation, justification, and a rational case. "The gift of the gab" is associated with the salesperson who has an enthusiastic answer for everything. Negotiation does not. Although relationships can be important, as is the climate for cooperation (without which you have no discussion), the behavior of the Complete Skilled Negotiator also involves **silence**, where appropriate. That means listening to everything the other party is saying, understanding everything they are not saying and working out their true position.

Silence

Silence can serve to strengthen your position during negotiation: the other person may seek to fill that silence with offers, or information, or in some cases simply capitulate as the silence becomes too much to bear.

Negotiation involves planning, questioning, listening, and making proposals, but it also requires that you recognize when the selling has effectively concluded and the negotiation has begun. If you find yourself selling the benefits of your proposals during a negotiation, you are demonstrating a weakness and probably giving away power. It suggests that you don't feel that your proposals are strong enough and that they require further promoting. Once the negotiation has begun, the more you talk, the more you are likely to make a concession.

So, recognizing when the change from selling to negotiating has taken place is critical. You are now negotiating. It is simple enough to shut up, listen, and think, whilst exercising patience. If this silence feels uncomfortable, it is, because you are now negotiating.

PERSONAL VALUES

Values such as fairness, integrity, honesty, and trust naturally encourage us to be open. Personal values have their place within any relationship but business relationships can and often do exist, based on different value sets.

Values are usually deep-rooted and many people feel defensive about them, as if their very integrity was being challenged. The point here is that they are not right or wrong. I am not suggesting that effective negotiators have no values – we all do. However, in negotiation, when you are involved in a process, what you *do* and what you *are* need not be the same thing. This is not about challenging who you are, but it is about helping you to change the things you *do*.

If you want to remain loyal to your values during negotiation there is nothing wrong with that. However, others may not be as faithful to theirs, which could leave you compromised. In other words, if you choose to be open and honest by, for example, sharing information with the other party and they decide not to reciprocate, guess who will gain the balance of power? And how appropriate is that?

Where natural economic laws, such as supply and demand, result in people doing business with each other, a cooperative relationship can help to create greater opportunities but it is not always critical. Trust and honesty are great corporate values: they are defendable and safe, especially when you have a business involving hundreds or thousands of people buying or selling on behalf of one business. They also help promote sustainable business relationships. However, in a negotiation, these values can be the root of complacency, familiarity, and even lazy attitudes that end up costing shareholders money. I remain a strong believer in collaborative relationships but with the emphasis on optimizing value whilst ensuring the best interests of *all* involved.

The case for collaboration

If you prefer collaborative negotiations it could be because:

- you need the commitment and motivation of the other party in order to deliver on what you have agreed,
- you prefer to work with a range of variables that allow you to include all of the implications and the total value in play,
- you regard it as a better way of managing relationships, or
- you simply fear conflict and the potential negative consequences of the negotiation breaking down.

Whatever your reason, you should ensure that it is because it's more likely to meet *your objectives* rather than simply a style preference that provides for a comfortable environment. How appropriate this is hinges on how honest you are with yourself about your motives and the benefits that collaboration will bring.

HONESTY WITH YOURSELF

It is often difficult to work out how good a deal you have actually secured following a negotiation. This would be far easier to work out if, when we reviewed our performance, self-justification was left out of the equation. Have you ever asked yourself: "If I had performed differently or taken different decisions, could I have secured a better deal?" It is easier to move on rather than reflect on our performance and consider the what, the why, and of course, the resulting quality of the deal we finished with. Learning something from each negotiation ensures that, where unplanned compromises have taken place, you take away some value from the experience. This requires honesty with yourself. The following four areas provide a useful frame of reference for review, and as preparation for your next negotiation.

The four challenges we face

Challenge 1: This is all about you

Negotiation is uncomfortable. It sometimes involves silence, threats, and consequences that many find difficult environments to perform well in. If you are to perform well, you will need to accept responsibility for your actions and recognize the significant difference your performance can make to every agreement you are involved in.

The art of negotiation can be learned and applied, but you must have the self-motivation for change and the ability to be flexible. That's easy to say when you are not under time pressure or there are significant consequences for not pulling the deal off but it remains fundamental to not capitulating when the pressure is on. This is not just about being tough or being prepared. It is primarily about being motivated by the prospect of creating value and profit from well-thought-through agreements. You should therefore recognize that your past performance is no indication of your future performance, especially as every negotiation is unique, like every basketball or football game.

So, the first challenge is you. It is *people* who negotiate, not machines or companies. We all have prejudices, values, ideologies, preferences, pressures, objectives, and judgment, as will the other negotiating party. So one part of our journey will involve your understanding of why your greatest challenge in negotiation is yourself and how, by nature, you see the world from your perspective rather than that of the other party.

The simple process of an exploratory meeting, and seeking to work *with* someone rather than to assume and then impose ideas on that person, is key to understanding how others see the world and what their objectives are when you are both selling and then negotiating. With so much change happening in the world, the concept of curiosity, not knowing all the answers to start with, is ever more important to engaging rather than competing. As an effective negotiator you need to be able to understand the dynamics of any situation from "inside" the other party's head. Without this insight, you will remain in a state that I call "being inside your own head," which is a dangerous place to be during a negotiation. If you really want to negotiate effectively, you first have to get your thinking this way round. If you don't know what you don't know, how can you know what you need to know to be able to negotiate effectively.

UNDERSTANDING THE OPPORTUNITY FROM THEIR PERSPECTIVE

A German electronics firm, ETD, who specialized in Bluetooth technology had built a successful relationship with a number of suppliers to the German auto industry. They had developed software that enabled them to program their "in-car module" to operate with virtually anything Bluetooth-enabled without interference from any other signals. It was a real breakthrough in being able to offer a reliable high-quality solution for those fitting electronics into vehicles. It meant that as well as media, mobile, and other devices, wiring in vehicles could almost become a thing of the past. The lighting, fuel flap, windows, and even ignition could be actioned via their Bluetooth device. Although the electronic hardware was not unique, the software itself was, and ETD had set about educating the trade and selling the benefits.

ETD Sales Director Thomas Schnider held a meeting with the procurement team at Brionary, a main components supplier to the auto industry. He presented a carefully planned business case, which justified the premium price point by demonstrating how savings could be made elsewhere as a result of using their proposition.

(*Continued*)

(Continued)

ETD understood that this type of change would at best be considered for the next generation of vehicles. Their excitement for this potential prevented them from getting inside the head of the buyers at Brionary. The questions asked by Brionary were:

1. "Can we buy access to the software and program ourselves?"
2. "We purchase most of the electronics through suppliers who we are co-invested in. How can we overcome this challenge?"
3. "How long do you think it will be before this type of software is copied?"

The answer: probably before the next generation of vehicles comes to market.

Thomas and his team retreated to their office in Cologne to reassess their strategy. They had approached the opportunity and the potential to negotiate terms from inside their own head. A month later they agreed a deal which provided Brionary access to the software as a concession for a longer-term contract on their existing range of hardware components. Had they been in the heads of Brionary, who clearly had an open mind to long-term co-investment, their approach and the outcome may have been quite different.

Challenge 2: There are no rules

In negotiation there are no rules. No set procedures, no cans, or cannots. Negotiation is often likened to a game of chess – the difference being that in most negotiations you are not necessarily trying to beat an opponent, and you are not restricted to alternate moves. Although there may be no absolute rules in negotiation, there are parameters within which we can operate. Most negotiators are empowered by their boss to negotiate but only to a certain level, beyond which discussions are usually escalated. Total empowerment results in exposure and risk, which for obvious reasons is usually inappropriate.

Challenge 3: Knowing when you have performed well

How will you know how well you have negotiated? You won't, because the other party is unlikely to tell you how you might have done better or how well you performed relative to their other options.

So, without the benefit of feedback from those we negotiate with, we have to rely on previous precedents (the outcome last time round), or absolute measurements (our profit and loss sheet), and have the humility to face such questions as:

- What might I have done differently?
- Might I have timed things or managed time differently?
- Might I have included other issues?
- Might I have tabled proposals that were better thought through?
- Might I have not agreed so easily at the end?

Questions that simply challenge how honest you are being with yourself. A good deal has to be defined, taking all of the circumstances into account. Your ego will result in blaming your circumstances when agreeing becomes difficult and you end up making unnecessary concessions. By the time a deal is done, you may just want to get on with implementation rather than reflect on your performance and what might have happened had you done things differently. Let's face it, who wants to carry regrets and think about the negatives when we have "successfully" secured a deal!

Measuring the quality of your agreement, without acknowledging some of the risks or concessions that have allowed for **the price** to appear like a "good deal," is not measuring the total value, thus failing to provide a true reflection of your performance. It is your honesty in self-review that needs to be encouraged if you are to truly measure the real value of your deals and learn from your performances.

The price

A single issue that offers only one measure and is usually not representative of the quality or total value of the agreement.

No good, bad, right, or wrong

In negotiation there is no good or bad, right, or wrong. If you want to conform and be popular you may argue you did "the right thing." That does not make it wrong, it just means the rationale you are using to justify your actions has been influenced by your revised view of what "right" is.

The economies we work in are dynamic, as are our suppliers, customers, and competitors. What they will and what they won't agree to and why. What was a great deal last week may be less well celebrated this week because circumstances are continually changing. Negotiation is about doing things that are appropriate to each situation you face with the information as you see it at that moment in time.

Appropriateness

Knowing how a car was built and how it works does not make you a good driver. When driving with so many obstacles on the road, the challenge is to be able to maintain confidence, navigate, interpret, and, where necessary, respond to situations in the most appropriate way when there is no absolute answer that suits all situations.

The same applies to negotiation:

- Should you set out to compete or to work with the other party?
- Should you seek to manipulate the situation or collaborate instead?
- Should you trust them or work on being trusted by them?
- How will your or their options influence the balance of power?
- Is the perception of power and dependency between you and the other party based on reality?

In so many cases the answer is based on *appropriateness;* that is, the ability to adapt and respond, depending on your circumstances. This requires an objective, rational, balanced mindset: a state that few human beings can maintain at all times, especially when faced with degrees of perceived conflict, rejection, and demands, all of which needs to be accommodated within the negotiation. So, am I saying that most human beings can be irrational, emotional, reactive, and predictable? Yes, and these are the people you are negotiating with!

Challenge 4: Nothing happens by accident

If the essence of negotiation is doing that which is appropriate for your circumstances your challenge starts with being conscious of everything that happens before, during, and after your negotiation. In negotiation, nothing happens by accident; everything happens for a reason. Being in control of yourself, your emotions, and the relationship is a critical attribute for a negotiator. Your challenge is that these qualities do not, for most of us, come naturally. Effective negotiators develop their awareness to the point that they do not lose touch with the human sensitivities necessary to manage relationships, and that they do not compromise for the sake of personal gratification for their own comfort, or to remove the stress they experience when challenged with the prospect of deadlock. It sounds like a psychological minefield! How can I be all these things at once?

The answer is that you must first **slow down**, give yourself space to think, minimize the time pressure you are placing yourself under, and take time away to recalibrate where you think you have landed.

NOW DO THIS!

Before you start, understand what is important to them:

- Proactively take responsibility for the issues that need to be negotiated.
- Take personal responsibility for managing your circumstances rather than blaming the circumstances for the deals you secure.
- Take time to review "what happened" and reflect on what you might have done differently, every time you negotiate.

CHAPTER 2

Virtual Negotiating

I'm in a new negotiating room! Where you make your own coffee, dial in on time, and ensure your team is briefed. There are bookshelves in the background as far as you can see assuming that is what they want me to see. Dress code? Gone are the ties and the smart suits. Attendees of this meeting are "working from home." We have an hour booked so we need to confirm the agenda and present our thoughts. The sense of pace, purpose, and formality take on a different tone when the negotiation is to be handled virtually. Or do they? The company tells their buyers to "turn off the cameras" so as to promote a more adversarial tone to the meeting. The account manager with a picture of their dog in the background aimed at "common values or ice breaking" conversation as they attempt to build rapport with their buyer. In negotiation, nothing happens by accident.

Virtual negotiations involve different yet subtle changes in communication with very real implications. This is not simply an extension from the meeting room. Discussions tend to be more linear, your turn, now my turn, who will summarize?

The days of face-to-face meetings may be far from finished as the roles of human relationships and building trust play in successful deal making should not be underestimated. And yet during virtual negotiations expectations of personal chemistry which are lower, unlike as the physicality of communicating in the same room which brings with it a sense of a shared investment in effort and respect. In the online virtual room or on-screen, negotiators have more energy to focus on reading into the words used (and those not used) as well as anxiety and stress levels through the language used. As you can only see their head and shoulders you now need to focus even more on the dialog. If the deal is important or at its final stages, if you can, make it a face-to-face meeting.

The screen offers an environment where the etiquette is adapted, the language used ever more literal and considered. This is a meeting where you may even be recorded! Gartner predicts that 75 percent of meetings will be recorded and analyzed by 2025 so the conscious competent negotiator needs to be prepared, clear thinking and totally aware of everything which is said.

Without the surrounding sounds, lighting, heating, seating, and other distractions, the screen is now your world, and the quality of communication is channeled in a more direct fashion. Language, signals, silence, rejections, patience, and qualifications are amplified, and you need to be ready to perform.

Teams of negotiators are now using group chat, set up on their organization's internal messaging platform enabling them to communicate independently throughout the negotiation in a way not possible when all attendees were sat in the same room together. Their meticulous planning and preparation can be monitored through a live collaborative, shared document. They can monitor live, the value of the agreement as proposals are tabled. And, if they are instantly calculating the value of the last proposal tabled, who has control?

AND WHAT OF TRUST?

Following the pandemic, virtual meetings and negotiations featured during many more deal making processes and sometimes the entire process following the explosion of cheap or free on-line, high-quality platforms, which present convenience and near zero cost.

However, expectations of trust run lower as communication differ between face-to-face, face-to-screen, and the written word resulted in different nuances during our dialog. Without the opportunity to "break bread" with others and connect, dialog will nearly always be more formal and although entirely possible, creative options are less likely to surface.

During face-to-face meetings it is easier to read their reaction, provide immediate clarification, judge the tone of response, and employ the appropriate level of assertion and reassurance. We have both invested more time, so now that we are together, we will share thoughts and seek to optimize our time spent together.

During a face-to-screen meeting, there is a greater reluctance to be as direct unless the consequences have been carefully considered. If communication is perceived to be too adversarial, the other party could simply conclude the meeting there and then! So, naturally there is a tendency to consciously tread a little more carefully. Language should be chosen more deliberately and aware that the potential for frustration is never far away.

THE RISK OF THE WRITTEN WORD

During negotiations when emailing or messaging, be careful not to be more direct than you intended. Try to remain aware that the point you are making need not come with you also outlining consequences and implied threats counter to the tone you are trying to convey. The power of the written word can also help provide the clarity that hours of conversation struggle to achieve and to summarize progress from your perspective cementing your position. Read your email and read it again before sending. We all have experienced at some point in our lives the consequences of autocorrect typing, which happens to have adapted the very word(s) and meaning we were trying to convey. With the written word, the fear of immediate rejection will not exist in your mind. Writing summaries and proposals with the right tone needs careful preparation and even proofreading by a colleague. Furthermore, what's written is "on the record", may be copied to others, and may well be referenced at your next meeting for all the wrong reasons. Be careful so consider how your counterpart might use your message. It's now in writing, can be referenced in future correspondence, so be careful about what you send, especially during early conversations when there is still a lot of scope to work through.

Mahav had a great relationship with his electrical retail buyer, Ishaan who worked for Tendelli Electronics based in Delhi. Mahav repre-

(Continued)

(*Continued*)

sented one of the most innovative manufacturers of home security cameras; there were always new models and features worth discussing. They had monthly meeting to discuss new lines and terms and had built a strong relationship over three years of trading together. Mahav would buy coffee, talk with other members of the busing team when he visited the offices, Ishaan would respect the fact that Mahav had travelled 150 miles for the meeting. Apart from the business, they would discuss the important cricket match with Sri Lanka at the Feroz Shah Kotla ground, and needless to say they had an understanding and their negotiations were generally collaborative. In March 2020, Delhi like much of the world was hit with covid and imposed a lockdown. Mahav and Ishaan took up Zoom meetings. Online sales of home security cameras were still good so it was business as usual. In September 2020, Tendelli Electronics changed their buying structure, Ishaan was moved on to a new category and Mahav had the task of starting a new relationship from scratch, virtually. It proved tough. What used to be a 10 o'clock negotiation, now felt like a 4 o'clock negotiation (see chapter 3, The Negotiation Clock Face). The agreements started to yield less value as price seemed to be the only issue on the agenda the new buyer wanted to discuss. Multiple attempts to invite other more senior members of the buying team to the virtual meetings failed to materialize. They came to realize that maintaining a relationship virtually was entirely viable. Building one based on trust from the outset was much more challenging. Today, the account yields 60 percent of the sales Mahav was achieving at the start of 2020.

TIME:

With virtual working increasing, it is becoming more usual for virtual to be the only way some meetings can take place due to the availability of those who need to be involved.

How much cost and effort is there in joining a meeting online rather than booking a day out? In taking a flight and taxi to arrive at 9 a.m. in some far-flung city to finally sit down in an unfamiliar environment?

The answer is of course, it depends but most account managers will understand this investment in time only too well.

With no travel implications, negotiations can be spread over many shorter meetings giving time to reflect prior to responding. Don't expect the agreement to come together in one meeting. There is always the opportunity to reconvene when the cost of doing so is negligible.

With virtual meetings, time has a subtle if not different meaning. Time allocated for meetings, the option of time outs, to invite others from different destinations all present new possibilities and opportunities. Time pressures of old become less critical. There is no plane or train to catch and as long as overall time constraints are understood, virtual access provides greater flexibility.

With higher levels of energy levels required for "screen concentration," meetings of more than an hour can often promote personal distractions.

The temptation to multi-task, answer a text message, or check an email as your mind wanders presents a real risk. It's worth scheduling several shorter meetings, allocating each a time slot allowing for a "time out" for or you to consider your position.

MESSAGING IS EASY YET CAN PROVE COMPROMISING

Often, between meetings there are the inevitable emails and messages, usually aimed at clarifying positions or making requests. The Complete Skilled Negotiator will consider who is the best person to send the message and to whom (assuming you are working in a team). Who should be copied in, and when is the best time to send it given the timing of your next meeting (assuming there is going to be one)? Is there a "best way" or "better way" to send the communication based on how sensitive the message is?

> Sunglasses wholesaler, Arona were experiencing a high level of staff resignations from their finance team during February 2022 following an extensive period of being asked to work from home during the pandemic. As life started to return to normal Madalina the Finance controller had a team meeting via MS teams. The purpose was to
>
> (*Continued*)

(Continued)

brief them on how the business planned to formalize their flexible working arrangements. Beginning at the end of March 2022, the team would be required to work from the office for at least two days a week with three being the preferred level of commitment. She also invited any questions and added that they could make direct contact with her if they had any queries or issues with the changes. Brian, a Finance administrator, followed up on the meeting with a Teams message seeking clarity on two days being acceptable, which Madalina efficiently responded with a "yes."

The entire finance team returned during March and agreed to work from the office on Tuesdays, Wednesdays, and Thursdays. Madalina asked Brian why he would not be in the office on the Thursday and that it was important as she was planning to hold their first in-person team meeting in two years. Brian quoted the email and forwarded a copy of her response at the time stating that his personal commitments now meant that he was unable to travel on Thursdays. The spirit of what Madalina was trying to achieve was rejected because of one message she had sent which was now 'on the record. Be careful about what you put in writing. Brian left the company in June 2022.

NOW DO THIS!

- Make the time to plan out your online meetings as if they were face-to-face.
- Keep negotiation meetings to an hour so that you can maintain your focus.
- Brief your team on their roles and agree on how you will communicate with each other during negotiations.
- Adopt a negotiation tool (pro forma) so that you or your team can all monitor progress and all positions, live.
- Summarize your position in writing immediately after the meeting, anchoring your position along with next steps.

CHAPTER 3

The Negotiation Clock Face

"There is no right, no wrong, no good, and no bad way to negotiate. Only that which is appropriate to your circumstances."

—Steve Gates

Robert and I are probably *similar people*. We may live in the same town, perhaps on the same street, with similar aspirations. If asked about our pension provision, we each might consider how much we should save, how much we can or want to afford in the short term, what our retirement aspirations are, and how we feel about risk. Our profiles are likely to diverge as our circumstances and attitudes are put to the test. The importance we place on our decision may be influenced by our partner but is almost certainly going to be different from one another. So, although we are probably *similar people*, we will see each opportunity differently and as negotiators need to get into the head of others to understand their priorities and interests and how our approach to negotiating will best serve each unique situation we face.

To make sense of how different approaches to negotiation could serve us, and because each negotiation presents unique challenges, I developed a model simply called the Negotiation Clock Face (see Figure 3.1). This model was born out of a commercial project I undertook to research and explore the many philosophies being advocated by so-called gurus, universities, authors, consultancies and, importantly,

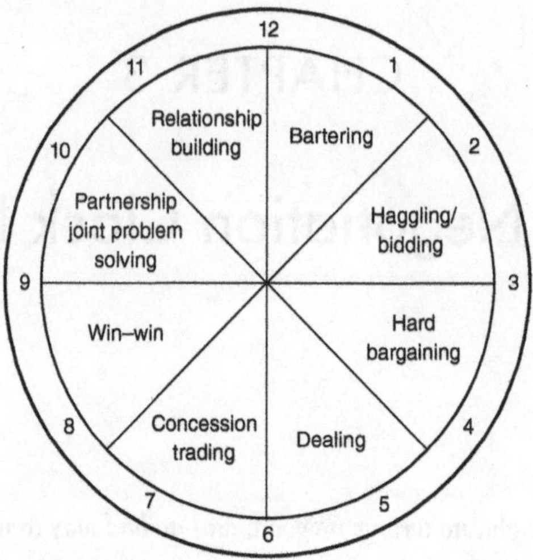

Figure 3.1 The clock face.

the group of organizations that I represented at that time. To define what is meant by "world class negotiation."

The definitions on the right-hand side of the clock face represent competitive negotiations based on those involved in distributing a finite amount of value between them. It symbolizes transactional dialogs with lower levels of trust and fewer issues regarded as important enough to negotiate. This means that those on the right are tougher to negotiate in nature and are either win–lose or competitive forms of negotiation. So the process is going to be positional and potentially confrontational. The amount of value available to share is finite, and it's simply a case of how it gets distributed.

Those definitions on the left-hand side of the clock face provide for more cooperation where collaborative negotiations lead to the creation of incremental value (creating a bigger pie). They reflect negotiations which are more commonly promoted in business-to-business situations (though not always). There is more dependency, higher levels of trust and a broader agenda around which to negotiate value.

However, these definitions are only a guide, in that within the same meeting, many negotiations can and do move from one position to another on the clock face. The Complete Skilled Negotiator recognizes this and will move the discussions into the area that suits their objectives depending on those considerations which are important to them (relationship, sustainability or, if they choose, short-term value).

The "engineering of variables"

The opportunity to build value through the "engineering of variables" and each party's relationships with the other is more likely to take place where there is collaboration in play, i.e., on the left-hand side of the clock. Collaboration of course requires some degree of common purpose, interest, or dependency between those involved. No matter how proactive or committed you are to developing a joint agreement, creating more value opportunities through negotiation requires the commitment of both parties, and such power on one side that the other has no option but to collaborate. Maximizing value through the engineering of variables need not be detrimental to the other party. They remain responsible for their actions and decisions as you remain responsible for yours. However, you should never allow complacency or the idea of fairness to affect your drive for improved terms as you will inevitably face resistance and challenges along the way, however you build your agreements.

The clock face, then, is a model for helping you, to determine what is appropriate for each of your situations. One way or another it reflects how most deals "get done." This model was designed to help negotiation practitioners differentiate between negotiations and to consciously adopt the appropriate approach to each of their negotiations.

The clock face model is not good or bad, right, or wrong, any more than north, south, east, or west is the right direction for any journey. It just "is" and wherever negotiation happens, the clock face serves to offer a simple range of definitions within which your agreements will take place. It is important to remember that the direction you take, decisions you make, and results you achieve still remain *your* responsibility. The clock face is simply a compass.

WHY ARE THERE SO MANY DIFFERENT WAYS TO NEGOTIATE A DEAL?

Capitalism and market pressures motivate and manipulate people to operate in the ways that they do. For example, account managers frequently become frustrated when trying to build relationships with buyers who they perceive to have more power within the relationship. The buyer (and this often works both ways) will negotiate competitively to drive every last cent of value out of the deal. As a result the buyer can become so focused on one issue that they are prepared to forfeit any other benefits whilst in the pursuit of the best price. Meanwhile, the account manager, desperate to build value through a range of variables (payment terms, volume, quality, delivery, and other offerings), tries to progress conversations on a collaborative basis resulting in proposals, which in this case go ignored.

So what is the answer? There is no one answer. How you negotiate will nearly always depend on the specific circumstances you face. This is why to understand negotiation, you first need a basis for differentiating the many ways in which negotiation can and does take place (the Negotiation Clock Face). The above situation, however, is certainly manageable. Escalation to a higher authority, introducing more variables onto the agenda, conditional movement from your position or even introducing time constraints could offer a start.

When asked to describe their preferred negotiation style, many negotiators have openly described to me how they get the best results, the way that best suits their industry, or the way their business does business. The response is rarely "it depends." The importance of relationships or dependency will often feature as the primary motive for preferring collaborative negotiations. This view of how negotiations can best be managed usually results in the individuals being effective in only one type of negotiation or relationship situation. The Complete Skilled Negotiator has a much broader understanding of the options available and is able to adapt to each situation as they find it.

WHEN ONE APPROACH DOES NOT WORK FOR ALL

Bright Light, a California-based PE firm had a designated team responsible for investing in high potential technology businesses. It was high risk investing but they had a good track record of nurturing on average two out of five investments through to maturity (selling it on) with substantial returns. It was and remains a competitive market with valuations in 2021 particularly high. Deals were designed with a combination of structured debt attracting different levels of interest, equity, and board involvement together with clauses covering warranties, covenants voting rights, share classes, and enough legal contracting to fill many hundreds of pages of subclauses. Working alongside advisory firms, legal counsel, other banks, and of course a timeline, the deals were high pressure with substantial amounts of work to be completed before agreement was achieved and the deal "crossed the line." This intensity was cushioned by a well-versed team of Partners, analysts, tax experts, and lawyers who had fine-tuned the process allowing them to close out five deals a year. Every deal was different, and they had built a process allowing them to work through each stage and any required negotiations, reducing slippage against agreed timelines as long as everyone (which included a lot of support services) did what they said they would.

In the first half of 2022, three deals were lined up and each one in turn failed to get across the line. By June the Partners held an inquest. Why had the momentum stalled? The market and the interest were all still strong. After three days of examining in detail the potential deals that had folded, they concluded that the very efficient process they had developed had in fact turned into a rigid process that they had come to rely on. Negotiations became stifled, and prospects were walking away. They conducted a review of their processes and the lessons learned resulted in

(*Continued*)

(*Continued*)
them introducing a wider scope for future engagements, greater levels of empowerment within their own team to take decisions and more regular progress reviews during the critical stages of closing out the deal. All necessary because each deal is unique.

Although there is no right or wrong way to negotiate an agreement, there is an appropriate way. This will invariably depend on the circumstances of the other party, rather than any set rigid terms that you decide to operate by.

HOW THE NEGOTIATION CLOCK FACE WORKS

The Negotiation Clock Face offers a visual representation of negotiation styles ranging from the toughest form of market manipulation through to high-dependency relationships. Each stage around the clock face offers more complexity, more opportunity, and more required collaboration. It helps us to understand and determine the most appropriate approach to negotiate, depending on your circumstances.

The negotiation environment

If we are going to control any negotiation, we first have to understand the environment within which we operate. For example, imagine you are responsible for managing a particular customer on an ongoing basis. You feel that a relationship is going to serve your long-term interests, which requires you to build some level of trust and an understanding with your customer. However, your customer has significant market power and exerts pressure on you to improve your terms. This makes your relationship difficult and transactional in nature as their behavior suggests their interests are in short-term gains only.

Do you choose to spend your time at 4 o'clock hard bargaining and risk suboptimizing longer-term opportunities (ignoring other possible variables), or do you attempt to move them around to 10 o'clock to work on the relationship in an attempt to gain more mutually beneficial agreements?

The answer to this again is "it depends." So by understanding the different factors that can influence your negotiations, you can build a stronger awareness of whether you need to proactively change the nature of your relationship with the other party or the climate of your meetings during your negotiations.

Bartering: 1 o'clock

Bartering involves the art of trading one thing off against another and does not necessarily involve money. Trade bartering has taken place around the world for thousands of years before money even existed. Today there are many websites dedicated to bartering or "swapping."

Price bartering, as anyone who has ever bought that carpet at the Egyptian market stall will know, can be very quick and the final agreed upon price can be far removed from the market value. Our satisfaction is from securing the carpet for only $XX when back home it would have cost $YY, regardless of the implications of getting it home or even whether we needed one at all. Both the culture and rituals employed in the Middle East make this form of negotiation process "normal" and comfortable for locals. There is a ritual, a process to go through where we establish the value of something between us. Indeed it is usual for locals to insist on getting to know each other before business can even be discussed. It's common for entire families to be involved in this process. It's how business gets done: it involves trust, personality and, yes, capitalism. It is a process those from the Middle East are far more comfortable with than those conditioned differently in Western cultures.

There need not be any relationship, trust, or even respect, simply a ritual to agree on the price. When bartering, the parties try to pretend that there is respect or trust in what each other is saying. At least when we move around to 3 o'clock and 4 o'clock there may not be much trust but there is enough integrity in place that the pretending has stopped. However, when it comes down to conducting business, this is the rawest form of capitalism: how much you want something and how much I need to trade something within our own micro-economy. Nothing else matters. In negotiation terms it's raw, basic, and yet effective. It's at 1 o'clock because it represents about as basic a form of negotiation as you can get. Until money was invented, it was the only way to negotiate items or services of value.

Haggling/Bidding: 2–3 o'clock

Websites such as eBay have helped create new industries in the way products and services are traded around the world. The days of the sleepy antique auctions, although still in operation, have been taken over by a vast online bidding industry. Today you can trade almost anything online via designated business auction traders or business to consumer (B2C) sites. Even the stock market operates using the process of bidding where ultimately the market (supply and demand) will define the value of the transaction. You can even bid with Virgin to upgrade your flight seat up to two days prior to your flight, providing Virgin with greater certainty of filling their premium offering and the public the chance to bid what they can afford.

This basic means of agreeing to a price demands the greatest of all self-disciplines: being prepared to walk away. The risks of becoming too competitive with no alternative options before entering into a bidding war are well illustrated following a bidding process in the early 2000s when the business world was experiencing the years of the "dot-com bubble." In 2000, Time Warner's bid was accepted by AOL for $165 billion. The two firm's combined stock market value at that point was $350 billion. Within a year of the deal AOL couldn't maintain its superior market position. Subscription and advertising revenue dried up with the shift from dial-up modems to cable broadband. A goodwill write-off resulted in AOL Time Warner reporting a loss of $99 billion in 2002 — at the time, the largest loss ever reported by a company. The total value of AOL stock subsequently went from $226 billion to about $20 billion.

At the same time, the UK government sell-off of the 3G mobile phone licenses involving multiple mobile phone operators ended up paying many times the value for the privilege of gaining one of the four licenses up for auction. You may have thought that these multi-billion-pound businesses would have used sales projections and profit forecasts to work out the limits beyond which they could not go. The other consideration was that there could only be four winners and these were going to be the players who would be around to compete in the future. The view was held that those without the licenses they would not be able to compete in the future. So the limits the competing companies were prepared to pay became greater than the commercial reality suggested at the time. The "winners" ended up paying £22.5 billion in what became the biggest auction of its kind in modern business. It took a further eight years before 3G technology took hold of the market and financial returns could start to be realized.

Businesses that use **tendering processes** are effectively using the bidding process to attract a price-based, best offer from a range of potential suppliers. Local government contracts widely use this process for subcontracting purposes as part of the procurement process, to ensure that competitive pressures are maintained and that taxpayers are getting "good value." However, where the nature of the contract is based on a performance-related service, for example the building of a road, price alone, even against a well-specified brief, can prove a restrictive means of agreeing to all terms and can lead to poor "total value" agreements. However, without such transparent, competitive procedures, government contracts would be more susceptible to illegal forms of bribery.

Tendering processes
An invitation to tender for the contract by submitting your best proposal against a briefing document. The organizers then use this either to narrow down a shortlist or to select the winners of the contract.

Many businesses use this 2–3 o'clock approach and build in a post-tender negotiation process with those who have effectively qualified to the final stage of potential suppliers. This allows the negotiation to move around the clock face to a win–win situation at 8 o'clock or beyond, providing for greater opportunities.

Hard bargaining: 4 o'clock

Hard bargaining in its purest form is not typically the preferred approach in business-to-business negotiations, but even complex negotiations such as those that involve the acquisition of companies frequently move to 4 o'clock on the final issues. This is typically when all the remaining issues have been exhausted and one final issue remains unresolved. It is under these pressured conditions when the skill, mindset, and confidence to hard bargain are both necessary and critical.

"What I get, you lose, and what you get, I lose"

For those who believe in fairness, hard bargaining provides the greatest of tests. It is not fair, it is uncomfortable: it requires nerve and it will make you question whether the discomfort was worth the benefit that came from it. Your opening position is likely to be rejected (if not, it would have been inappropriate), and you are likely to be facing someone who is attempting to understand how far you will go.

Of course, hard bargaining for yourself is a different experience from doing it on behalf of the company you work for. Although it may not be your preferred approach to negotiation, it has to be understood in order to avoid leaving yourself vulnerable. Where people or companies have power, they will use it to their commercial benefit, and if you are not equipped to perform under such circumstances you will pay more than you need to.

Bargaining range

The bargaining range is the difference between the most you will pay and the least the other party will accept.

The two most important disciplines in any negotiation consist of asking questions and making proposals. Information is power and, at 4 o'clock, power will play a part in how the **bargaining range** is divided. This is rarely transparent. If you told the other party what your breakpoint was (your bottom line), would they be prepared to pay a cent more?

The art of hard bargaining is, of course, to work out what *their* breakpoint is – that is, negotiate from inside their head.

Once you understand their interests, priorities, time pressures, and options, you are better positioned to gauge how far and hard you can push. You can assume that the other party is responsible for their own interests and are unlikely to agree to anything they cannot or don't want to agree to. Your questions should be designed to provide you with ever more forms of information and as a result, help make your position more powerful. When you have the insight that you need you are ready to make your proposal(s) (see Figure 3.2).

Delivering a proposal

When stating your proposal, you should set out to create an anchor from which the other person feels that they need to reassess their own expectations. It should be extreme and yet realistic. Too extreme and they may just walk away from any further dialogue. Your opening position is simply the start of a process during which you set out to manage their expectations. Everything becomes relative to this position, even your own concessions, in that you know you will have to move if you are to agree on a deal. Yes, they are going to reject it so get used to the word "no." Yes, they will be emotional as they express their shock and surprise. This is to be expected and is all part of the process. However,

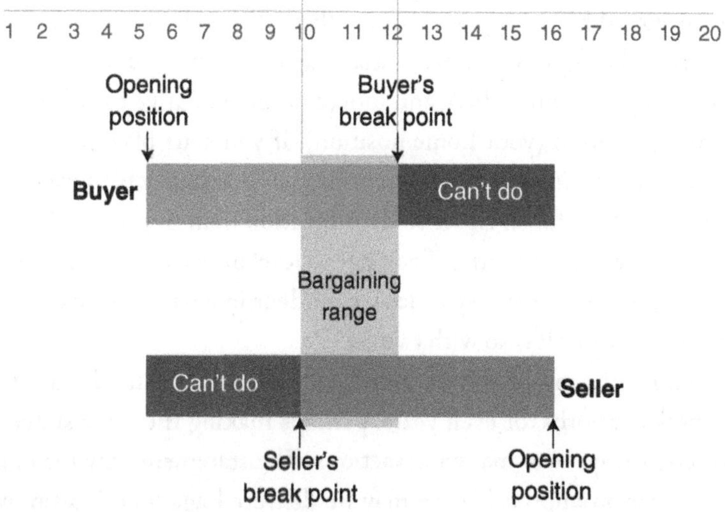

Figure 3.2 Hard bargaining positioning.

if you antagonize or insult the other party, for example by opening at too extreme a position, you risk losing the chance of maintaining a conversation and ultimately completing the deal, even if you have significant power. So the art of hard bargaining is gauging your opening position and then being tough on issues like price, whilst remaining respectful of the people you are negotiating with. This means:

- appropriate positioning,
- holding tough, and
- conceding on fewer occasions and by lesser amounts than the other party.

In the majority of cases, negotiators who make their offer first will come out ahead.

Another characteristic of hard bargaining anchoring consists of stating your position as a fact early in the dialogue. It can be one of the most powerful tactics available to you for gaining psychological power. In situations where there are no clear market value indicators and there is scope for the perception of value to be different from market value, first offers have an incredibly strong anchoring effect. This relative positioning of what I call "playing at home" exerts a strong pull throughout the rest of the negotiation as counter-offers and moves become relative to the opening anchoring position (your home position). If you start playing away you run the risk of trying to move them from their position, which means you are more likely to finish closer to their position than to yours. Of course, this is much easier to control if you have a level of real transparent power. For example, it's pretty easy to look confident in a game of poker if you have four aces, but less so with two 3s.

Medium- or long-term positioning can be more subtle. It can occur over weeks, months, or even years, perhaps making the same statement in different ways over many interactions. The statement may firm up as the negotiation approaches, or may be delivered again and again, with the negotiation only occurring when the negotiator deems the anchoring positioning to have created the right conditions and timing for success to be more likely.

Dealing: 5 – 6 o'clock

The timing of the contract (the sooner the contract can be completed) may have as much benefit to me as it has a downside to you: bonus payments may be as costly for you to achieve as they are for me to provide. So although each agenda item needs agreeing and perhaps even trading, they may not necessarily provide any incremental benefit. Where you are faced with simply agreeing on terms, which provide little by way of any real incremental benefit, a deal-like climate is likely to exist and the need to be considered, conditional, and tough during your dealings is critical to protecting your position and the value of the deal.

The process of deal-making is usually made up of trade-offs and compromises rather than of low-cost, high-value trades as found in classic win–win situations. This is because, where time pressures are in play and there is a need to make the deal work, trades tend to be made up of "necessary" moves to make the deal work rather than value-adding activity, although the two are not mutually exclusive. Deal-making can involve few issues, which means the style and dialogue can sometimes be little more than hard bargaining, although the climate tends to be more respectful. The difference is that you can offer to move on one issue, providing them with some satisfaction subject to a reciprocal move on another allowing for the deal to be completed. Price, as we know, is the most contentious and transparent of all variables, which is why, when negotiated alone, it tends to lead to competitive forms of negotiation. When dealing is in play at 5–6 o'clock there can be three or four issues involved, each of which are transparent and, although they need agreeing, they provide little by way of opportunity for mutual gain.

Concession trading: 6 – 7 o'clock

This is the first of the collaborative approaches where both parties recognize that some level of cooperation is required if mutual interests are to progress. The more common interests that can be identified between the two parties, the greater the potential for creating value. The process can involve conditional trade-offs across a broad range of issues from a pre-agreed agenda.

The negotiation climate is usually constructive but still guarded. For example, saying "if you place the order today, we will guarantee your required time slot," would seem to be an offer to move things around to accommodate the other party. It could, however, be the case that you were going to do this anyway, that there is no cost implication in offering the time slot or that you have very few orders so they could have had any time slot without any implications to you. All that matters is that you were seen to offer a conditional concession (in this case, the condition that the order is placed today) and were providing some value (convenience and security of securing an important time slot), leaving the other party with the satisfaction that they have agreed to a "*good deal*" with you.

Now that you are on the left-hand, collaborative side of the clock face, your focus should be on working "on the deal." Nothing is agreed until everything is agreed, which means that you can park issues or variables and come back to them if not agreed on. An unresolved issue does not mean there is a deadlock, but that other issues need to be examined in order to help resolve the current impasse.

Win–win: 8 o'clock

Win–win implies by its very definition that both sides in a negotiation win or come out ahead. The rational process of trading low-cost, high-value issues in such a way that the total value opportunity can be enhanced was popularized in the 1980s in the book *Getting to Yes* by Ury and Fisher. The concept of win–win assumes that both parties will make decisions based on the fact that, if one party offers you something of greater value than that which they seek, in return leaving you with an incremental gain, then you are more likely to accept it. If your aim is to build value, it's difficult to argue with the theory. However, as Ury and Fisher later went on to write in *Beyond Reason*, the emotional side of a relationship plays a significant part in how agreements actually come together. People are not always rational in their behavior (see Figure 3.3).

During 2015 Facebook progressed a strategy of building relationships with publishers including the BBC, Bild, NBC news, and the *New York Times*, amongst others. The concept (called *Instant Articles*) attracted nine publishers who committed to provide news information to Facebook. This in turn attracted audiences to their own monetized solutions, of which they were able to keep 100 percent of those revenues. It was apparent to the publishers that Facebook was in fact competing with Yahoo, Google, and Twitter, securing exclusive social media feeds. The negotiations resulted in the publishers taking control over which stories appeared and ensured that, by embracing social media, their own online business model would not be undermined. The agreement facilitated by Facebook sought to build on the mutual interests of those involved, focus on the longer-term picture and measure success through the synergy and strengthening this would bring to their own users. The win–win agreement had only been made possible because of the collaborative approach this engendered.

From 8 o'clock onwards you have the option of sharing some information in order to help the other party help you. This, of course, requires a higher level of trust than when simply concession trading. Trust takes time to earn and can be more easily nurtured when the balance of power is

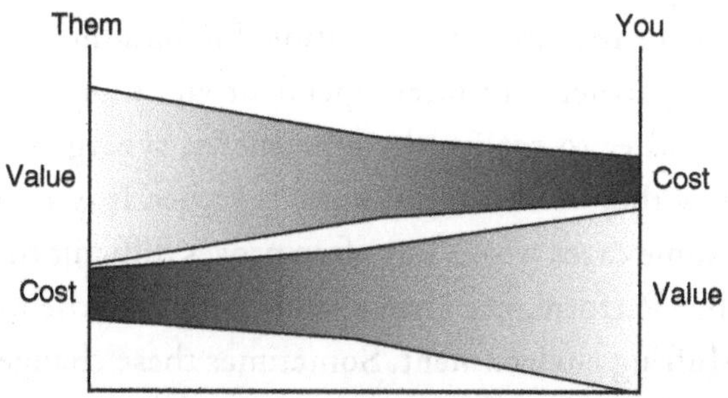

Figure 3.3 Low-cost, high-value win-win trade-offs.

more even or when the dominant party has a genuine motive for securing your commitment to an agreement.

Partnership joint problem solving: 9 – 10 o'clock

When building an agenda for a 10 o'clock negotiation, your mindset should be focused on forming a sustainable agreement that covers all areas, including:

- performance
- compliance
- risk

Take the concept of total value agreements that are central to win–win negotiations and extend the possibilities through building more dependency between parties. For instance, if this benefits us, it will benefit you; if it harms us, it will harm you. Focus your attention on what issues could create problems during the lifetime of the agreement for both parties. Take your time working through the level of risk and responsibilities that both of you are prepared to take. Then build an agreement ensuring that responsibility is transparent and clearly stated and that risk is clearly compensated for.

Relationship building: 10 – 12 o'clock

The value of partnership in business cannot be underestimated. It often represents the optimum position for building agreements – when trading partners are interdependent and there is a clear need to help each other to realize the efficiencies, synergies, and savings as part of how they work continuously together. It is an "ideal" situation and in some cases works but often proves difficult to achieve and sustain. Why? Performance change and changes in the market result in an ever-shifting environment. Sometimes these changes have been factored into the agreement and sometimes they serve to expose one party or the other. At 10–12 o'clock, risks will have been considered as part of the original agreement. However, if one party suffers as a result of change that could result in the trading relationship being affected, both parties are more likely to reappraise the trading arrangement and sometimes even renegotiate the terms. The degree of interdependency in play means both parties are implicated if one is affected by change.

When negotiating past 10 o'clock your agenda should be designed to encourage transparency, creativity, and possibility. In essence, the broader the agenda the greater the scope for building robust deals with added value. Examining longevity, intangibles (things that are not material), risk, sustainability, information, resources, and so on, allows for highly creative agreements to be built that reflect all of the interests, need for flexibility, and potential opportunities for both parties. However, this ideal requires understanding and patience and in some cases, an acceptance that the reduced risks achieved by longer-term agreements may have to come at the cost of short-term margin or profit maximization. If that is desirable, then the partnership approach may well prove appropriate. Much will depend on the circumstances and objectives of those involved.

Back to bartering (1 o'clock)

In Tim Harford's book *The Undercover Economist*, he explains how the cost and value of a cup of coffee can vary and why the average commuter is prepared to pay a premium for a cup of coffee at the train station or airport when time is at a premium and supply and demand are in favor of the well-positioned coffee kiosk. Although you may be a regular customer of the kiosk as you rush to the office and may have become loyal to a particular brand of coffee as a result, your relationship is not a partnership. Indeed, the balance of power as a result of supply and demand is still firmly in favor of the strategically positioned coffee kiosk. Your ability and your motive to negotiate in public over a few cents is removed. Also, the kiosks with loyalty scheme cards effectively constitute a proposal made to their loyal customers: a retrospective discount, a loyalty incentive, more coffee rather than a lower price, a trade barter and low-cost, high-value incentive, which takes us past 12 o'clock and back to where we started: bartering.

Exploring the reality of partnerships

Partnerships provide the necessary veneer enabling many agreements to be progressed in business. Some corporations believe so strongly in partnerships that their values and ethics strongly promote them through and across their business.

Ethical partnerships carry a sense of righteousness about them. Few companies would openly admit that they are out to screw every last cent out of their customers or suppliers, and yet they are required to provide statements about maximizing shareholder value. Again, this cannot always be achieved without someone else paying and, the larger the organization, the more leverage they have for doing so. I am not suggesting that partnerships do not exist, but in all my experience in business they are rarely as idealistic or as reflective as the true definition of partnership might suggest. Formed partnerships take the form of unions, marriages, cooperatives, societies, confederations, alliances, associations, and institutions, and there are many more entities based on common interests, values, and motives for investment. By their very nature, two or more businesses working together are going to be challenged – they will have independent interests to consider, and you must always remain mindful and aware of these considerations.

Co-investment also has its risks, as you also need to understand who else is backing the venture and what risks or exposure they carry.

Renault owned two-thirds of Avto Vas the Russian based car maker that makes Lada. Many of the parts used to make the Lada were sourced from Europe. A minority stake was also held by Rostec, a state-owned Russian business that made weapons. Russia was also Renault's second biggest market after France. During the War with Ukraine, in March 2022, the Russian government threatened to take over companies that were at least one-quarter owned by "unfriendly states." Avto Vas value dropped by 40 percent and was revalued at €3 billion. What was operating as a successful partnership was undermined by geopolitics, a risk that would have been impossible to factor into the shareholder agreement.

During the pandemic, some pharma companies, notably Astra Zeneca, sold their vaccine at cost price while others adopted a more commercial view. While wealthy countries could afford it and were more focused on simply obtaining enough for their needs, they were unaffordable for others who relied on home-grown alternatives or even herd immunity strategies. Amongst these countries, those pharmacy companies taking the short view came under pressure from governments for their patents to be removed on other drugs. Some governments in poorer countries took the view, if you price us out when our need is at its greatest, and you currently have the power to do so, we will review the privileges afforded by your patent protection. Where serious amounts of investment had to be recouped, the notion of partnership and examining the broader landscape was not a strategy adopted by many pharma companies. The implications of this strategy are still unfolding.

Where partnerships work effectively is where the relationship is of *strategic* importance, i.e., where the businesses could easily be compromised if the relationship were not to "perform" and that the investment in time and effort delivers obvious mutual synergy benefits. Although partnerships perform better with trust, trust can take time to earn and requires the glue of dependency. Once it exists, it can also be harmful in that it can serve to disarm, promoting familiarity and complacency. So a continued balancing act needs to be "policed" through measurement and performance reviews for the partnership to be sustainable. These considerations should feature early in the negotiation agenda as being critical to the sustainability of any agreement that you may build.

There are no right or wrong ways to negotiate, and no fixed way of ensuring that you will always get the best agreement. The clock face helps to differentiate and recognize those behaviors and strategies in play and how these are likely to affect value, rather than simply suggesting a right way of negotiating, which would be highly exposing.

NOW DO THIS!

- Work out where you are on the clock face and adopt the appropriate approach for each of your negotiations.
- When the negotiation gets tough, recognize that you are moving around the clock face and adjust your stance accordingly otherwise you will become compromised.
- If you want to build value in your agreements and there will be dependency in the relationship, plan to negotiate between 6 o'clock and 12 o'clock.
- Where the balance of power is strongly in favor of one party, the tendency is for the negotiation to take place or end up in the 1–6 o'clock environment, so be prepared!

CHAPTER 4

Why Power Matters

"You only have power over people so long as you don't take everything away from them. When you've robbed a man of everything, he's no longer in your power – he's free again."

— Aleksandr Solzhenitsyn

WHAT DO WE MEAN BY POWER?

You are as powerful as others perceive you to be, so you need to understand how they see the situation. Power can be real or perceived, or as subjective as it is objective in that it exists in people's heads; even though the other party may be dependent on you or independent of you. Power can shift, can be created from timing and circumstance, and can be used to nurture or exploit, so clearly it needs to be understood and respected.

Why the balance of power matters

So why is power so important in negotiations? Quite simply, it provides you with options and, if understood, will enable you to control where on the clock face your negotiation will take place.

- **Holding the balance of power.** If you hold the balance of power in your relationship(s), you have greater scope to control the agenda, the process, and ultimately influence the negotiation in your favor.

- **Power to influence the climate, style, strategy, and possibilities.** Power provides you with the opportunity to choose between being competitive or collaborative, depending on which suits your objectives.

Creating the perception of power *before* the negotiation begins can be achieved through demonstrating indifference, outlining your options, or the other party's lack of options. All are designed to manage expectations and suggest that you are negotiating from a position of strength. Trying to do so once discussions have begun is transparent and can prove futile. The Complete Skilled Negotiator understands the value of clearly framing the facts surrounding the circumstances of those involved so as to enhance their perceived power.

Holding the balance of power

History has taught us that those with power will at some point seek to exercise it. Therefore it is vital to understand the balance of power, be clear where the negotiation is likely to take place on the clock face and prepare accordingly. The type of relationship you have with those you negotiate with will directly influence how and where you choose to negotiate on the clock face.

One of the most important considerations when gauging power will be the amount of *information* available relating to each party's circumstances. The degree to which time and circumstances are transparent directly affects the power balance within your relationship and the style of negotiation that is most likely to follow. That is not to suggest that those who enter a negotiation from a weak position enter as lambs ready for the slaughter: very often the more powerful party will use the situation to gain other forms of value such as loyalty, exclusivity, or greater flexibility rather than just beating the other party into agreeing to a lower price. Where you negotiate on the clock face will have an impact on all these possibilities and on the total value opportunity that will be created from your discussions. So we need to treat power respectfully if we are to make the most of it. The purpose of this is not so that you can win or beat the other party. They are not your competition. It is to help you optimize value from the negotiations you are preparing for.

HOW DOES POWER INFLUENCE NEGOTIATIONS?

Influencing factors

Those factors which have the greatest influence on where negotiations take place on the clock face are made up of the following:

1. The level of dependency.
2. The power of the brand and the relative size of both parties.
3. History/precedents.
4. Competitor activity and changing market conditions.
5. The party with more time.
6. The nature of the product, service, or contract.
7. Personal relationships.

1. The level of dependency

Who needs who the most, or the level of dependency between both parties, directly influences the balance of power between you and those you negotiate with. If you don't need to do a deal and are not dependent on the other party, your position of "indifference" provides you with a greater level of power, assuming that you both know this and believe it to be true. Any need to form an agreement is usually influenced by your circumstances, whatever they may be.

In economic terms this is referred to as **supply and demand.**

- If there is an abundance of supply and little demand, the buyers, assuming they have a need, will have more power available to them.
- If the product or service is in short supply yet demand is high, the seller will more likely have greater power.

Bitcoin is a good example of how the supply of new bitcoins, which can be mined is intentionally reduced over time (every four years) to ensure that a reduced supply will support the price or value it attracts. If the market were saturated with ever-increasing volumes of the coin available, like any currency printing exercise, the value would simply collapse. This does not guarantee the value but is designed into the model to promote relative scarcity. Quite simply, if there is a shortage or difficulty in acquiring something, assuming that demand is stable or strong, then the value will increase. In times of no demand or when there is an oversupply, the value or price will generally drop. Although this is the case in most market situations it is not always so apparent. Asking the right questions will help you to clarify this:

- How is your supplier performing generally, and how important does this make you to them?
- How many options, other than you, do they have to achieve their strategic objectives?
- If demand for the product has slowed, how much more important has this made your agreement?

The more demand you are able to create, the more options you have, and the more powerful your position will be in just about any type of negotiation.

Although not always possible, one of the most effective ways of building power for yourself is by developing BATNAs (Best Alternative to a Negotiated Agreement), because the more options you have, the stronger you become.

The clearer your options, the more definitive your own break-point will be.

Understanding and building options or BATNAs is fundamental to establishing power. **No options = no power**, or at least from inside your own head.

The supply of money on the money markets influences the best mortgage rates available for home buying. These rates are regularly published in the media as banks compete to lend money against the security of property. Some take the time to talk to a mortgage broker who will provide a range of options based on their circumstances; some will approach the bank or mortgage company who will outline their latest offer, or they may simply be advised of the cost of extending their current mortgage without providing any other options. However, those who genuinely shop around, research on the internet, and talk with a number of suppliers effectively get a feel for what the best on the market is. Along with a BATNA, knowing that you can go elsewhere ensures that the time invested in research pays off. The best deals are not necessarily the ones advertised. In the world of private banking there are many deals available for the right person at below high street prices, subject to the right relationship and broader circumstances. With a high-street BATNA in hand it's worth progressing such discussions.

Qualifying the other party's options, and therefore their power, requires us to question objectively the viability of the options they say they have. In some industries there are substantial costs in implementing an option. For instance, the set-up costs of switching manufacturers may be considerable: re-tooling, resourcing materials, new safety inspections; not to mention the disruption, ongoing training, and relationship-building that needs to take place. The other party may be able to employ their BATNA, but they may be unwilling to actually implement it.

So creating power where you can control supply and demand can be a highly effective way of strengthening your negotiation position. It is important, then, to understand power and how it impacts your expectations and those of the other party. The way most people gauge power is from instinctive, subjective insights formed from observations of the other party, or more often on clear factual market evidence. If you are the only supplier who can deliver what your customer cannot do without, they are likely to pay as much as they need to get what they want.

For example, the oil industry or in some cases governments controls its output in terms of how many millions of barrels of oil are produced or made available in any given period. This has a direct impact on the price of petrol at the pumps.

Where the balance of power is strongly in favor of one party and the need for cooperation during the negotiation is not necessary, that party can drive very tough negotiations. **Dependency imbalance** can result in the negotiation swinging around to the right-hand (competitive) side of the clock face.

In a business-to-business (B2B) context, absolute dependency leads to absolute power, which can promote corruption and make for poor business. This is why governments have competition and monopolies acts to manage extreme cases of non-competitive market manipulation. Creating options or a best alternative before entering your negotiation is an effective way of reducing dependency and, in doing so, of reducing the power of the other party. Creating a BATNA is therefore an important element of preparation (see Chapter 9). For as long as you have total dependency on one supplier or buyer, and assuming that they know this, you will be negotiating from a position of weakness.

Dependency imbalance
This occurs when one party has a greater dependence on the other, reducing their negotiating power.

Of course, few relationships are so one-sided or remain so for very long. Power is often measured in a subjective manner, meaning that feelings, instinct, circumstance, and behavior also contribute to the way you weigh any given situation.

On the many occasions I have facilitated negotiation planning sessions across teams with various clients, I ask the question about power: "Who has the balance of power in your business relationship, you, or the buyer/seller?" Approximately 70 percent of the time, the first response is "the other party!"

Why? Because most of us live inside our own head. We find it difficult to see, feel, or understand the pressures that the other party is experiencing, so we focus on those to which we are exposed, which of course undermines our own position of power. Negotiating from inside your head is a dangerous place to be. The balance of power between those involved in the majority of negotiations is much closer than most will allow themselves to believe.

As a Complete Skilled Negotiator it is important to recognize that, even where the market power is clearly stacked against you, you can set out to change the dependencies between you and shift the balance of power.

CREATING OPTIONS

Launching a new product onto the market takes a lot of careful planning. Agreeing to terms and commitments comes pretty high on the list and the way your plans are communicated can significantly change the attitude of others. Who needs who the most here? Your options could be who you offer what levels of investment to. Those to whom you offer exclusivity, marketing, extended ranges, or terms protection based on volumes. You may even enjoy market power where you have several supplier or customer options so can create competitive tension. The key is that whatever the environment, you need options or best alternatives.

One challenge for account managers who manage only one customer is that the customer is aware of this and knows just how important they are to the account manager sat in front of them. You may even be part of a team dedicated to managing the one account and the buyer knows this only too well.

So who has the balance of power in this situation? How do you calculate power and does it really matter? As always, it depends. However, what I have found is that in a majority of cases the balance of power is not as fixed or as one-sided as most are prepared to believe.

Even where you can't choose your customers, you can choose which ones to invest in, which ones to partner with, which ones to work more proactively with, to strategically differentiate and then ensure they understand that your business has options to offer this elsewhere.

Whether you sell insurance, energy, engineering parts, consultancy services, or tins of tomatoes the same dynamics apply.

Make the time to be proactive, plan out your options and, where appropriate, make them known. Make the time to create alternatives and you will be able to manage the balance of power more effectively.

2. The power of the brand and the relative size of both parties

Imagine you are responsible for selling an established mega-branded soft drink. You know that any retailer will sell more of your brand than their own brand or a lesser branded soft drink. The retailer accepts that margins will be lower due to the high investment in the brand itself, but this is offset by being able to sell higher quantities.

The retailer will probably sell their cheaper, higher-margin own brand as well, resulting in their overall product and margin mix being optimized.

Significant amounts of money are invested in building brands. As part of establishing the brands some manufacturers have even, for limited periods, supplied products to the distributors or retailers at no margin at all, or even below cost. The aim here is to expose their product to the market as part of creating demand, brand awareness, and attracting market share. In the long term, brand power and the terms that can be negotiated with a strong brand will more than outweigh the market entry costs.

In some cases, retail buyers need to stock certain lines in order to make their product category credible to their customers and also to remain competitive with other retailers. In doing so, they will list branded products despite having to operate at lower margins. So both extremes are in play here: brands are built and represent power within a negotiation in that the buyer needs them, but the same brands with which account managers need exposure to maintain their market share position can carry limited power. Who needs whom the most and why? What brands bring to the broader business case in terms of their reliability, quality, and customer loyalty, will have some bearing on the considerations of the buyer, as they seek to optimize their profitability, starting by objectively weighing up the balance of power within the relationship.

THE PERCEIVED VALUE OF THE BRAND

The year 2022 marked the end of a 30-year collaborative relationship, FIFA (footballs world governing body) and Electronic Arts the owners of EA Sports deadlocked on a deal after months of negotiations. It was to signal the end of two brands who had successfully served each other and benefited greatly. FIFA, apparently wanting to capitalize on digital revenue streams and EA Sports releasing the FIFA game which was delivering 29 percent of its entire revenue stream, not that it believed that it would without the FIFA branding. EA Sports believed their best alternative was to build their own variant of FIFA's model and that brand loyalty to EA Sports would limit the loss of subscribers to their gaming platform as the FIFA license cost them approximately $150 million a year.

With EA sports offering covered NFL, National Hockey League, Formula One, UFC it had significant brand power, user loyalty, and reliable revenue streams. There is only one FIFA although there are many other football awarding bodies covering Europe, the Americas, and Asia, which were prepared to continue supporting EA sports. So, the balance of power? After 30 successful years and months on negotiating they still managed to deadlock. Was it due to differing agendas and visions of the future? Was it due to the value that each placed on what they brought to the relationship? Was it the personalities behind the brands? Over the months as discussions unfolded the conclusion was that the glue that had help these two brands together had softened.

(*Continued*)

(Continued)

The glue was dependency based on the power of the brands. Once both held the view that their brands and their opportunities could be better served elsewhere no amount of negotiation was able to prevent them from dissolving their relationship. No matter how powerful the brand, it is only as powerful as its relevance to the other party.

3. History/precedents

History and precedents also play a part in influencing how people seek to rationalize and legitimize their position: "Last time we agreed to a discount of 15 percent on volumes in excess of $3 million so let's start at 15 percent." Current terms can serve as the rationale for an **anchoring position.**

Anchoring position
An opening position that serves to anchor the relative expectations and movement of the other party.

All else remaining equal, previous positions serve to shape expectations. Many organizations work hard to address this through the continuous innovation of products or changing the nature of the service they offer: they seek to remove the "apples for apples" comparisons. To achieve this, many may decide to:

- change the people responsible for the relationship;
- move historical understandings; or
- change the package, service offer or product being supplied.

It is quite normal for organizations to do this as part of ensuring that trading remains competitive.

Often when change occurs and a new person or team is assigned an account, or when a competitor has been acquired and new personalities enter the picture, the objectives and motives of the new players can shift quickly, moving the business away from what it was before. Many organizations systematically move their buyers around to ensure that historical dealings can be ignored more easily.

In other cases, such as in corporate banking, great value is placed on established relationships and mutual experiences that have taken years to build, and the value that these relationships offer can add to the collaborative way that the relationship is managed. In each case there is the knowledge of how business has been conducted in the past, which is used to influence how it should be in the future.

4. Competitor activity and market conditions

During the credit crunch in 2007/2008, a period of unprecedented uncertainty was experienced by most industries in the US and across Europe. Commercial property prices, business values, future earnings forecasts, and ultimately earnings multiples, were all severely hit. Companies with high debt levels became more vulnerable and even companies with strong forward order books looked less secure. Market assumptions relating to risks were challenged; cash became king as commodity prices hit record highs along with the cost of oil and the radical shift in behavior of the banking industry. Literally within months, long-term commitments were difficult to attract as risk aversion became critical to survival. These changes tested just about every forecast assumption, resulting in many contracts being negotiated or renegotiated in an entirely different climate and style to that of the original agreement.

The unpredictability of change affects the degree to which people are prepared to commit and the level of risk they are prepared to accommodate. In other words, stability and certainty promote a basis for longer-term commitments. In our ever-changing and fast-paced world, the issue of change plays an important part in any negotiation, in terms of what is being discussed, the length of any agreement, and which party is more exposed to the influence of uncontrollable change.

Although change affects risk and value it can also affect power. Your competitors' innovation, marketing, and strategy will have some bearing on what your customers regard as their options. The very fact that your competitors are competing provides your customers more power during negotiations. For example, in electronics the exclusive launch of a new high-end, 80-inch, 3D, HD plasma TV that attracts 10 percent of the retail sales in its target market will directly affect the sales of its competitors' TVs. This in turn will influence their trading performance and the power they have to negotiate with their retail and wholesale customers.

5. The party with more time

Time and circumstances offer the greatest of power levers in negotiation. If you have been effective at getting inside the other party's head and understand their time pressures, you will probably have more available power to exert. How you choose to use this will depend on your objectives, your relationship, and the overall shape of your deal.

Any company operating under pressure, whether it is to make a decision, place an offer, or conclude a deal, can become compromised by time pressure, and will already place a premium on doing whatever is necessary to meet their deadline. Your job as a negotiator is to test and qualify the priorities and interests of the other party all the time, as the value or perceived value of just about anything is constantly changing. A party who is prepared to pay more today as a result of time pressures may not be in the same position next week. So if you leave the opportunity too long, you may lose the power you had as their circumstances change.

But what if the deal's timing is not naturally in your favor? The other party could have many options and can reject your ideas and proposals. The answer is to orchestrate events in such a way that you build power by taking control of time and circumstance. But how can this be possible?

If time and circumstances affect options, then, by creating circumstances through the sequencing of events, you can effectively take control and negotiate from a greater position of power.

TAKING CONTROL OF TIME AND CIRCUMSTANCES

Sequencing events by mapping your negotiation process can be used to create momentum and power. Sequencing allows you to proactively manage events and communications aimed at helping you remain in control of the overall process.

In was March 2020 and the immediate surge in demand for PPE (personal protection equipment) following the outbreak of Covid resulting in Governments across the globe offering contracts to those that could provide/produce volume in short timescales. The political pressure to act and spend as necessary was extremely high. One at a time across Europe, countries were locking down and health services were under immense pressure. Meyer, a sourcing company that at the time specialized in sourcing handbags from China, had access to good contacts and five factories that were versatile and decided to seize the moment. Their "head start" on others meant they were able to deliver on a range of products within days, subject to flights, they were able to secure incredible terms, and the deal they achieved maintained their business (a handbag company) through the entire Covid period. However, before they had even won a contract to support the UK's NHS with 1,000,000 aprons, they contacted each of their five suppliers with specification sheets and offered 12 hours to respond. Four did. That day they sequenced their preference of supplier based on historical reliability and scale and contacted the bottom two. Between them they could deliver, and the terms were good. On day two with their BATNA in hand they then contacted their next two (preferred suppliers) offering each an order of 250,000 units. Once they had secured equivalent terms, they increased their volume offer to their preferred suppliers for a further discount, which they secured. It cost them two days but they managed to secure the items on time and at a great margin.

6. The nature of the product, service or contract

Negotiating a complex construction deal or business merger is, by its very nature, more challenging than buying a car from your local garage. Alternatively, agreeing to a contract for IT services, by its very nature, requires a different type of process and agenda than, say, agreeing to a settlement following a marriage breakdown. Due to the different relationships at play and the nature of the outcomes, most negotiations are unique.

Example: Buying a car

If you were buying a second-hand car privately, you would probably set about agreeing on a price with the current owner. Two pieces of information would help set the parameters for discussion. First, the price that the owner is asking, which is effectively their opening position and, second, what the model and age of car would typically sell for in the market. Both parties are aware of this and usually end up negotiating around the price. The buyer may seek to lower the seller's aspirations by pointing to some work that the car needs to bring it up to scratch. The seller may try to increase its perceived value by promoting the reliability of the car and the fact that it had one-owner. Neither argument need make any difference to the negotiation unless you choose to listen to them. There is no prospect of a relationship following the deal, few issues to negotiate around, so a Hard Bargaining or Deal Making negotiation is likely to follow (4–5 o'clock on the clock face).

Now imagine you were in a position to spend more money and decided to purchase from a local dealer. Can the worn tire be replaced? Will they tax the car? Can they provide competitive finance arrangements? Both the possibility of a relationship beyond the immediate agreement and a broader agenda to discuss could result in the negotiation being more appropriately conducted in a Concession Trading or even a Win–Win environment (7–8 o'clock on the clock face).

Finally, consider the same transaction, but this time you are considering buying a new car from a main dealer. Servicing, depreciation, and future trade-in guarantees, extras on the car, and even insurance now start to feature into your discussions. Total value becomes a greater consideration and the deal may well take place in a Joint Problem Solving or even a Relationship Building environment (10–11 o'clock on the clock face).

What has changed over these three scenarios is the breadth of issues which can be discussed and the possibility of a relationship that goes beyond that of the transaction. The item, a car, remains broadly the same but in each case the appropriate style of negotiation changes.

There is no right or wrong. Your responsibility as a negotiator is to weigh up what you are trying to achieve and decide which process is more likely to cover the broad range of risks and benefits involved.

7. Personal relationships

In every culture, relationships and trust play a part in the climate of negotiations. Building an understanding of each other's position and needs through exploratory meetings is critical if broader agendas other than price are to be entertained. Most people prefer doing business with people they trust and respect. The degree to which trust exists will almost always influence the climate of openness and the position on the clock face where the negotiation takes place.

Respect has to be earned and is more likely to be achieved through being consistent and reliable rather than by being over-flexible or agreeing to make unconditional concessions. In my experience, even if you feel others are being unfair, inconsiderate, unyielding, or even arrogant in their dealings, you need to look beyond behavior and make a rational, sober, unemotional assessment of the balance of power. But if trust is built through meeting people, and spending time with people, how are virtual meetings going to impact your ability to build trust though face-to-face dialog allowing for "human interaction"? Email promotes a more direct form of communication, one where positions can be stated, threats can be more easily made, and proposals misinterpreted. Without being able to read reactions to what you have said, or the ability to adapt or show through immediate silence the seriousness of your offer, you are effectively operating with fewer sensors at play, which has a direct impact on your relationship, especially if it is a tough or complex deal.

Without some degree of trust, your negotiations are likely at best to feel transactional and difficult. Equally, with too much familiarity complacency kicks in and the total value and opportunity become compromised. The challenge for you is to find the right balance to serve your interests.

INFORMATION IS POWER

If you could read the minds of the other party you would be able to see the available options, understand their actual cost base, their time pressures, the real implications of having no agreement, and so on. Unfortunately, such transparency does not exist. However, you can still unearth some of this information by questioning, exploring, and listening to various stakeholders in order to understand their circumstances.

Information about the other person's options or circumstances certainly provides power, so for the same reasons you should seriously consider how much information and what type of information is appropriate for you to share with them. Building power requires you to think and operate like a barrister, but not an interrogator, questioning appropriately to glean those "information nuggets," or insights as to where the nuggets are. Approach the issues from different angles. This is not about interrogating, as we have to manage the relationships involved. It is about understanding the whole situation; using your curiosity, inquisitiveness, and desire to clarify the issues as they see them. The more you invest in understanding their motives, desires, and objectives the more powerful your position becomes.

It is for this reason that questioning and listening are critical negotiator behaviors. Negotiating in a vacuum (not understanding the market around you) can only result in you operating inside your own head and therefore suboptimizing your opportunities.

Quite simply, information is power.

ITS WORTH IS WHATEVER THEY WILL AGREE TO

Supply and demand is one of the more straightforward economic levers, but it is used universally through the stock exchange, auction houses, the cost of an airline flight, or one of today's roller coaster crypto currency values. These are all driven by demand and how much the other party is prepared to pay. Of course, when negotiating, this can only be helpful if you understand the circumstances of the other party: their options or best alternative, their means to pay, and their specific circumstances. Without this information, you risk simply guessing and negotiating from a blinkered position. If you have no understanding of the level of demand, you have little power to play with, even if there is an actual demand.

During the pandemic, many organizations cut back on their staffing levels and restructured their business models as a means of surviving the uncertain era. Fast forward two years, these same organizations noticeably in leisure and hospitality were left not only vastly understaffed but unable to attract back the workforce who had moved on to new careers or retired. As a result, cruise ships could only operate with a fraction of their capacity, restaurants operated at suboptimal levels, airlines reduced the number of flights they operated, and the list went on. Now they had to compete for the same skills as before, resulting in a shift in power.

Companies were forced to revisit their budgets and working practice requirements. The demand was apparent. The capacity to deliver the business offering was not. How much is it worth to operate at full capacity rather than at 60 percent? The answer is usually the difference between profit and loss.

Seaview, a hotel chain, was suffering from a severe staff shortage. One of their hotels needed a general manager and they were offering the role at a salary representing a 25 percent premium on the market. The executive team led by the COO was desperate to fill the role. At this level, they managed to attract candidates, principally from their competitors. The final interviews resulted in an offer to the preferred candidate.

Arielle was offered the position. Within hours she responded to an email thanking the COO for the offer and placed a counteroffer with them. The offer was for a further 15 percent in salary, three more vacation days, the right to work flexibly on one day each week, and not being required to be in the hotel on both weekend days. This was a new dynamic that the COO was not accustomed to. Seaview had the right candidate and remained confident in their decision to offer. There followed a meeting during which the exec team agreed to the terms. Again, an email to Arielle was responded to with one final request. That the companies pension contribution be increased from 7 percent to 12 percent. She understood the market, had listed throughout her meetings about the challenges the company was facing, understood that her value had risen, and she was worth whatever they would agree to. The option for her was to stay where she was. Their option? To take second best. Her demand was agreed to that same day!

THE POWER OF A THREE-TIERED STRATEGY

Mateo is the procurement manager based in Tijuana, Mexico, for La Nestas internet bars. There are 1500 Nestas bars spread across Mexico, and for several reasons, the business was adapting to credit card payments over cash. Mateo was set with the task of procuring 1,500 card readers and a backup service that would be durable, reliable, and stable with the Microsoft Finance system already in use across the business. Following his research, he engaged with three potential suppliers, each of whom had provided a proposal to support the business and each offering similar levels of support. One such supplier, Pay Up, was his preferred vendor. They offered a free trial, free hardware, no minimum charge on transactions, and their equipment could handle contactless and Apple Pay. They did, however, have a 2.75 percent transaction charge.

He advised the Sales Director that he was impressed with Pay Now but the transaction terms needed to be 'reexamined.'

He had set out a three-tier, three-week strategy to engage in discussions and to first negotiate with Credit Now. They had a transaction rate of 2.25 percent although there were start-up costs involved, and the relationship and reputation were not as strong. He advised his PR team that he was in advanced discussions with Credit Now and checked to ensure that an online tweet to this effect would not be an issue.

In week two, he progressed conversations with Blue Pay who were offering 2.05 percent transaction costs but again with high start-up costs. Again, this was leaked to the market as almost a given that the deal was done.

On the Monday of week three, Mateo had a conference call with Pay Up who were based in Mexico City. They were aware of the announcement. Mateo started the conversation with an apology for not being able to conclude the deal with them and that they were his preferred vendor. He added that he was not authorized to not move above 2 percent and others were able

(*Continued*)

(Continued)

to offer those rates. He closed by saying that he had to sign by Wednesday as it was a condition of the offer on the table.

On Tuesday he had a call back with an offer of 1.95 percent from Pay Up. The deal was concluded and turned out saving La Nestas 5 million Pesos in their first year of operation.

TACTICAL PLAY

Tactics can be used as a way of delivering implied threats or consequences used to manipulate a situation. This is sometimes done through introducing false timelines or ultimatums, which have been imposed by a "higher authority" such as the other party's boss. These are used when trying to apply pressure or to create urgency. If the other party attempts to apply these, qualify them. Ask them what will happen next without asking the types of leading questions that could result in you digging a hole for yourself such as "so you have no movement on this issue then?" The idea behind qualifying such claims is to attempt to establish if gamesmanship is in play. Of course, they are never going to admit to this so it is your role to gauge the likelihood of risk, given all the information you can gather.

Although transparency helps to wipe away some of the "mist" when deciding the difference between real and implied threats, you need to gain as much clarity as possible. Without clarity, you will be operating from an unclear if not compromised position, regardless of what the balance of power might suggest.

If power is directly affected by circumstance then supply and demand represents one of the main issues that influence it. If there is a shortage or difficulty in acquiring something, assuming that demand is stable or strong, then the market value will increase. That does not mean that it has to increase for you. That depends on their situation. In times of no demand or when there is oversupply, the value or price will generally drop. Again, the market rule need not always apply. It depends. Power influences strategies and tactics employed, provides one party over another with more options and therefore advantages, yet should not be assumed. With the right strategy, those with the power stacked against them can still negotiate excellent deals.

NOW DO THIS!

- Understand how time and circumstances or supply and demand dynamics change and can impact on your agreements.
- Workout where the balance of power sits in your relationships.
- Don't credit the other party with more power than they actually have. If you do, you are operating from inside your own head.
- Develop time-based plans for your negotiation ensuring time is working for you not against you.
- Create credible options (BATNA's) and be prepared to use them.

CHAPTER 5

Time – The Distinct Advantage

"Time is to negotiation what oxygen is to life. When time runs out, the game is over. The one thing you can always be assured of is that with time comes change."

— Steve Gates

"Time is precious. Time is Money. Time is the stuff of which all life is made."

— Benjamin Franklin

Any person who is genuinely indifferent about the consequence of time holds the balance of power. But of course, you are not, are you? The value of working flexibly, working from home with reduced commuting, conditioned from our period through the Covid pandemic, introduced a value to life that many have sought to maintain and justify based on their ability to work more efficiently from home. The value placed on time and many who seek more of it, is a reminder of the value that it carries. It is precious, finite, and cannot be refunded. In negotiation, it offers the greatest of levers and provides us with even greater insights.

Now, continue reading if you are going to be honest with yourself, if you are prepared to change something, and if you accept that you may not be the world's best negotiator – yet. Yes, your time is precious, and reading this chapter will require some but my role here is to help you realize an ROI that will last a lifetime. We can only achieve this if you are prepared to change your thinking and when negotiating, adopt a set of practical principles focused on *time*. If you do so, I promise that your negotiation possibilities and outcomes will improve dramatically.

Like many things in life the notion of time is simple and obvious, yet when understood and applied is the most powerful focal point and differentiator of any negotiation.

Tomorrow will come whatever. The world will keep turning, the tide will flow, daylight will rise, night will fall, and you will be one day older. It is one of the few accepted entities or measures that no one can stop. It is universal throughout the world, and the only thing upon which we can be certain is that time will move forward. Every negotiation strategy is in effect a process managed over time. Every tactic becomes more powerful when used with time; every communication will mean different things at different moments in time and every deal, deadline, implication, from inside the other party's head will be influenced dramatically by the implication of TIME.

I have witnessed teams conclude deals which they would not if it were not for the circumstances they face due to time, the value of agreements rise or fall because of timelines passing, dependencies changing, options dissolving, or new options emerging.

What creates pressure? Usually, time and consequence. With no time pressure we can seek options, continue dialog, ignore threats. However, there is usually some deadline in play. There is always a clock ticking and understanding the implication of this is fundamental and yet informative in providing you with the power to execute the best strategy for your situation.

Why do negotiators place a time limit on an offer? The answer is not necessarily to put you under pressure to decide but often because this same moment in time has an implication for them. Perhaps financing, availability or need to hit internal targets. You may already be familiar with the weekend, month-end, year-end syndrome that results in a more flexible salesperson seeking to close the deal. Often, they will even tell you this is why they are authorized to make a concession. Imagine if you had the same level of transparency around the agreements you are involved in. If you can control time, you can control the deal.

The purpose of *The Negotiation Book* is to help you become an infinitely better negotiator. Not by assuming that you are not already effective or that by studying a philosophy on negotiating will help you further, but by linking everything you do in your negotiation to Time. Knowing how to take control of your negotiating environment gives you options and a means by which you are more likely to optimize your agreements. Those who become victim to time and circumstance usually attribute these factors to why the deal didn't work out as if to suggest it was not something they had any control over.

It starts with planning, mapping, sequencing, scoping, researching, and questioning so as to take control and starting with what time means to the other party. You may have heard the phrase that information is power. Well, understanding everyone's time pressures is a power lever that we should all understand.

Power in negotiation can be both real and perceived. When you link information to time and circumstance it can offer the opportunity to create power that never before existed.

Time and circumstances are as powerful as supply and demand, which generally influence costs and prices.

The pressure and often stress experienced in negotiations come from the implication of time. Time is finite. Time can be negotiated as can deadlock. "If we are unable to agree to all the clauses by the 15th, we agree that subject to clauses 1-5 being signed off, we will allow a further two weeks for legal to complete the final contracting." Do we have a deal in principle?

Every plan or strategy, and you will need one, should have associated timelines, which allow you to take control. Even when mutually agreed, the art of the Complete Skilled Negotiator is to engineer implications to speed up or slow down progress. The first question or piece of information any negotiator should establish is how much time do you have or what are the implications of a delayed decision?

THE TIME MACHINE

Transparent time frames, or the implications of non-agreement are often used consciously as power generators.

Onus of transfer allows you to impose or imply that it is, in fact, the other party who has the time pressures, otherwise they will face those implications you have highlighted.

Pressures, created from time, drive people into their own head. If there is a risk to continued dialog, contract renewal, or deadlock, the tilt in pressure can create a momentum. If enough of the other party believe the timeline to be true and the implications to be real, then the pressure will build unless they have a strong BATNA (Best Alternative to a Negotiated Agreement).

If you begin the negotiation collaboratively yet explain the time restriction on them, it will much more likely to be believed.

By introducing a process for discussions with detrimental implications if a step of the process is not completed within the timescales, offers you power. When introducing time limitations late in discussions, it will more likely feel tactical and therefore attract suspicion or lack credibility so being proactive is important.

The stress of being late for the train or the flight with the obvious implications of a wasted day, a client obligation not met, a ruined holiday, all for what can amount to a few minutes, offers us an understanding of what time pressure feels like and how cutting the implications can be impactful.

MANAGING WITH TWO CLOCKS AND SOMETIMES MANY MORE

The starting point for any negotiation should be with planning, wherever time allows. As much as possible, strive to understand the other party. Whether through collaborative dialog or research, their circumstances are your business. Information is power and understanding what time means to them is fundamental to understanding where the balance of power sits between those involved and their interests. So, the first step of any negotiation whether competitive, collaborative, transactional, or partnership is to understand and monitor the meaning and value of time to all parties involved. If you achieve nothing else, you are already better informed than most people entering discussions. Understanding their clock allows you to decide the best time to commence negotiations, assuming you can influence this, the optimum time to conclude, stall, delay, or postpone, and in doing so, manage timing to create power.

Creating power is not to suggest that negotiation is a power struggle and that it is our job to attract as much as possible so that we can optimize our position. It is simply a fact that the more power you have in negotiation the more options you have. The ultimate strategy you adopt will be governed by the power in play.

Do you think you understand the value of time? A hospital bed, a ringing alarm, a heart attack in progress, and the rushing feet of nurses. I stand and watch helplessly as each minute, second passes in hope that the situation will be dealt with. The value of each second is highlighted as never before. Comforted by the urgency of the nursing staff, the value of each minute becomes ever more apparent. Another year, another month or week. Yes, time can mean life or death. For now, as the law of relativity sets in, the patient would settle for another hour just so that the situation can be managed.

Time, like all aspects of negotiation is subject to relativity. It is Dynamic and ever changing rather than a constant. The value of an hour at this moment in time has become priceless. At another time in another place to another person it probably carries a different interpretation. Our different clocks meaning the circumstances we face, the pressures and dilemmas we can see change the way we view and measure things and that includes time.

My friend survived his heart attack, and happily for all of us is living a healthy life today. Each day valued more than before because we have learned to value how precious and fragile life is. Private medical, pharmaceutical, insurance, and hospitals around the world ensure that this value is optimized. We all have a clock related to Maslow's number one need, health and in the world of negotiating contracts, capitalism is alive and flourishing.

Today the world's imagination and obsession appear to be with convenience. Catch up TV, smart phone apps for just about anything, and ultimately the largest companies in the world Apple, Google, Facebook, Netflix, Amazon, Uber all providing their version of convenience. They all offer services, which are time saving that you will pay for. Sometimes the predictability of time is used by entire industries to maximize value. Christmas and Thanksgiving land on the same dates each year. The Turkeys don't know this although if they did, I'm confident they would count the days down like a sentence. The farmers and retailers know that each Turkey will sell at a relative premium during one period in the year compared with any other. It is they who plan and contract to maximize value using the predictability of a moment in time and supply and demand. Why is a flight far more expensive during the school holidays? Supply and demand and the predictability of time allow the flight operators to maximize value. Using the exclusivity and predictability of time, recognizing the importance of time to those with whom you contract can quite literally change everything.

By understanding and making use of your understanding of what time means to others, you are already a significantly better negotiator than most account managers and buyers that I have met who negotiate for a living. Driven by objectives, targets, incentives, and competitive pressures, many more than would be prepared to admit, are driven by their own clocks. They will make concessions and sometimes even capitulate to get the deal closed when they are operating inside their own head. When was the last time, under time pressure you made a concession to close the deal and thus meeting a deadline? So, we need some curiosity and questioning skills. We need a little bit of charm rather than a competitive attitude. We need to get to know the other's circumstances. To do this, we need to be proactive and use time to fact find, research, and prepare leading up to the negotiation dialog to qualify their circumstances. If you can afford it, you need patience. To rush through the process of exploring with those you want to do business with will bring with it risk. Moreover, if you do come to understand their circumstances you will significantly enhance your options.

Of course, this line of enquiry needs to continue throughout as you get to know them and their specific and changing circumstances.

As the children's game plays out "what's the time Mr. Wolf?" they would cry, never knowing if they would hear the words "dinner time!" The fear of being chased as the wolf who has decided that it's time to eat resulting in everyone scrambling for safety. The wolf's time to eat was never a good time for those playing the game and working out when that time was going to be was a lottery.

Not knowing or understanding time creates a tension, an uncertainty, and ultimately an unnecessary level of ambiguity. Great if you want to play a game but then negotiation is not a game.

Time is not only one of the most underestimated dynamics at play in negotiation, but it's also the one many believe they can navigate without really understanding, which results in many failed deals.

In almost all cases, time and circumstance mean different things to each negotiating party. They have a clock, you will have a clock, and both will mean different things. The end of the day, week, month, and year will bring different implications to each party. An absolute deadline to one party can represent a mere moment in time to another. What you understand of their deadlines yesterday may be different today. Circumstances as options are open to change so we must never assume the constant.

One key piece of information as a negotiation practitioner is the implication or criticality of time. "What would be helpful to them, why, and by when?" When signing the contract, completing the deal, or renewing the agreement, what timing means to them should be of upmost interest to you because they will be operating by a different clock. Of course, there may be many clocks in play, as for different stakeholders the agreement may carry different implications. The Salesperson is measured by the month, the Sales manager by the quarter, the Sales director by the year. From when does the year run, the quarter, and what does the deal mean to the different stakeholders? When would be the best time to engage and who can you gain access to?

When engaging in negotiations you need to understand the practical nature of how time affects value or the perception of value at any given point in time. What I have witnessed is that understanding the dynamics of time and what it means to the different stakeholders involved significantly enhances both your power base (you will hopefully come to know more about their deadlines than they will understand about yours) simply by understanding what questions you need answers to as you work toward an agreement.

Who will be involved in setting the deadlines? Why is this?
What is this dependent on? Why is this?
When do you need to have the contract in place? Why is this?
What arrangements do you currently have in place, and when are these due to expire? Why is this?
When would you hope the contract to start? Why is this?
You will notice the following question in each case; Why is this?

Understanding a time related issue at a given point is useful but understanding why the issues are important or what they are subject to provides a far greater level of understanding when considering how the current status might change in the near future. For example, knowing that the contract needs to be signed off by the procurement function even though you have been in discussions with the general manager suggests that the contracting is more likely to be conducted via a rigid process (Procurement functions have a reputation for channeling discussions and promoting competitive tension via RFP processes). However, when asking the question Why? and getting the answer "because the potential value of the agreement will exceed $500,000", provides an insight in how you might restructure your agreement to avoid this necessity. Now, couple this with a further understanding that contract commencement is urgent and the procurement process slows this down, you are ready to negotiate a collaborative agreement, which meets the deadlines for your client by structuring the headline terms below the thresholds of a policy.

Time brings uncertainty and risk, which is why it's important to understand what "clocks" are in play and how you can use this information to your benefit.

At The Gap Partnership, we have seen many deals close prematurely because of a sudden change of circumstance. It could be funding options running out, other parties in the process withdrawing, a change of politics following an election, a sudden change at the top of the organization, and even a divorce settlement, which resulted in a director agreeing to a deal as part of the terms of a settlement. Some are irrational and bizarre and most unforeseen yet all related to specific circumstances, which changed over a short period of time. Conversely, we have seen even more deals collapse through fatigue, new options surfacing, or financing being withdrawn following diligence exercises. In other words, where the implication of time changes, an unpredictable response may be the result.

Tracking the meaning of time can be like tracking the weather. You can never assume a constant, which is why certainty, early agreements, and long-term commitments all carry a premium. They reduce the notion of risk and therefore are often desirable.

The closer you can get to understanding the circumstance of those you negotiate with, the better your understanding of those issues, which are most likely to impact on their importance on time. This requires dialog, patience, sometimes diligence, and qualification. Agreements on contract length, break clauses, vesting, performance bonuses, completion penalties, renewal clauses, notice periods, and many more are all affected by the length of time associated to the specific clause. Time is often the differentiator around whether or not a clause is acceptable. Let's take one single area as an illustration. Contract length, which may be fixed or variable, may be linked to performance triggers, quality, or even market conditions. A one-year contract may limit the scope for investment whereas a five-year contract opens up a wider range of investment opportunities. The positions taken up by both parties relating to contract duration in itself may reflect attitudes toward risk, a value placed in flexibility, or a whole range of internal dependencies, and your job is to find out.

If you think about the notion of two clocks in motion rationally yours and theirs, it's an easy enough concept to grasp. However, the psychology of what it does to those of us tasked with negotiating provides evidence of the amplified impact on behavior.

When you understand deadlines and consequences, you read behavior and witness that what may have started out as a firm, inflexible position better by the other party softens as the deadline approaches, assuming the deadline is real. In the final stages of most negotiations where a deadline looms, decisions get made and quickly. Football transfer windows offer an example of headline grabbing figures negotiated up to the last possible moment with the clock being legitimate (set by the governing body), both parties understand the prospect of no deal is real.

Curiosity, inquisitiveness, and questioning are fundamental attributes of an effective negotiator. Use them to work out their clock, their pressures, and the value they place on time. Understand their clock and what time means to them. Make it your number one mission. All information is important about the other party's circumstances but understanding time is the key to negotiating from a position of power.

PLACING A VALUE ON TIME AND FLEXIBILITY

Time is linked to just about every variable and will have a direct impact on the value of that variable and should never be overlooked. These variables can include minimum timelines, order times, lead times, contract period, cancellation times, notice period, guarantee times, delivery times, collection times, contract triggers, and payment times. It's possible to secure what looks like a great deal, the right product with a great specification at a great price, but if it's nowhere to be seen, requires 100 percent payment upfront, and you have to commit to a 10-year supply, the agreement starts to look unpalatable. So not only considering time alongside every variable is important but calculating the risk versus benefit on a sliding scale can offer some sobering thoughts.

What's the value of flexibility? It depends. The value they place on time today for a contract that may not start until sometime in the future may be different to the value they place on the same arrangement next week. Why? Because often time, circumstance, choice, and options are a changing dynamic. The risks that they are seeking to mitigate are often subjective, attitudinal, or based on current circumstances or lessons learned from the past. If next week they attracted another large order from elsewhere, the dependency and dynamics with you could be quite different. So we need to remember that even the timelines and flexibility signed up to today may carry a different value if and when they are called upon. So, from inside their head what value, what price would they be prepared to make or concede to attract greater certainty or flexibility? And for that matter, the same equation is one that you as a negotiator should be asking yourself. If you've ever had a mortgage, you may recall the time you chose an option that you felt best suited your needs. Apart from interest only versus repayment plans, you will have had fixed interest versus variable, 5-year versus 25-year plans, and clauses for early repayment or overpayments. Given your circumstances, you probably chose what you felt offered the most flexibility relative to what you thought might happen in the future. More flexibility will have come at a different rate and all the time, the uncertainty of future interest rate changes provides a constant uncertainty of how much your home will end up costing you. It depends.

It's a one-year contract. Why one year? Why not a rolling contract with a termination clause? Why not a renewable three-month contract? Why do notice periods have to be the same for both parties if the risks of moving are different for both? So, it's one year at $500 a month for your service. "I will pay you $525 a month with the ability to cancel offering four weeks' notice at any time." "Our terms are $500 a month for a minimum of 12 months." "Under what circumstances would you be prepared to offer a flexible contract?" "Why do you want a flexible contract?" Because I have a customer who is due to renew their contract in six months.

I have no certainty that they will, so you need a six-month break clause." "Let me see if we can accommodate that." The early assumption was to buy out the fixed contract period driven by uncertain circumstances and the need to manage flexibility in the light of uncertainty. As soon as the supplier had identified the cause of the uncertainty, they adopted a joint problem-solving mentality. The uncertainty of what might happen in the future created the need for this dialog in what was a simple agreement.

Time is linked to every variable you may choose to negotiate with either directly or indirectly. If you understand how to attach time to a variable, any variable, you can change the value or perceived value either way. It can however increase the complexity of the agreement and relationship between issues agreed, but will as a result, significantly enhance the total value of the agreement over the contract lifetime. The offer is available for a set period of **TIME**. It comes with a guarantee for a set period of **TIME**. Payment has to be received within a set period of **TIME**, and delivery will take place within a set period of **TIME**. The amount of time in each case becomes the negotiable.

For example, a penalty clause for late completion could trigger at one month, two months, or three months. Each will have different implications and a different level of risk associated to each of them. A notice period is an arbitrary period, agreed by both parties and can carry significant cost or value when triggered. It's usually specified for a set period of time. As we seek out certainty or the ability to understand risk, we can negotiate with specific timelines associated with each variable.

Today we live in a world where people and organizations increasingly value convenience and flexibility. The disruption to retail created by Alibaba and Amazon and many other on line retailers is testimony to society valuing convenience. The expectation is that it comes at the same price. So, although these companies have soaked up incredible market share, they do so without yet making a profit. Dynamic pricing with airline or train tickets based on when you book them and which are changeable will cost more than a non-changeable or non-refundable one. The flexibility factor is built into the price.

So how do you build time flexibility into your agreements and protect your margins, price, or the profit you seek? And, if I leave them with open-ended choices, how will I know what the delivery cost of the contract will be? How do I offer flexibility around time when it could carry an incalculable cost?

Firstly, it depends on how important flexibility is. Most will state that it's important but will not want to pay for it. So, the first rule is to create choices which are linked to corresponding terms based on your assessment of their needs. They will most likely highlight the risks they carry that they cannot control and therefore the risk via flexibility should be shared. Again, I would suggest that this passing of accountability should not be accommodated. By being proactive, the extent to which your commercial position can cope, you are offering choice with conditional terms. I have often used a scaled framework, which offers flexibility and yet always with a reciprocal requirement.

This can be in the form of banded discount levels, payment plans, volume requirements, delivery timescales, delivery venues, and the list can be applied to any variable. Each band they choose comes with a stated cost or benefit.

THE CONSUMER SEEKS FLEXIBILITY

But what if the contract is not flexible? What if we are one of 1,000 and we have to get in line? What if we want to work with them and they have limited supply, so we have to work with their availability? What if they are not empowered to negotiate their standard terms, and they appear to have far more options than I? These are the common challenges faced by consumers. Individuals within the masses who do not fit into the stereotypical "perfect customer" for whom the service provider has created their contract. They might include the cable TV service, the bank, the mobile phone service, the insurance company, the utility service, or even the retail service. How do you negotiate flexibility in this environment? I don't want the standard contract, do not want to be tied in for three years, and don't need all these extra channels. I only need car insurance for one week for my son. The consumer has a tough time determining the value of the contract versus the time and effort it will take to talk with a senior enough person who will listen. Who has the time to invest in generating other credible options as leverage, all of which will cost you the time. Which is valuable to you? B2C organizations depend on apathy, sweat, and effort to negotiate and to wear down a majority of those wanting something different.

TIME LINKED DYNAMIC PRICING

Uber, Air BNB, Booking.com, airlines, holiday companies, train companies, and car hire companies all utilize the dynamic of supply and demand through dynamic pricing. The price right now for a given service is based on availability and demand. It may well be different 90 seconds from now. Also, now that you have looked at our website you are captured within an algorithm, which will further predict your level of interest and change the price accordingly. But when negotiating can you integrate such models into your proposals? I will charge you £15 a bag, although that may change each day as my supplier and customer base activity fluctuates! Who can manage a business with such dynamic pricing? The same dynamic is at work for organizations working with foreign exchanges, values changing each moment and impacting those who have not hedged their currency. Buying out risk of further fluctuations is standard practice in the airline industry when buying fuel. As the biggest operational cost, medium-term visibility of pricing is critical to forecasting and planning so regardless of the market price, agreement to terms is critical to their operation. So, certainty of cost is important and comes at a price.

TRIGGERS AND CHANGE

Accommodating for changing circumstances within your agreement sounds like common sense. It carries the risk of diluting the value of your negotiated agreement or protecting what you have worked hard to agree on. Many renegotiated deals involving suppliers improving their terms result in reduced compliance and other performance issues, which when not stipulated at the time of the re-negotiation serve as a backdoor way of reducing the cost of supply. So, the buyer may have improved their cost price only for the value to seep elsewhere unless of course they re-negotiate the entire contract.

Too often time implications result in managers accepting the standard terms of the supplier. Every aspect of a "standard agreement" is negotiable, and this should be sought from the outset of discussions. Otherwise time and momentum will be used against you, as will higher authority to limit their flexibility and the time you have to tackle all the potential issues.

What if? What if our circumstances change, and I need to change the terms of the agreement? Depending on the size or complexity of your agreement, you can develop any number of clauses and triggers which stipulate who takes responsibility, meets the cost, needs to exercise flexibility, and under what circumstances. Having them agree to them all of course is another matter, so one must remain realistic when drafting such clauses. However, when creating an individual one-off contract, risks can often be overlooked and as a result, seriously impact the value of the agreement. If there are no implications on termination of contract, if order sizes fluctuate, if payment is late, when is the point at which the clause triggers, and what are the penalties or remedies against which parties are obligated? As a rule, I set contract performance time reviews in the contract. I stipulate how often the contract will be reviewed and how deviations in performance will be remedied.

TIME CAN REPRESENT RISK AND UNCERTAINTY

The cost of time goes far beyond that of labor and materials. The one dynamic in life you can be sure of is that time (over the lifetime of a contract) brings with it changing circumstances and risks. Whatever terms you may agree on today based on your understanding of the current situation, will be exposed to all manner of changes over time. So how do you accommodate the known? What are the uncertainties in your deal?

How do you build agreements which are effectively "future proof?" What if your performance commitments are not delivered on and the contract you thought you had agreed on simply doesn't deliver the value to which you thought you had agreed? Just about every variable that may feature in your negotiation will be subject to this dynamic. By protecting against uncertain events that can happen over time can have you can plan in new clauses and variables designed to protect the value of your investment. And if you can't, there is always insurance.

Trellocom, was a Spanish provider of "home of the future" technology for new apartment complexes. Their proposition involved cloud-based services to new build complexes, which provided for multiple services to be shared by all residents. Security cameras, broadband, electricity management, air conditioning, broadband, TV streaming, mobile phone, and the list went on. Contracts had been agreed with the main developer for four sites and all were excited about the offering providing a clear differentiator to each of the 120 apartments on each site with a premium price point. The installation went smoothly as did the service for the first nine months. The main contractor who remained the freeholder of the property would charge for the service as well as ground rent and other maintenance items and were invoiced by Trellocom quarterly. During month 9, a platform software update took place, which went horribly wrong. It brought the first site to a complete standstill for 16 hours. Back-ups had failed and after multiple attempts Trellocom failed to reboot the system. Some residents could not access their properties, freezers stopped working, and the "home of the future" was no longer. For all the contractual reassurances and phases of back-ups, the situation could not be managed in the moment. The compensation negotiations which followed were as a result of a lack of clarity in the protection clauses in the original contract. It cost Tellocom 750,000 euros in compensation and a further 700,000 euros in legal fees. The original deal was worth 20,000,000 euros over 10 years. The negative PR across Spain resulted in a further three pending sites due to receive the operating system being cancelled.

So, if we assume time and its uncertainties have a value, how do the best negotiators use this lever to create value? Link time to risk, understand the degree of risk the other party is prepared to take, compare that with your interpretation or ability to offset the same risk, and you instantly have a tradable that has a different perceived value to both parties.

All things being equal, a debt outstanding for six months has less risk than a debt that has been outstanding for two years. Again, all being equal, long-term fixed loans cost more in interest than short-term fixed loans.

When, when, when? This is the question that could be critical to your needs but will come at a cost to deliver. I need installation to begin by Thursday and may be possible by air freight, which will cost an additional $1,000. The job being completed by Friday-week may be possible if we double the engineers, which will cost an additional $1,000. I need all 16 working, and I had priced for an initial eight but it can be done for an additional $1,000. You say service response is 48 hours, I need it in 12. If it can be done, that will be another $1,000 per machine. You get the picture? The timing around a variable adds or subtracts the cost or value so increase the complexity of the negotiation (see Figure 5.1).

Uncertainty or certainty are linked directly to risk and risk is multiplied by time. The longer the risk, the more likely it is to be triggered or to happen. Risk is a negotiating variable that is calculated by insurance companies and banks based on formulas used by underwriters. It is typically accommodated across a range of clauses much like any contract that stipulates responsibilities and assumptions. Each is a negotiation variable, and each can be expanded or limited through the use of time. Time triggers and qualifying periods are all aimed at controlling the level of risk in play.

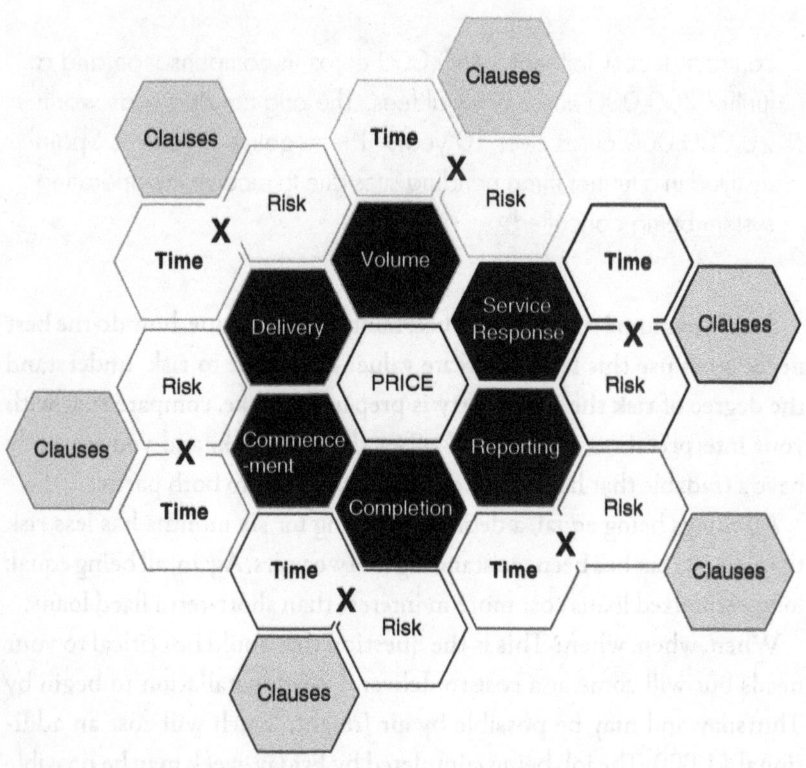

However, in many negotiations risk is a subjective issue based on past experience, appetite, personalities, natural risk aversion, and entrepreneurial empowerment (how much you want/need this to happen). The point here is that very often the value associated with risk varies considerably between negotiators and as a variable that is linked to.

People like certainty. John and Mia were, via their lawyers, negotiating a divorce settlement. It was complex with properties, children custody, future earnings, investments, pensions, and a multitude of other issues, which had so far taken two years (and much legal costs) and yet with no absolute conclusion. The inability for either to move on and plan their own futures was slowly grinding away their resolve to secure a fair or a better deal depending on how you saw it. Having held tough on numerous issues, John made a significant concession that provided Mia with what she needed (or thought she needed). He offered her the family home, a lump sum, not connected to earnings or investments, and custody of the children subject to access. The deal was affordable from John's perspective although was partially dependent on his investments delivering. It was a risk he was prepared to take to break the impasse; besides, the lawyers' fees were really starting to bite into the estate. Mia wanted certainty and John was prepared to accommodate the implications of time before getting his share of the split. Although he was now dependent on his investments being realized, he was prepared to trade this against the uncertainty of anything being resolved in the foreseeable future.

NOW DO THIS!

- Make use of time, risk, and certainty, how to value it, and how to trade it.
- Find out what time means to the other person.
- Design a plan that uses timelines, limits, and deadlines to schedule your plan around this.
- If the time period of your contracts present a risk, ensure you build in enough protective clauses.

CHAPTER 6

The Ten Negotiation Traits

"Until you make the unconscious, conscious, it will direct your life and you will call it fate."

— C.G. Jung

Self-awareness comes from knowing and being honest with yourself about who you are, what you do, and how you perform.

Most people like to regard themselves as good negotiators. Yet when asked why they think they perform well, they can only usually describe a few of their strengths, or things they believe make a difference to their performance. If the clock face has taught us anything, it has demonstrated that different types of negotiation require different skills. In other words, Hard Bargaining at 4 o'clock on the clock face requires strengths that are different from those required to perform effectively when Joint Problem Solving at 10 o'clock. However, before moving on to examine how to adapt your behavior as you move around the clock face it is worth understanding how personal traits can influence your overall ability when trying to secure the best deal. To a sports professional, examples of relevant traits might be stamina, agility, speed, and flexibility. These will be important to different degrees, depending on the sport they specialize in. They help to define a player's potential and those areas that require further development as part of improving their overall performance. Some traits are innate and some can be learned or improved on. Importantly these traits underpin the player's ability to behave and perform to the highest levels in competitive environments.

The ten traits

1. Nerve
2. Self-discipline
3. Tenacity
4. Assertiveness
5. Instinct
6. Caution
7. Curiosity
8. Numerical reasoning
9. Creativity
10. Humility

You might argue that these traits will mean different things in different cultures, and you are right. What may be regarded as requiring nerve in the US may come more naturally in India. The one common language I have witnessed globally throughout my 25 years of negotiating is **respect**. Whatever these traits may bring you or mean to you the one common connection that people relate to is respect, regardless of what is happening in the negotiation.

Traits directly influence the actions you take and can be developed through a more conscious approach to how you negotiate. They relate to those attributes that come more naturally to you or those you are more likely to gravitate toward. What is important here is that you think about how these traits influence you and your performance when you negotiate. The ten traits underpin your behavior. For example, maintaining your nerve supports your ability to think clearly when faced with conflict and to open a negotiation with an extreme and yet realistic position. If you handle pressure well and have the nerve to maintain self-control comfortably, your performance in tougher negotiations where competitive behaviors are required will come more naturally. Your traits are neither good nor bad; they are just a reflection of who you are. The important point is to understand yourself well enough to compensate for that which does *not* come naturally and, of course, to use your strengths to your advantage.

1. NERVE

Believe in your position, never offend, and always remain calm

Nerve helps us to exercise patience and to remain calm when the pressure is on. Anyone operating under pressure is reliant upon controlling their nerves as part of being able to perform. The pilot, golfer, police officer, barrister, to name but a few, rely on their nerve to be able to carry out their duties, as will you when you negotiate.

Exercising nerve during negotiations involves handling both perceived and real conflict, being able to read the sensitivities around the situation and to calculate the risks before responding. Nothing happens by accident in negotiation, so having a clear head that allows you to operate as a **conscious negotiator** is essential to staying in control. Nerve also allows you to introduce challenging opening positions where appropriate in the knowledge that you are taking a risk that could compromise the potential of a deal. It allows you to demonstrate conviction when taking up a position more easily with confidence.

Opening with an extreme position and remaining silent where appropriate might be described in some contexts as aggressive or even arrogant. Yet when combined with humility, and remaining calm, exercising nerve can make for a highly effective, if not tough, negotiation stance. Without nerve you are more likely to become a victim of your own discomfort, lose respect, and ultimately concede more readily. With nerve

The conscious negotiator

In negotiation, nothing happens by accident. The conscious negotiator is aware of everything that happens in the room and their every action, comment, or interaction is intentional and considered.

comes the ability to move your position when you are ready and only when it is appropriate.

2. SELF-DISCIPLINE

To understand what to do, and to do that which is appropriate

Self-discipline: it's an everyday term, yet in negotiation it requires you to separate your behavior from your feelings and emotions.

It allows you to be what you need to be and what the situation demands of you, rather than behaving in a way that satisfies your own emotions and levels of comfort. Self-discipline does not require you to be a different person, but to fulfil the role requirements at the time to help you perform. For example, remaining indifferent to the potential of a proposal that has been made may be more appropriate than showing any overt enthusiasm or excitement. Having the self-discipline to resist showing emotion helps you remain calm in appearance. This is not to suggest that you should remain indifferent to all proposals made in your negotiations, but to be disciplined enough that you present the signals you want the other party to read.

Patience and the ability to handle frustration are qualities found in most experienced negotiators. It is highly frustrating trying to get the other party to agree to something they appear reluctant to do. However, this can be achieved by the use of:

- good timing;
- summarizing;
- repackaging the offer;
- remaining at ease with silence; and
- having the self-control to avoid selling your position or talking inappropriately.

Having achieved this within yourself you need, of course, to ensure that where you are negotiating in a team, the remainder of your team need to be equally as well-disciplined.

3. TENACITY

The negotiator's equivalent to stamina

The times you hear the words "no, can't, won't" are the occasions where you will have to turn to "how." Rather than simply conceding on the issue, you should examine the rejection from different perspectives to find out what other conditions or circumstances you could introduce as part of maintaining control and managing their expectations. For instance, in tennis if your opponent breaks your serve, you don't give up on the set, you work harder in the next game to regain your position.

There will be times when it is appropriate to hold firm and test the other negotiator's resolve. Tenacity is not only about holding firm on your position but also being prepared to be persistent where you deem it appropriate; perhaps even to employ the "broken record" tactic. This is a tactic to employ when you need to repeat your position time after time until it registers.

It is about having the courage of your convictions when faced with challenges from the other party, which are often used tactically to make you question your own judgment.

Tenacity helps negotiators to work on deals rather than being driven to close on them and conclude agreements prematurely. The more time invested in a deal the more likely you are to create or extract value from it. Few people genuinely enjoy negotiating or can see the value in continuing discussions when the deal is seemingly done. Attitudes such as "We have reached agreement so let's agree now while we're ahead" are held by those who miss the point. It is at this time that you should ask, "How else can we ensure the contract is delivered?" With ever more considerations around how the deal can be tuned, the tenacious negotiator will find the extra value or risk reduction that would otherwise go untouched.

Tenacity helps you to resist capitulation: it's the part of you that enables you to hold your position and not be worn down by the other party. It's an attitude that requires stamina, helping you to seek value right up until you finally agree to conclude the deal.

THE POWER AND VALUE OF TENACITY

In 2019 the city of Seville (Spain) was experiencing a surge in business growth. This had largely been anticipated with the opening of seven new office complexes being completed within a three-mile radius and all were pre-let totaling 170,000 square feet of new office space. Owned by seven different development companies, lease contracts to 32 companies varied between 5 and 10 years.

In March 2020, the Pandemic hit Seville as it did the rest of the world, and workers were consigned to working from home. During 2020 and 2021, seven of the 32 prime office property companies defaulted on their bank loans.

Following the take up of Zoom, Teams, and other online video communication platforms the average office space utilization in Seville was running at 35 percent.

By June 2020, one of the companies that was hit especially hard, office complex owners Solorus, decided to offer their tenants the opportunity to renegotiate their leases offering up flexible working space with shorter term commitments but with higher prices per square foot for the flexibility.

Manuel Gurcha, one of the tenants, held a meeting with the account team at Solorus. His company had 35,000 square feet of space and desperately needed to downsize to 5,000 with an additional 2,500 feet required on an ad hoc basis for team meetings. With radical changes in working patterns many of his team were being prepared to work remotely. Manuel had four years to run on his lease agreement. At the first meeting with Solorus, he framed the issues that he imagined Solorus had regarding the loss of tenants and income. He realized that the situation was an issue they both needed to work on. He asked for a rental reduction of 75 percent. It was rejected outright.

A week later, Manuel returned to hear what Solorus's offer was. They offered a 50 percent reduction. Manuel countered with a reduction on the lease to two years and a 67 percent reduction for the newly defined space requirements. It took three further meetings, eight emails, and four weeks of lawyer activity to finalize the other terms and conditions. Manuel's tenacity finally paid off. He got a 62 percent reduction with the high-quality flexible space that he needed.

Meanwhile, Solorus saved five of their eight tenants who released between them 50 percent of the total space available. They then quickly marketed the balance as an exclusive offer to the area before their "competitors" could respond. By playing the exclusive flexible workspace offer. They filled the space within a month. New prospect tenants were keen to negotiate terms but the short-term power, Solorus's exclusive offer attracted both premium rates and full occupancy within months. Meanwhile, manual's tenacity had got him the deal his company desperately needed.

4. ASSERTIVENESS

Tell them what you will do, not what you won't do

The best way to determine the future is to create it.

Being in control of the negotiation primarily comes from being proactive and demonstrating confidence from being prepared and having a well-defined strategy. Then it's about how well you perform.

The Complete Skilled Negotiator comes across as being firm and in control. Not obnoxious or disrespectful but simply able to say what is necessary in a calm, authoritative manner. This is not about being parental or patronizing in your communication style, but simply being confident in your assertions. This can be a fine line to tread. As an assertive negotiator you need to facilitate the development of the agenda and set out your position. You should focus on the deal and remain open about what is, as well as what is not possible.

It is worth considering that the outcome of any negotiation can only be influenced by the proposals that you make and flexibility you offer. Therefore, ensure that it is you who is making the proposals. As an assertive negotiator, you will not wait for the other party to make their proposals first. Yes, of course, listen to what they have to say to understand where flexibility exists, but ensure that it is your proposal that they are responding to. As an assertive negotiator you should also resist the temptation to conform. You should regard yourself as being "in charge" and yet respect the attitudes, feelings, and views of those with whom you are negotiating. Being assertive helps you gain respect. Being firm is not to be confused with being rude.

5. INSTINCT

Trust it – you will be right more often than not

Experience and "gut feeling," or what some refer to as a "sixth sense," are traits that effective negotiators refer to as instinct. Instinct helps the Complete Skilled Negotiator:

- to hear not just what is being said but the *meaning* behind the words; and
- to gauge honesty, and sense if the deal is too good to be true, or if there is more scope to negotiate.

Your ability to read any situation will allow you to judge your response and respond with counterproposals. If it seems too good to be true, it usually is. You should trust your instinct when you are faced with such a situation.

Most people have good instincts, yet under pressure do not always listen to them. They choose instead to accept the case placed before them and conform rather than challenge. As an effective negotiator you should have the courage of your convictions, challenge anything that does not "feel" right, and always demand clarity before being prepared to proceed.

Trust your instinct, otherwise too narrow a view on the bottom line could ultimately provide you with a suboptimized agreement. Price can be incredibly seductive, and those who shut out other considerations, even when the opportunity feels too good to be true, fall foul of listening to and acting on their instinct. The very need to feel as though you got a great deal can be enough to distract you from the logic you might otherwise exercise and has led to some negotiators agreeing to disastrous deals. Great deals are only so if they are honored and delivered against. Instinctively, you know if you are offered a cheap Rolex watch in a bar by a stranger that the item is unlikely to be from a reputable source. However, how sure would you be if they were in an office dressed in a suit offering a timeshare apartment in Panama? Still suspicious? OK, how about the real estate agent from a reputable agency who tells you they can sell your house in under a week if you sign with them today?

Instinct usually comes from both experience *and* knowledge, as well as your subconscious observations. The instant evaluation and judgment most people make when they first meet someone are based on subtle assessments of nonverbal communication and language. The Complete Skilled Negotiator has the ability to make these assessments more consciously as they deliberately analyze the behaviors of the other party.

6. CAUTION

If it seems too good to be true, it probably is

The "action" or interaction, once a negotiation has begun, comes in the form of proposals and counterproposals as the deal starts to take shape.

Picture the high levels of mental energy and the work rate taking place *inside* the heads of two teams of negotiators around the table. Both parties seeking to create or distribute value in the knowledge that if they are too hasty they may miss an implication. By being seduced on price, they could be entering into an agreement that could carry more risk in the long-term. It is during these critical exchanges when reality checks should take place. This is when patience is needed and time should be taken to calculate what has changed.

IF IT SEEMS TOO GOOD TO BE TRUE . . . IT USUALLY IS

With the likes of Serena Williams, Lana Del Ray, Kim Kardashian, and Michelle Obama amongst hundreds of keen celebrities, the nail bar industry has boomed, becoming a $10 billion-per-year industry. California alone employs 100,000 nail technicians. Philip Montone, a Paris-based entrepreneur, hastily set up five bars across the affluent suburbs of Neuilly-sur-Seine. With his experience in the beauty salon industry he was well-versed in how middle-class Parisians liked to pamper themselves. Working with a team of nail bar specialists he set about investing. Within a long list of equipment needed were the ultraviolet light units used for curing gel. By his calculations, he needed to purchase 20 of these. Following some online research, he had three suppliers respond to his enquiry. All claimed that there was a supply shortage and there was a three-month waiting list, such was the surge in growth in the industry.

That evening Philip received an advert pop-up on his phone screen from a supplier direct from Hong Kong. Obviously, AI had been at work. The supplier offered to supply units within 10 days and at the specification Philip was asking for. He called them and negotiated guaranteed delivery and a 20 percent discount on the prices before placing the order for $4,000. The units arrived four days before opening day. They were everything he had been offered except for one oversight. They were wired for Taiwan at 110 volts and, although they could work with transformers, they would not meet French health and safety regulations.

Philip attracted a great price and delivery, but in his haste and because of a single oversight, he ended up writing off the total cost. Today you can buy these units on Amazon for as little as $20 each.

7. CURIOSITY

Asking why because you want and need to know

Gathering information both prior to and during your negotiation is the ultimate way to create power. Even if you think you understand your market well or you have dealt with someone for many years, it's still possible to assume far too much. Some negotiators get caught up with what they need to achieve and the pressures they face, rather than seeking to understand what the other party needs or how things may have changed for them in recent times. Effective questioning used to seek information and uncover facts, data, and circumstances, which may not be obvious or may even be concealed, *must* be a precursor to making any proposal.

- What are their priorities and why?
- What are their time pressures and why?
- What are their options and why?
- How might any of these be changed?

Understanding the situation does not just come from questioning. Researching the other party, talking to others, and obtaining credit checks are activities that those who want to know and those who are naturally curious will be involved in. It's not an interrogation, but information is power and without insight you will be a weaker negotiator.

8. NUMERICAL REASONING

Know what it's really worth, know what it really costs

Numerical reasoning allows you to consider more easily the "what ifs." Your ability to engineer different trade-off scenarios by performing quick calculations allows you to expose opportunities that might otherwise go unnoticed. This involves linking the value of a risk with the benefit of an opportunity by calculating the incremental upside and then tabling it as a proposal. Although it's a good idea to prepare some proposals ahead of your meeting (following initial discussions), calculating counterproposals and providing alternative solutions during the negotiation with similar or even improved outcomes will come more naturally to those comfortable with numerical reasoning.

Unfortunately, for many, this is not the case. Using simple "ready reckoners" to work out the financial implications of movement is one way of preparing yourself for this. For example, working out the implications of each 1 percent discount or one-week extension, or each increase of 500 in unit volume requirements, and having this prepared on a spreadsheet can help you calculate quickly and respond to proposals with a clear understanding of the units and values involved.

Numerical reasoning helps you to calculate options or consequences and prepare and ready to respond with possible alternatives. It helps discussions and ideas to flow, and also minimizes the number of times the meeting has to adjourn while one party reworks their figures. If you are in doubt, it's highly appropriate to adjourn. If you are ever in doubt about how the value of the deal has or will change as a result of a proposal, you should take whatever time is necessary to understand the implications of entertaining the proposal before moving on.

US President Joe Biden entered office with a pledge to increase US offshore wind capacity from virtually nil to seven gigawatts by 2030 — enough to power about two million homes. In April 2022. A federal auction for six wind power development leases was held by the U.S. Bureau of Ocean Energy Management.

Wind farm plots were made available positioned off the coasts of New York and New Jersey. The auction raised a record $4.4 billion.

CNBC reported that the one of the top bidders was Bight Wind Holdings, which paid $1.1 billion for a 125,964-acre tract off the coast of Long Beach Island in New Jersey.

David Hardy, chief executive of Orsted Offshore North America, one of the world's leading offshore wind developers, said,

"What does that $4.4 billion do for the industry? It goes into federal coffers. Maybe it helps pay for Social Security or helps us defend a country in Europe that needs help. But it doesn't help offshore wind." Orsted withdrew from the three-day New York Bight auction as prices escalated. His view of the commercials resulted in him resisting the temptation to compete beyond that which for Orsted, made good business sense.

9. CREATIVITY

Exploring and building on possibilities

Creative solutions not only help resolve deadlock situations but help us to trade off ideas as part of creating more value. By using a creative approach you can link and package variables (volume, timing, specification, etc.) in different ways. Nothing is agreed until everything is agreed so the creative negotiator is comfortable with degrees of ambiguity as the shape of the deal evolves. It provides you with the chance to introduce options and opportunities in a disciplined, linear fashion rather than trying to work through only those issues in front of you.

Many negotiations involve a broad range of variables and the way these are linked together and are traded against one another provides for the art of creative deal-making. Even when it appears that there are few variables – let's say price, timing, and specification – the creative negotiator will identify other value-adding considerations and turn them into variables ready for negotiation.

Imagine you are buying 50 acres of land from a farmer. The price asked for the land will be important and transparent to both parties. The timing of the availability of the field will allow you to plan how you intend to make use of the space. Other considerations may include access to the land, fencing, and what the land has been used for in the past. However, the creative negotiator will look at an even broader set of variables as they consider the possible trade-offs. What about options in the future on adjoining land, drainage, conditions on how the surrounding land may be used, and contamination? What about letting the land back to the farmer, access for local huntsmen that the farmer is involved with, and so on?

The creative negotiator examines risk, longevity, performance, and the interests of the other party to "fully" scope the parameters of the lifetime of an agreement. The creative negotiator also looks beyond the variables that they are measured on as they realize that incremental value may come from elsewhere and often not all components are visible at the outset.

10. HUMILITY

It is people who make agreements and humility which breeds respect

Exercising diplomacy and empathy during negotiations to help manage the appropriate climate sounds like common sense. However, with the tensions that can exist, it's humility that often serves to bring discussions to an adult-to-adult level, cutting through the tactics and competitiveness in play. Humility removes the need for ego to surface and helps you to demonstrate your intention of working with the other party, rather than against them, to create a mutually beneficial relationship. Reciprocity ensures that if one party becomes competitive, the other party will mirror this behavior and, as a result, both will find themselves being drawn into positional arguments that become counterproductive. It is your humility that will allow the other party to "win" the argument as they concentrate on the climate and maximizing the total value of the deal from their perspective.

Ultimately, it is not you who is important; it is what is best for the relationship and for the agreement. It's not about competing or about how you feel. Humility requires the removal of personal, emotional considerations other than the need to maintain mutual respect with your focus on the agreement. The skills associated with managing climate are well-documented under behaviors later in Chapter 7, "The 14 Behaviors that Make the Difference." Humility is what sits beneath the behavior. It is a trait that allows you as a negotiator to focus on the quality of the agreement rather than being preoccupied with personalities and personal agendas.

Although it carries risks, having the confidence to admit that you don't know something (where your credibility would not be completely ruined), being open to ideas without appearing influenced, and making the other party feel important are all indicators of humility in play. It's all right not to know all the answers. It is knowing what questions to ask and demonstrating integrity and gravitas that allows those with humility to build the appropriate relationship for the more interdependent deals.

Some traits will be more reflective of you and your strengths than others. No individual trait will ensure better results but understanding them and you offers the opportunity to become a truly outstanding negotiator.

NOW DO THIS!

- Control your nerve, stick with your plan, demonstrate respect, and remain calm.
- Keep your self-discipline and only act as you had planned.
- Take control of your negotiation by exercising your assertiveness and self-assurance. Remain firm and yet engaging.
- Trust your instinct. If you think it could be too good to be true, don't continue blindly. Recognize it, and act accordingly.
- Before agreeing to any new terms, exercise caution by working out the potential consequences, hidden risks.
- Information is power.
- Use your curiosity and **ask questions** throughout your negotiation.
- **Make the time** to calculate options and alternatives using your numerical reasoning before and during the negotiation.

CHAPTER 7

The 14 Behaviors that Make the Difference

"If all you have is a hammer in the toolbox, everything looks like a nail."
— Bernard Baruch

The 14 behaviors make up the framework I developed over 25 years of client engagement for supporting the development of negotiation capability. It is time to consider your capabilities as a negotiator. Your versatility, adaptability, humility, and a range of skills to ensure that you can optimize not only ever-changing opportunities, but each agreement or relationship differently. The clock face in Chapter 2 provides the basis for differentiating the many ways to negotiate. The role of power in Chapter 3 helps us understand how situations and relationships can be manipulated or influenced, meaning that we have to continuously reassess our assumptions. The ten negotiation traits we examined in Chapter 4 provide a framework for self-awareness, enabling us to do that which is appropriate. In this chapter, I present the 14 behaviors that enable you to exercise the right behaviors at the right time. Together, the traits and behaviors support the competent performance of the Complete Skilled Negotiator.

The 14 negotiation behaviors capture and describe what it is that you do when negotiating. They make up the varied skills required to perform at different points on the clock face and when employed, enable you to be versatile enough to perform in all types of situations. They have been used as a framework for assessing, developing, and supporting negotiations in over

700 corporate businesses around the globe in over 60 countries employing the clock face as their "standard" negotiation reference (see Figure 7.1).

1. Thinking clearly when faced with conflict
2. Not allowing your sense of fairness to influence your behavior
3. Maintaining your self-control, using silence, and managing discomfort
4. Opening extreme yet realistically to shift their expectations
5. Reading their break point
6. Listening and interpreting the meaning behind the words
7. Planning and preparing using all information available
8. Questioning effectively
9. Trading concessions effectively and conditionally
10. Applying analytical skills to manage the value of the deal as the negotiation unfolds
11. Creating and maintaining the appropriate climate for trust
12. Developing and using your agenda to help control the negotiation proceedings
13. Thinking creatively to develop proposals that help move the deal forward
14. Exploring options to help gain agreement

Figure 7.1 The clock face.

The first five behaviors are more commonly, although not exclusively, used on the right-hand side of the clock face (1–6 o'clock negotiations), yet the self-control associated with them can also underpin those behaviors used further around the clock face.

The next three behaviors are based on listening, planning, and questioning, and relate to all positions on the clock face.

The final six behaviors, which build on the former behaviors, help us to perform in more complex agreements where relationship, dependency, and total value are more important.

THE 14 BEHAVIORS

1. Thinking clearly when faced with conflict

Everything you do in negotiation requires you to think: if you can't think clearly your performance is going to be compromised. In some ways, it is similar in its definition to the personal trait of nerve (see Chapter 4). The extent of conflict, real or perceived, within a negotiation will vary depending on the strategy being adopted by both parties. The ability to think clearly when faced with conflict is one that will serve any negotiator well at any point on the clock face.

Imagine that you receive a letter outlining a price increase of 10 percent. It is unexpected and comes with a limp excuse citing market conditions. Your first reaction is disbelief and then anger. You reach for the phone and then place it down as you reflect on your approach. You need to think clearly and consider your approach. You need to control your emotions and commence negotiations in control of yourself. The risk is that your emotional reactions could confuse or cloud your ability to perform in such circumstances, which clearly are not in your best interests.

Thinking clearly involves clarity of thought; not allowing the other party to make you feel as though it is you who does not understand the market and who needs to concede. Never agree to anything unless you understand it. In negotiation, nothing is agreed until everything is agreed, so make sure you have not missed anything before agreeing. It also means standing up to anyone exercising arrogance as they attempt to manipulate your thinking – unless you want them to think they are doing so because it serves your interests.

When there are major consequences at stake, or serious time pressures in play and there is an obligation on you to perform, you will inevitably experience pressure. Depending on how much pressure, your ability to think clearly may be affected. It's your ability to hold your nerve and accommodate pressure that will differentiate your performance, especially in hard bargaining negotiations.

MANAGING CONFLICTING POSITIONS

Grabashoe (Graham Bashel) was a top online influencer with a following of 35,000,000. Behind Grabashoe was now a small support team of analysts and bookkeepers managing a business, which was now attracting $4.5M in revenue a year globally, mainly from sports trainers brands but also other start-up sports brands.

Grabashoe typically attracted a 2 percent "Like rate" and a 0.7 percent engagement rate so they had a large and loyal global following.

Utilizing influencers has become a primary part of online retailer, Sports Clothing's marketing budget. Typical posting rates were running at $1,200 a shot. The annual agreement with Sports Clothing was set to be worth $275,000 a year to Grabashoe.

Negotiations had been progressing well. Payment terms, release dates, product context, and a range of other variables had all been agreed. Sports Clothing's new trainer range was due to go live in 21 days and the Grabashoe agreement was set to be a key component of their marketing plan. Discussions were already three months in. During this time, Grabashoe had increased their following by 2 million. Final negotiations had moved from email to virtual discussions via MS teams.

Sports Clothing's Marketing Director said, "We are excited about working with you, but you need to help us here. We need the level of activity already agreed, which is 230 postings over 90 days, but you need to agree to $250,000 for us to sign." Kim, Grabashoe's representative immediately left the MS Teams meeting leaving the three Sports Clothing reps stunned. A message then appeared on-screen requesting five minutes to reconvene. When they did, Kim opened the meeting with: "We will agree to $6,750 discount subject to an agreement now and a 50 percent up-front payment of $134,125, to our bank account today. All other terms remain the same." There was silence. Both nerve and silence remained as the Marketing Director Clinton, had to make up his mind. Was he going to conclude or walk? They had not even come halfway from the $275,000 to $250,000. They had however secured a concession. A further time out was called, this time by Clinton, who followed up with a counter proposal of £262,500 with 50 percent up front. Kim took a further 2 hours to reflect before finally accepting the deal. Rather than deadlock, she had thought through the situation and decided she had provided enough movement to demonstrate that she wanted the business and at this rate it was still good business. By managing their own egos as well as recognizing the consequences of deadlock, they both got the deal across the line.

In practice

- Gather your thoughts and remove any emotion from your thinking; if you do not do this you will lose composure and will more than likely underperform;
- Demand clarity as a condition of continuing;
- Remain focused on your purpose at all times;
- Control the negotiation by restating your position and letting them do the talking; and
- If you are not sure about the deal or what it adds up to, then take time out. You can always return once you have taken time to consider your options.

2. Do not allow your sense of fairness to influence behavior

Fairness has no place in negotiation as it cannot be measured objectively. What's fair to you may not seem fair to the other party so it cannot be relied on as a basis for seeking agreement.

However, the perception of fairness is important where you need balanced cooperation with the other party and where you need to work with them on an ongoing basis. But "fair" is a subjective word and a relative term. You offer one person a price of $40 and they think that's a fair price. You offer another person a price of $40 and they think it's unfair. The first has been used to paying $45 elsewhere and thinks they have a good deal and the price is fair. The second has never purchased before but is expecting a price of $35, so is not happy.

Similarly, fairness is not the answer to conflict. Opting to split differences straight down the middle, for example is not negotiating: it is compromising. The need to exhibit fairness often leads inexperienced negotiators to accept the 50:50 offer. This is because it feels "fair," when they should make further counterproposals to provide less costly solutions. So rather than grabbing the deal with the final 50:50 split, for example, why not offer a further conditional proposal that costs you far less than 50 percent of the difference?

The more you try to be fair, the more your "generosity" will be taken advantage of. Most people will not live by the same value set as you. They may simply be more callous or irrational about how they go about trading. One thing is for sure: they are out to maximize profit and, if you make it easy for them, it will be to the detriment of your interests.

Perversely, people who do operate in a fair way during negotiations can in fact be perceived as unfair. For example, in a hard bargaining situation at 4 o'clock someone may decide not to ask for more than they expect in the first instance to avoid offending the other party. Their sense of fairness results in them feeling uncomfortable with the prospect of rejection, which would be likely in the event of them opening with an extremely high or low offer. The other party, however, expecting to negotiate, will want them to move from their opening position in order to gain some satisfaction. The first party is left with two options: either to give away value that they cannot afford (because they have already opened on their break point); or to say "no" and not move. This in itself could lead to a perception of stubbornness, unfairness and, potentially, deadlock.

Firm is not rude, tough is not nasty. Liked is not respected. When hard bargaining, nice people don't get good deals.

In practice

- Aim to look for the optimum solution rather than simply a fair one;
- Remember that the easy, fair route to splitting the difference is rarely the optimum way to the best deal for all concerned;
- If the other party offers to split down the middle, it usually means that they would probably accept less; and
- If you give concede they will want more – all trade-offs should be conditional.

3. Maintaining your self-control, using silence and manage discomfort

This competitive behavior might be regarded as unacceptable in many relationships, but when you are trying to move the other person's position, self-control and silence are the most powerful of behaviors to conduct.

During a hard bargaining negotiation at 4 o'clock, for example, there is inevitably a conflict in positions: Tension and sometimes even emotion can run high. For most, it's uncomfortable but for the trained negotiator it is part of the territory. The stronger your self-control, the more power you will attract as the conversation unfolds.

Negotiation has less to do with talking and more to do with listening. You should let the other party:

- sell their position;
- explain their position;
- promote all the benefits; and
- explain why they need an agreement "today."

Negotiation is silence and to master this is to maintain self-control and manage the resulting discomfort. Information is power and the more they talk the more powerful you will become.

Conversely, if the other person remains silent and you feel obliged to respond, don't. Don't pay the price by instantly conceding as you attempt to remove your discomfort, because if you speak too early, that is what will happen. *If you have nothing to say, say nothing.* They are thinking. Let them think. If you speak to fill the gap, you will probably end up compromising your position by offering further information or even by implying that there is room for movement.

What you think is important and need to say will usually work against you. A local café always offered a window display full of delicious cakes sold by the slice. People rarely walked past without admiring the range of cakes presented in the window. Trade was always good due to the reputation of the cakes. The cakes were sourced from a local cake maker who supplied 15 large cakes each day. The margin was quite healthy for the café. The price they paid for each cake averaged £20. The supply agreement was informal, with orders placed each week and daily deliveries arriving by 8:30 a.m.

The cake maker asked for a meeting with Mark, the café manager who was authorized to purchase all stock requirements. The relationship was a strong and a familiar one, which was by now in its third year. The cake maker demanded a 15 percent price increase with immediate effect and handed over the new price list to the manager. Mark examined the note and said nothing. The cake maker then started to explain why, citing ingredient cost increases. Mark continued to say nothing. The cake maker then said that there had not been a price increase for over a year. He agreed with her. It was a fact. "I provide you with the highest quality cakes, which keeps your café busy all year 'round," she said. Mark agreed. He finally turned to the cake maker and said, "If you maintain your current terms and service level we will renew our agreement with you for a further year. Please let me know what you want to do by tomorrow morning."

He did not argue with her case or seek to negotiate over the 15 percent. He listened, remained calm, and restated his position. With no justification and without being rude. He remained "in charge." And she ultimately accepted the deal.

In practice

- Let the other party do the talking and focus your attention first on what they are saying, rather than thinking too much about how to respond;
- Listen to what the other party is saying in order to establish how far they will move from their current position; and
- If you are not ready to make your proposal, either ask a question or say nothing.

4. Opening extreme yet realistically to shift their expectations

To open extreme is simple enough, as you just state your proposal. The fear of the predictable rejection, however, results in many feeling uncomfortable with stating it in the first place. Because of the fear of the reaction we are expecting, we risk losing our composure. Rather than saying "my price is $50," some will say something like, "I'm looking for around $50," which instantly suggests it's negotiable. If it's worth $100 to you, offer $50. We know they are going to reject the offer but that's part of the process.

You can't change or remove this feeling of being uncomfortable so you need to get used to it or find ways to accommodate it. To do this, think about it as a process that you are involved in. The process will do three things for you:

1. First, it will help you to position your offer appropriately.
2. Second, it will help you to counter the position of the other party.
3. Third, it will ensure that you provide the other party with the satisfaction of having got a better deal than they believed was originally available.

Your opening position or proposal should be extreme enough for them not to accept it, but not so extreme that they choose to walk away, concluding the conversation there and then. If your opening position is too extreme, the other party may conclude that you are wasting their time, are not serious or credible, and move on. Your offer also has to be realistic if they are to stay engaged.

For example, if you wanted to buy something for $200 and they are asking $300, you might negotiate them down, depending on the circumstances. But if you were attempting to finish at $200 by opening at $25, then they would probably walk away.

The purpose of opening extreme is to create an anchor from which to move. If you have control over your own sense of fairness and can manage your discomfort, then you can do this. Assuming the other party is still talking to you, you are now in a proactive position that allows movement on your part, given that you will have taken up an opening position outside of their break point.

You can wipe their extreme openers off the table by attaching equally ludicrous conditions to their price. Imagine if a seller said to you, "The price is $500." You respond with, "I can agree, subject to payment installments over three years and that the item is guaranteed for the duration of the payment plan." In negotiation you never need to say no. You can always reengineer the variables in such a way that you can say yes and yet with your terms, which offset or counter the offer being made. Simply attach conditions that offset the implications of saying yes otherwise known as wiping their proposal off the table with an equally ridiculous response. Also, you never have to, nor should you, lie in negotiations. There is no need to if you understand the process you are involved in. The process of opening extreme is simply that – a process – and is usually employed in the hard bargaining context. By offering $275 you are not lying, you are simply making an offer by telling them what you will agree to.

During tough one-dimensional negotiations, it is important to recognize that you can get a great price and yet a lousy deal. Never resort to attacking their position. It will usually result in you losing sight of your own position. An antique clock collector negotiated an amazingly low price on a clock at an antiques fair. The seller said that it needed "some attention" as it was not working. However, the buyer was seduced by the price the seller agreed to and bought it. That was five years ago. The clock has now been through three different repairs, costing the collector the asking price over and over again. After each repair, the clock worked for less than a week. It now sits at the back of his workshop.

If it appears too good to be true, it usually is.

In practice

- Ensure your opening position is extreme enough for them not to accept it – but not so extreme that they will immediately walk away;
- Make your position credible by cutting out any soft exposing statements: avoid the use of words like "around," "in the region of," "I was hoping for . . .," "we were expecting . . .;"
- Use a non-verbal reaction to their opening position – tactically known as the professional flinch, this is designed to clearly demonstrate to the other party your surprise at their position;
- Apply self-control when making your offer, state your figure – then shut up; and
- Learn to be at ease with silence.

5. Reading their break point

In any hard bargaining negotiation, you should define your break point first. That is:

- The point at which you have other options that you could take.
- The point at which the deal is not viable.
- The point at which you will walk, rather than do business.

This is not your objective or a measure, just a fail-safe position. Its only purpose is to prevent you from agreeing to a deal that, in the cold light of day, is just not viable. Your job when hard bargaining is to finish the deal as close to their break point as possible. So therefore, your first task is to work out where you think this is, and then open extreme and yet realistic on the other side of it assuming, of course, you are hard bargaining.

You can read the other party's limits through:

- the types of proposals they make;
- the language they use to justify their movements;
- the timescales they are working to; and
- the size and frequency of their concessions or counterproposals.

This can help you to identify their break point. Their opening position and response to yours will help you plot where you think they may settle. Under pressure people often say (without realizing) the exact opposite of what they actually mean to say. For example, if they say, "We once paid $60 an hour for this and would not do it again," they are saying this not to you but to themselves. Even *they* do not believe it. It's their denial that drives this behavior so listen to what they are saying. If they were not prepared to go to $60 an hour they would not feel the need to state it.

Reading their break point is about reading the situation based on a combination of information, questioning, and reading of their actions. All should help you to establish how much they need the deal and how far they will go. Time can play a role here. Where negotiations go on for weeks and months, many will agree to offers that would have been totally unacceptable during the earlier stages of the negotiation. Sometimes the negotiation process serves to wear them down; it could be that other options they thought they had dissolved or that the time and energy spent negotiating would be better spent elsewhere, so they conclude the deal. Sometimes circumstances change over the duration of the negotiation, throwing up more options or alternatives and therefore influencing the flow of events.

Under great pressure some have even been known to capitulate and forget their break point altogether. How many times have you heard of people who have come out of an auction having paid far more than the limit they had set themselves because they got caught up in the heat of the moment?

In practice

- Remember you are negotiating with a person, not a company, and each will carry a set of circumstances that will be unique to them;
- Assess where their break point is by examining previous agreements (if you have dealt with them before), researching the market and speaking to competitors;
- Identify the issues of high value to them and try to establish the issues in which they are prepared to be more flexible;
- One way of working out your own break point is to define your Best Alternative to a Negotiated Agreement (BATNA); and
- Test your own assumptions by stating them as facts and waiting for their response.

6. Listening and interpreting the meaning behind the words

There is so much to be learned through what we see and hear. The phrase "getting into their head" has as much to do with getting *out* of our own head. Rather than concentrating on our own thoughts and feelings, we need to consciously turn our attentions to theirs.

Watch them, watch for the signals. This can include phrases such as, "Well that wasn't as much as we were hoping for," or "I can't go that far," or "I was looking for a higher figure," all of which suggest they are in the process of revising their expectations.

Listening to what the other party says is only part of the skill involved in reading and understanding them. Look for inconsistencies in the way they attempt to justify their position. The more they talk, the weaker they are feeling. If they start to sell the benefits of their offer during the negotiation, they are feeling weak. Remember that the same will apply in the way they read your behavior.

- **Establish how firm their offer or proposal is.** Try to observe the "soft exposing giveaways:" "I was looking for around $500, if that sounds OK?" This is not a firm offer; it's a very obvious example of someone feeling uncomfortable tabling their opening offer. Often we are given less obvious hints, yet there can still be clues within how their proposal is stated. Try to listen for what is said and how it is said.
- **Focus on listening to the questions asked.** For example, if they ask you if it is available today, or if you can pay cash, rather than simply answering those questions, you should think about *why* they are asking such a question, and perhaps ask in return why this is important to them. If you are wrapped up in your own head, then you will miss the opportunity to qualify the things that are important to them.
- **Once you have listened, stop, and interpret what the information offers.** This should be before you feel obliged to respond. For many, the time taken feels uncomfortable, but the new information needs time to be considered. If they are selling and are opening with $500, where might their break point be? Think about this before you respond. The ability to actively listen for information that may help progress the negotiation, rather than using the time available to think about what you want to say next, leans heavily on the negotiator's trait of curiosity (trait 7, Personal Relationships, Chapter 4).

In practice

- As a Complete Skilled Negotiator, understanding their position, priorities, interests, pressures, and needs is a critical part of your job.
- The value of listening is far greater than that which can be achieved by what you have to say.
- Listen and interpret their true position: How much do they need this deal? How many options do they really have? How dependent are they on an early decision?
- Think about *why* they are asking a particular question and ask in return why this is important to them.
- Actively listen for information that will help you to progress the negotiation, rather than thinking about what you want to say next.

7. Planning and preparing using all information available

There is a direct correlation between successful negotiations, however measured, and the time invested in preparation. Planning can be as simple as building an agenda, or as complex as managing many stakeholders involved in multiple negotiations around the world requiring a detailed strategy and tactical analysis for all concerned. It is important to emphasize just how critical planning is as a discipline and as a behavior, as so few managers I have met take enough time to plan properly, taking the attitude that they can still perform without it. (This is explored in greater depth in Chapter 11, "Planning and Preparation that Helps You Build Value.")

Insight, options, confidence, direction, knowledge, and control can all be gained from preparation using all available information. An attitude of familiarity with the situation or relationship can result in no or poor preparation. You should never "wing it." We all work under pressure and the task of planning can often be minimized or even forgotten in favor of "more urgent" tasks. You need to take the time to plan. It has been proven time after time that effective negotiators plan in advance.

You should plan:

- what questions to ask;
- what position or statement to open with;
- what type of agenda to use;
- how to present your opening position;
- how to respond;
- what information they will need;
- when and where the meeting will be held;
- who needs to be involved; and
- when will discussions commence, and much more.

Some negotiations can take weeks or even months of preparation. When the stakes are high, each and every possibility should be considered. Even routine negotiations should be given as long as necessary to work through the issues, values, and possibilities. Your planning should help you develop insight, options, confidence, and structure. All of this will help you take more control of your negotiation.

THE POSITIVE EFFECT OF METICULOUS PLANNING

Paul, the General Manager of Paris Hotel, Bernard Jean Lucrecci, was asked to take responsibility and manage the lighting upgrade required throughout the hotel. The move to LED lighting through the 300 bedroom hotel was in line with the hotel's sustainability strategy, which impacted on its rating and was a key focus of the owners. There was also pressure on energy costs and the refit offered an estimated electricity cost saving of 175,000 euros a year. The Hotel Bernard Jean Lucrecci had contracted with their own electrical contractor two years earlier, a five-year contract giving all electrical works, maintenance, and upgrades to Genite Elec. The specification and proposal had been received by Paul, which came to 1m

Euros. This was no surprise; however, the 18-month work completion timeframe offer, access requirements, and in some cases compromises on lighting levels due to the shift to LED, highlighted the need for subsequent negotiations. Genite Elec was a mid-sized company run by the two Genite brothers. Their work was well regarded with health and safety always the top criteria, which is part of how they came to win the original contract. Paul and his team decided to take a day out to better understand the Genite Elec business, how many clients it now served, what contracts they had secured, what this contract would mean to them, employee numbers, etc. During this time, they designed a three-phase strategy for negotiating the 1m Euro contract. A first meeting was called to discuss the proposal. In this phase both brothers attended the meeting at the Hotel and Paul stated that unless the work could be completed in four months, he would put the contract for the lighting upgrade out to tender. Genite responded by referencing the contract they already had with the hotel, which meant that was not possible. Paul simply shrugged his shoulders, referenced the owners' wishes and told them to think about it. Although not happy, Hotel Bernard Jean Lucrecci was still their client, so they needed to maintain respect for the conversation. As planned, a week later they met again, this time the brothers focused on the five-year contract that stated they held the right to all electrical works and maintenance. Paul, as planned moved to his 2nd phase by outlining the start date, if they wanted the work, the payment terms for this specific piece of work, again different from the umbrella contract, and the specification required for the banqueting rooms, which was higher than that stated on the proposal. . .for the same total cost. Frustrations were starting to show as the brothers felt that Paul was being irrational and was acting outside of the contract

(*Continued*)

(Continued)

that had already been agreed. Meanwhile, Paul had two competitor proposals in hand as his BATNA's. Ten days later, a third meeting was called. Paul opened the meeting by referencing the two other offers he had. He then went on to describe how strong the relationship with Genite Elec had been and that by reallocating their team of electricians onto this contract, the timescales were achievable. He then offered to extend the remaining three-year contract back out to five years, effectively adding a further two-year commitment if they were able to start the work within two months and finish within six. He had never intended to outsource the work but felt he needed the power from somewhere to motivate the Genite brothers to be more responsive. This was not a case of price issue but of lead times and specification. The Genite brothers agreed to the terms. Paul had employed a three-stage approach, which finally secured the commitment he needed, even if it meant stating options that he knew he could not easily carry out.

Having advised through this negotiation, I observed many hours of time and effort that went into the preparation, including what could be said and what could not be said at each meeting. This ultimately resulted in a re-drawing of the contract that traded off improved terms for The Genite brothers in return for the critical timings required by Hotel Bernard Jean Lucrecci. In turn, this enabled the hotel to initiate a Marketing campaign based on their sustainability credentials.

In practice

- The time to start getting into their head is during your preparation;
- Focus your attention on each variable you are likely to discuss and be precise about the information you need or questions you plan to ask;
- Keep a record to simplify future planning;

- Involve others in your preparation – it will strengthen your discipline to plan in the first place, as well as keeping you grounded and objective in your assessments;
- Plan the agenda and map out the variables you can employ; and
- Ensure you understand the values of the tradeoffs involved against each of the variables from inside their head.

8. Questioning effectively

In March 2007, a senior government official in the UK confessed that his biggest regret was not challenging the assumptions being made about the existence of weapons of mass destruction prior to the invasion of Iraq. He admitted that more questions could have prompted more answers, which may have altered the course of history.

The following approach, **STROB** (Scope, Terms, Risk, Options, Barriers), enables you to plan out how you can extract more information than might otherwise be forthcoming. It helps you to create five open-ended questions enabling you to open up or expand your knowledge and understanding:

1. Examine broadening the **SCOPE** of the agreement as part of broadening or narrowing your relationship. This could include considering the longevity of the relationship, dependency, risk, or other factors, which create greater scope for maximizing value.
2. List the **TERMS** you think will feature and their relative value to them. This could include their basic requirements, issues, or could be related to how the individual negotiator will be measured.
3. List any issues they or you may regard as **RISK** related. This could include timescales, third-party relationships, market assumptions, etc.
4. List any/all of the **OPTIONS** you believe they may have if your negotiations run into difficulties. In the event of deadlock what would they do?
5. List the potential **BARRIERS**, issues, or objections that are likely to be presented.

The **STROB** technique is used by converting your questions into order of importance, listing your top ten, and using these during the exploratory phase of your discussions.

For example, making use of "what if" questions to establish how the other party might respond to different scenarios and their attitude to risk can help during your exploratory meetings. They can also be used to help identify priorities and the value the other party places on certain issues. "What if we order 50,000?" "What if we order 100,000?" "So what if we order 600,000 then?" – these are questions that will help you to understand the economies of volume. Taken a step further, you can begin to question timings, payment terms, and all other variables with "what ifs" to help establish how their cost base is made up, what is easier for them to agree on, and where flexibility lies within their list of interests.

As the Complete Skilled Negotiator, you will have the confidence to be flexible and to use a combination of questioning styles in order to extract the most useful information (see the following box).

QUESTION TYPES

Contact questions help you to establish rapport: "How have you been since we last met? Did you have a good holiday? How is business?"

- **Probing questions** help you to seek further information: "What do you think about your competitor's latest activities?"
- **Interrogative questions** help you to encourage them to think about solutions for themselves: "Why is that important to you?"
- **Comparative questions** help you to explore in detail: "What has business been like since the introduction of product A? How have things changed since your new promotion began?"
- **Extension questions** to challenge: "How do you mean? How else could we do that? What are you thinking of specifically? What do you mean when you say . . .? How can you be sure of that?"

- **Opinion seeking questions** to test their knowledge and thinking: "How do you feel about . . .? What do you think about . . .? What are your views on . . .?"
- **Hypothetical questions** help you to test their knowledge and thinking: "What if we were to order 500 units? What if we included all the costs? What if I paid you in advance?"
- **Reflective/summary questions** to draw ideas together and test their understanding, and to summarize what has been said: "So, you think that we need to introduce this new range? You think that the product will achieve X? As I understand it, you reckon that you can deliver it?"
- **Closing questions** help you to secure agreement: "When should we start – during May or at the beginning of June? I can deliver on the first or second week of that month; which would suit you best? How much?"
- **Mirror questions** serve to reverse the question and confirm the point: "We think we can deliver this for you. You think you can deliver this?"
- **Leading questions** help you to secure a desired answer. "You can't deny that . . .? Isn't it a fact that . . .? You wouldn't say that . . .? It's a great offer, isn't it?"
- **Rhetorical questions** help you to prevent them from saying anything: questions that do not require an answer: "Do we really want to do that? And how did that happen?" *Implying that you already know.*
- **Multiple questions** help you to gain agreement to a package: "You did say that you could meet the deadline? Oh, and you will meet our specification and, ah, by the way, you can do this for us can't you?"
- **Closed questions** help you to establish specific facts and information: "Will you do this? Have you the ability to deliver? Can you meet our requirements? Do you need help with this offer?"

In practice

- Use the STROB technique to put your questions into order of importance;
- Make a conscious effort to work on the different questioning types in order to maintain control;
- If they are reluctant to answer, try asking your question in a different way;
- Be careful to avoid being seen as interrogating – you're likely to attract suspicion and resistance; and
- Also be wary that you can sometimes give away your own interests unintentionally by the way you ask questions.

9. Trading concessions effectively and conditionally

Every trade you make should be considered and conditional.

The aim of trading is to build more value for your business as a result of each trade. As there are no rules in negotiation, you can, in theory, offer anything that has a value to them, providing it is a reciprocated move. Whatever they want, they can have, in return for something you want. Each trade then should be designed to provide you with a net gain. In practice you will, of course, want to weigh any variable traded as the implications of trading it may be broader than simply its financial value.

In the case of a football club buying an international footballer in the transfer market about to move clubs. The negotiation involves the player's agent and the chairman of the football club. The agenda consists of a transfer fee, a signing on fee, length of contract, salary and bonuses, and a range of performance-related incentives and obligations the player has to meet. Variables could also include the phasing of payments in relation to appearances, number of goals scored, or whether they appear for their country. Each variable will feature as part of a set of conditional trade-offs. The club, having chosen their player, wants to ensure that they get maximum value from their services. Meanwhile the player may be looking for maximum income or flexibility within the contract, known as "personal terms." Each of the variables can be adjusted as part of the negotiation that follows, and the process involved is that of trading concessions.

When trading concessions you therefore need to identify through your planning and questioning what is important to them. This will help you to build proposals involving concessions that are the least cost to you but represent a greater value to them. In return, your condition is that they provide movement that improves the value of the deal for you. This sounds rational, fair, and transparent but usually it's not, in that what they offer will be no more than they absolutely have to and usually this is something of minimum cost to them.

Understanding the implications of their offer is critical if you are to assess what you want in return. Your creativity can work wonders when you move away from price only and focus on total cost or total value.

You can only trade effectively when you understand or gauge the value of an issue in their terms. Part of this you may know from understanding your market, and part may be from any history you may have with the other party. Remember, low cost and high value trade-offs should be worked through as part of your preparations before negotiating begins. Work out the trades. Work out your potential moves. Remember, generosity engenders greed. Nothing is free in this world, and if you start providing unconditional trades, the other party will either get suspicious or become just plain greedy.

In practice

- Identify what is important to the other party through your planning and questioning;
- Build proposals that involve concessions of least cost to you, but greater value to them;
- Use "What if . . .?" questions to explore the value and measure reactions to particular suggestions;

- Place your condition first, rather than the concession (i.e., "If you . . . then we . . .") as they will be less likely to interrupt you in order to hear what's it in for them; and
- Be creative when identifying options for trading – change the shape of the deal rather than focusing on what can't be done.

10. Applying analytical skills to manage the value of the deal as the negotiation unfolds

As a negotiation unfolds, the total value or cost of a deal often becomes more complex as the number of issues increase. This especially includes negotiations that involve a number of interrelated variables; each of which need to be agreed on and many of which will be interrelated. Let's say you are agreeing on a contract that involves office furniture. There are a range of issues you need to agree on. You make a proposal that consists of the shortening of payment terms in return for a lower up-front payment or deposit. In being able to track the progress of your negotiation you need to understand the cost or value of each variable to both you and the other party.

You need to calculate the saving for them if payment is settled over a shorter period of time and how they will value a lower deposit, sometimes literally as the negotiation is unfolding. Of course, this goes hand in hand with understanding these values or costs from your own perspective. Using your analytical skills enables you to understand the implications of their response and work out what your next proposal might be:

> "We will accept the lower deposit subject to you reducing your payment schedule from your proposed 12 months to 9 months."

How would this affect the total value of the agreement? Should you now park this issue and examine how other terms can be introduced as part of the conversation?

Understanding the implications of trades is critical to working through possibilities and opportunities as we effectively "engineer the deal." That is not to say that you have to be lightning quick with figures or that you have to be highly analytical to work through more complex agreements. You simply have to ensure that, through the time you take or the way you delegate or automate (sometimes using spreadsheets) such activities, you are clear about the decisions you are making.

The less tangible an issue is, the more difficult it can be to value the trade. Some examples might be:

- the changing of opt-out clauses;
- agreement to a testimonial recommendation;
- flexibility in completion dates; or
- the offer of exclusivity.

Understanding how to value these types of implications within an agreement is important if you are to trade them effectively. The cost may be little to you and yet hold a significant value to the other party.

During your negotiations, track your and their proposals by documenting them so you can monitor each issue's progress and movement. Track what their last proposal was and how the value of the deal equates for you. Make use of spreadsheets to analyze "what if" scenarios and for tracking proposals, especially when it's an existing contract being renegotiated and the issues under review are consistent.

If, despite this, you struggle with the figures, take your time. Take time out or take someone with you to the negotiation as your "figures person." If you become wrapped up in figures, you will not be in control of the negotiation. If you don't understand the figures, you are in danger of agreeing to something that may prove regrettable.

In the commercial arena, you are negotiating over resources, interests, priorities, preferences, even prejudices. There is a broad range of both tangible and intangible issues, all of which carry a perception of value. Then, of course, there is the money. If you are not aware of the consequences of your proposals, then you are not in control. Make it your business to qualify the worth of all the issues under discussion that you are responsible for negotiating.

In practice

- Ensure that you understand the implications of the other party's response in order to work out what your next proposal might be;
- Track your and the other party's proposals so that you can monitor each issue's progress and movement;
- If you struggle with figures, take your time, or ensure you take someone as your "figures person;" and
- Make it your business to qualify the worth of all the issues under discussion.

11. Creating and maintaining the appropriate climate for trust

This is critical if the other party is to accept your ideas as being genuinely collaborative and to consider the options you bring to the table. Remember, you are responsible for their feelings and the atmosphere during the negotiation. If they do not feel the ideas being tabled are in the interest of mutual progress, they simply will not entertain them.

Where real or perceived conflict of interests exists, trust can be difficult to come by as each party gravitates toward protecting its own interests. The other party may not be as open-minded as you or the balance of power (being in their favor) may mean that they do not need to be so. It takes two to tango. If they want to hard bargain, you must be prepared to backtrack and adjust your strategy. Drive at a broader agenda with the aim of building a sustainable agreement rather than engaging in a bruising battle over price.

In a sustainable relationship (9–12 o'clock on the clock face) it is critical to maintain a basis where constructive dialogue can take place without suspicion or the need to compete. Being cooperative, presenting creative proposals and using statements that help progress rather than antagonize discussions, requires humility, a broader perspective and an acceptance of the longer-term benefits that a relationship based on trust and respect will bring.

At 4 o'clock on the clock face you are hard bargaining and are without relationship constraints – you can be tough. However, when there is a high level of dependency between you, you not only need to be cooperative but should recognize what cooperation provides: a basis for creating more value. Your plan to maximize profits remains the same. The way you achieve this is by working with the other party, and changes as you move around to beyond 6 o'clock.

To gain trust, you have to earn it and this takes time and patience. One way to help achieve this during meetings is by offering information in a controlled and considered manner. The act of sharing information is important to both parties, as it demonstrates that you are prepared to be open and therefore, by implication, to be trusted. Therefore you need to organize and manage what information you are prepared to offer. This is an important part of any negotiator's preparation.

Creating the appropriate climate for trust may require you to do something or be someone you are not. This is where the "conscious negotiator" comes into their own. They recognize the egos involved, recognize how the other party wants to be treated, and present a cooperative front. They attack the problems and not the people by ensuring the climate in the room remains conducive to building the agreements.

In practice

- Trust takes time to build so patience is needed; yet it can be destroyed in a moment if you cross the other party;
- Offer information in a controlled and considered manner to demonstrate that you are prepared to be open and can be trusted; and
- Drive at a broader agenda with the aim of building a sustainable agreement rather than engaging in a bruising battle over price.

12. Developing and using your agenda to help control the negotiation proceedings

The agenda is effectively a working document for all parties involved, which helps to shape and control negotiation proceedings. It is there to provide transparency around those negotiable variables that will contribute toward the total value of the agreement.

Further, agreeing on an agenda before the meeting helps ensure that it is "owned" by all involved. Agreeing on the agenda alone can sometimes require a negotiation in itself. If you impose an agenda on the other party, they are more likely to be dismissive and challenging of the issues. Ultimately, both parties agree that all items in need of consideration are listed and agree that all parties will work from it.

Imagine contracting with a PR firm. Having narrowed down the options to the final two firms, you decide to enter into negotiations to find out from where you are most likely to attract the greatest value. Now, PR at the best of times is a challenging service to measure. However, the basic terms of any agreement will need to feature as part of your agenda. This could include:

- a retainer fee;
- notice period;
- length of contract;
- range of services;
- PR training provided;
- contact requirements; and
- payment terms.

Already we have seven issues to be discussed on the agenda and from these there will be further issues relating to performance, compliance, and risks linked to each of these seven. The broader the agenda, the more comprehensive your considerations, and the greater the scope for shaping the deal and ultimately building a higher value agreement.

Some parties choose to outline their entire offer from the outset. Some tendering processes demand your opening position across all variables. Even though you may be in possession of this information you need not be drawn into responding to them all at once. Try to trade off no more than three issues at a time. Any more makes it difficult for them to calculate and, worse still, confusing to understand.

Watch out for hidden agenda points or "red herrings" introduced by the other party with the aim of trading off against them. In doing so, they expect to gain some leverage on issues that are important to them. Where new issues appear on the agenda, set out to qualify their legitimacy. Conversely you may choose to let the other party win some of the lower-cost issues and gain the leverage you need to secure those issues that are both important and of high value to you.

Even if you list a draft agenda on a flip chart in the room minutes before your meeting, you have created the illusion that you are prepared. This provides a basis to explore the variables that will need to be agreed to with the other party in a more collaborative manner.

In practice

- The broader the agenda, the greater scope there is for shaping the deal;
- Aim to trade off no more than three issues at a time;
- Watch out for hidden agenda points or "red herrings" introduced by the other party with the aim of trading off against them;
- Position price, fee, or cost about halfway down your agenda – too early and it can promote unnecessary friction; too late and it could limit room for maneuver; and
- If you are going to "lose" or concede on an issue, then trade it conditionally and reluctantly – if it is truly important to the other party, they may give ground to secure it.

13. Thinking creatively to develop proposals that help move the deal forward

Thinking creatively – that is to say thinking around the issues and possibilities that might not have been considered or traded before – can move the negotiation forwards. Picture yourself as a sculptor: designing, forming, shaping in an artistic manner. Stand back and examine your progress from different angles and perspectives. You are involved in carving out something of much greater value than the sum total of the materials involved. The creative negotiator interprets the possibilities before them and regards the challenge in hand as one of creating value.

In an online consumer situation, for example, you are usually presented with pages of terms and conditions that consumers are unlikely to ever read. They are presented as a "take it or leave it" contract offering most with little real choice. However, in business, the same tactics are employed by procurement teams who often miss the opportunity to negotiate around terms more creatively in order to optimize value.

An English sparkling wine company was raising funds through a crowd-funding scheme, offering a return on investment through a five-year bond, with "fixed terms and conditions" attached.

As expected, I received the standard terms and conditions. It consisted of four pages of text in font size 6. The assumption was that I would not read it and that the terms were a given. It covered everything from liabilities, confidentiality, payment terms, contract amendments, copyright protection, and so on. From this, I identified 23 variables (apart from price) that I decided to discuss – some offering the potential for more flexibility and some for opportunity (for example, increased investment stake at a later stage).

The company owner agreed to a meeting. At first the owner was hesitant to engage. I am sure he had had easier conversations with other investors. However, after agreeing on the first two conditional trades, the conversation continued. The agreement we struck through some creative trade-offs offered me a deal that I was truly married to by the time I had finished and an opportunity for the sparkling wine company to sell their wines through another business I was involved in.

Sometimes you just have to tell the other party what is important; otherwise you are not providing them with the opportunity to make things possible. Detailed exploratory discussions can offer tremendous opportunities to build agendas, which reflect every part of the deal including the risks, performance, compliance, quality, opportunity, communication, and many other important components of the relationship.

The ability to remain open-minded and use creative or lateral thinking during negotiation is difficult for many people. It is competitiveness, pride, a need to maintain face, and even ego that prevents many from being open. This result can be a dogmatic approach aimed at minimizing risk and sometimes "winning."

In negotiation the lateral thinking patterns associated with creativity are at direct odds with those emotions experienced during moments of perceived conflict. Where conflict exists, we are more inclined to batten down the hatches and are more likely to focus on protecting our position. By adopting a mindset driven by "under what circumstances" we become much more able to explore and be creative rather than being bound by insecurity.

In practice

- Understand what is really important to them and why;
- Differentiate the people from the issues;
- Extend your mutual agenda to create more possible variables;
- Consider any risks involved and trade these off where possible; and
- Identify low-cost, high-value trade-off opportunities.

14. Exploring options to help gain agreement

Try to resist the temptation to say no. The challenges and frustrations presented in negotiations are there to test us. Deadlock is an option but only after every possible option has been exhausted. Where peace talks can take years, merger and acquisition negotiations months, the work involved in searching for common areas where agreement can be struck comes from the persistence of those involved. There has to be a belief that there is a solution to be found. The trait of tenacity (Chapter 4) helps the Complete Skilled Negotiator to explore options continuously, keep the agreement and relationships on track, and deliver the possible deal from what once seemed, at best, unlikely.

Although it's appropriate to remain on your guard, if you are able to park your suspicion and search for alternatives and other conditional options, you will surprise yourself at just how many times a last-minute solution can be found. By seeing the whole picture and the possible links that can be made, you can introduce possibilities and explore options that you may not have considered before.

Consider the merger of two software companies and it's a week before the final deadline. Documents are due to be signed, yet conversations are continuing over the management structure of the new enlarged business. Both CEOs believe they have the credentials to lead and could best serve the new larger group.

This leads to a deadlock situation, placing the merger at risk. Identifying with this situation, the advisory broker introduces a facilitator to "help identify a solution," who starts by saying, "I respect what you both feel, what may be at stake here, and the extent to which your respective companies will be looking for reassurances. However, if we are not able to resolve this issue, everyone will lose. It is your responsibility to explore options and identify a solution for the greater good. Can we agree on that to start with?"

They did. The situation was complicated. There were careers at stake. A list of interests were drawn up. None were financial. With interests revealed and both parties prepared for the better good to work on their interests rather than against the other, a deal was struck. One took up the role of Chairman and the other CEO. Egos were the issue and packages were used to overcome the impasse.

In practice

- Convert thoughts of "No," "Can't," or "Won't" into "HOW," no matter how frustrating this might feel at first;
- Take time to explore options and continuously consider the deal from their perspective;
- Use "positive energy" rather than "defensive energy" to explore options;
- Make use of the planning tools in Chapter 9 to help visualize possible or different relationships between the issues; and
- Ask the question "under what circumstances could we bridge the difference?"

- The 14 behaviors offer a framework for The Complete Skilled Negotiator to develop and perform across all types of negotiations effectively. The more conscious you become at using these skills, where appropriate, the more likely you are to optimize your negotiation opportunities.

NOW DO THIS!

- Work out what your behavioral strengths are and compensate for those that do not come naturally.
- Plan and prepare (number 7) it's the most important activity you will undertake so do it and don't "wing it."
- Be flexible and adapt to your situation.
- Be clear in your mind about what you are trying to achieve and the different ways of arriving there.
- Understand what patience, nerve, and power mean to you before you engage in your negotiations.

CHAPTER 8

The "E" Factor

"During a negotiation, it would be wise not to take anything personally. If you leave personalities out of it, you will be able to see opportunities more objectively."

— Brian Koslow

THE EFFECT OF HUMAN EMOTION ON NEGOTIATION

"How difficult can negotiation be? It's not rocket science." No, it is not. I would argue that it is more complex because it involves the most unpredictable of entities: human beings. You. And you are unique as is every human being, meaning there is no one piece of advice that will suit all. "Emotion," derived from the Latin word movere, meaning "to move" is fitting in that it is emotion that motivates us to act and move from our existing stance both in and out of negotiations. These "moves" often make negotiation highly unpredictable. The impact that this has on the dynamics found in negotiation is what I've defined as the "E" factor. Negotiators who are less self-aware struggle to control their emotions and, as a result, become readable and transparent to other negotiators. The more balanced, controlled, clearer thinkers use the "E" factor to their advantage, like seasoned poker players.

You can never assume the reaction you are going to attract when tabling a proposal, especially when it's not one they are expecting. So the "E" in

"E" factor is, you guessed it, *emotion*. It is a conscious state that allows you to manage, use, manipulate, understand, and control it, so we start with understanding what these "feelings" are going to do for you.

The Complete Skilled Negotiator develops an eye for watching your every action and reaction as they gauge what is really going on inside your head.

Experienced negotiators:

- are conscious of what they are looking for;
- are calm and patient in their thought processes;
- are aware of the sensitivities in play; and
- send you the messages they *want* you to read.

One interpretation on this is; am I describing stoicism? As Leonard Mlodinow writes in his book *Emotional: How Feelings Shape Our Thinking*, Stoics should not be psychologically enslaved to their emotions; don't be manipulated by them, be actively in command. But who can possibly live their life with the stress of being without emotion? Emotion matters as does your awareness as to how it will impact you.

Because every action emotionally charged or otherwise attracts a reaction. Trained negotiators work hard at calculating how you will react to certain actions, and which signal to send that will most likely influence you during your negotiations.

No matter how many tactics, strategies, or variables are in play, it is you who will make the decisions and it is you who will need to understand; in particular, how to behave in the heat of the moment. Unlike an engine, which is mechanically predictable and responds each and every time to the push of a throttle, negotiation and, importantly, you are not.

Negotiation requires an attitude of mind based on emotional self-discipline and self-control. In an age of greater awareness of mental health issues, how can I possibly advocate putting your emotions to one side simply to be a better negotiator? What makes good negotiators into Complete Skilled Negotiators is that they not only execute negotiations using skills, tactics, and strategies but also employ the attitudes and emotions, hidden or otherwise, like wearing a coat. You simply put it on when you need to use it then take it off when you don't. So I am not suggesting that you change who you are, simply that you do what is necessary in the moment. Like many professional sportspeople who exercise a skill for the moment which they would not use in their everyday life or may not reflect who they are but to perform, they recognize that some disciplines have to be adhered to.

It is emotional control that allows for clear thoughts, judgments, motivation, and decision making. Behavioral control, mental control, and emotional detachment are all needed to get inside the other party's head. But this is not easy when you are challenged with irrational behavior, a lack of trust for others who appear to be manipulating power.

Many negotiation decisions in business are still emotionally influenced, even during sizeable complex deals. I am also not suggesting that deals take place without careful diligence or clear criteria and analysis. What I am suggesting from observation is that during negotiations, proposals and considerations are not always dealt with in the objective manner you might expect because those carrying the consequences of the outcome will feel something about what is happening. Emotion and ego, as well as enterprise, have a significant role in influencing how decisions are taken.

The role of emotion

Emotion has its place when used in a considered and controlled manner:

- when the risks have been considered (walk out, outburst, deadlock);
- when its purpose is to attract a desired reaction; and
- when the seriousness of the issue needs conveying and you are confident that you will not ruin the chances of progress.

There is nothing wrong with a display of emotion during a negotiation, provided it is designed for effect and premeditated. The outburst in the middle of the meeting with a threat to walk away from the deal may appear irrational and hot-headed, but if the action were premeditated and the drama designed to attract a back-down from the other party, the emotional display can serve a useful purpose. This level of risk needs, however, to be a thought-through decision and one that is designed to attract a calculated response in an orchestrated manner. The real risks arise when we allow our decision making to be dictated by our own emotions, and we start reacting to their demands without thinking.

Understanding our emotions

Essentially, the emotion experienced by many in negotiation comes from uncertainty, risk, desire, and even fear: emotions that we have lived with for millions of years. But today we experience the types of dangers and risks that trigger these emotions less frequently than our ancestors and, more often than not, in a psychological context rather than in the physical form. As a result, we are less practiced and equipped to cope, meaning that even low levels of uncertainty for some can feel quite uncomfortable. For any emotionally driven negotiator, this can lead to inappropriate decision making and sub-optimized deals, which is why an understanding of these emotions is important as part of your make-up as a negotiator.

The emotions of fear, hope, anger, envy, and greed resonate in us as strongly today as they ever have. Today there are ever more psychological models available to help us define what drives emotion, how people cope with it and the effect that it will have on you. Yet, when faced with confrontation over a price increase in a negotiation, are we any more able to cope with what this does to our thinking and ability to perform? The answer is: only through greater levels of self-awareness and control.

Negotiation is uncomfortable and, when negotiating on behalf of your business, you are effectively being paid to be uncomfortable. If you concede unnecessarily or capitulate on a deal, you are effectively buying your own comfort which may not sit comfortably with those you are negotiating on behalf of.

THE TELL-TALE SIGNS OF STRESS

The pressures and stress that you experience in negotiation, however mild, are difficult to suppress and have their way of showing themselves through your physical actions. The stress you experience when tabling or rejecting proposals can start to exhibit itself through your body language. The act of touching your face, scratching your nose, brushing your hands through your hair, tapping your pen, folding your arms, or tapping your feet when making a proposal are all behavior changes, and will be seen by the other party who will be watching for them. You may not even be aware of it. Most are not. However, the other person will be watching every move you make. Whether they mean anything or not is unimportant. For now, you need to understand that the other party is watching.

More experienced negotiators learn to adapt to becoming more comfortable with being uncomfortable. This is achieved through heightened levels of self-awareness and becoming experienced in doing what is necessary from an objective standpoint, rather than allowing themselves to be victims of their emotion.

If you witness negotiators exhibiting these fidgety types of behaviors it may well mean nothing, other than an adjustment of their position. Body language, and its meanings, tend only to be relevant when change, speed, or the timing of movement correlates with something that has happened. If the other party responds to your proposal immediately, insisting that they will not or cannot accept the offer, observe their physical behavior as they respond. It is likely there will be some emotion involved. It is possible they mean it but it is also possible that they don't. Look for a correlation in body language or facial expressions if there is more than one of them negotiating. This is usually most recognizable when they are stating a position, rejecting a position, or making a statement.

- Listen to what they are saying, the way they are saying it, and what they do not say.
- Listen to whether they justify what they are saying.
- Listen to whether they go on to sell what they have just said.

The Complete Skilled Negotiator will see, hear, read, and interpret the meaning behind this as part of getting inside the other party's head.

If you, or those who negotiate on your behalf, experience high levels of anxiety, the resulting agreements are more likely to be compromised. The stress and anxiety of the process can lead you to concede or conclude agreements too early. Negotiating effectively requires nerve, as well as a mindset that recognizes it is not personal, it is business. Negotiators I have worked with who appear at least to have high levels of emotional control will and can mentally separate the people they negotiate with from the business of working on the deal.

WHEN THERE IS A NEED FOR A COLLABORATIVE SOLUTION

Partway through a negotiation involving the fees, specification, and timescales of an outsourced technology solution, the procurement team became frustrated at a lack of certainty, clarity, and absolute commitment to timescales. The "AGILE" system for managing the project offered the supplier more flexibility and less accountability to finish within the agreed specific timescales. The procurement team decided to impose penalty clauses in the event that the solution was not operational within six months. The clauses emphasized the importance of the timescales, transferred some of the implications of non-delivery, and promoted a more formal relationship.

Meanwhile, an internal agreement was being crafted between the finance and IT function of the same business. This, however, was an internal negotiation. A project involving the configuration of an online analytics tool used to measure sales conversion rates throughout the sales cycle was behind schedule. The CTO, ultimately responsible, remained evasive around the project completion dates. The CFO could not directly introduce penalty clauses within his own company and yet needed greater certainty from the CTO. He was an internal client. He needed a long-term collaborative relationship with his colleagues in technology, so rather than making threats he engaged in a meeting to better understand their short-term challenges. He approached the issues from the perspective of how and under what circumstances the deadlines might be met in a problem-solving manner. Ultimately the CFO then negotiated with marketing, asking them to agree to a four-week slippage on their website project (releasing the same programmers as needed for his project) for a relaxation on their budget phasing, which he knew was under severe pressure. He presented the new window of opportunity to the CTO, who agreed to meet his more tightly defined timescales.

In the first example, the supplier was expected to take responsibility and be held accountable with commercial implications. In the second example, the attitude adopted was to work with those involved, both in technology and marketing to question, listen, understand, and then propose solutions that helped to get the collaborative result needed. He had relationships to preserve so he adopted a collaborative, problem-solving stance.

CONSCIOUS COMPETENT

Any negotiator must become conscious of their own incompetency's before the development of the new skills or learning can begin. As you become more aware of specific negotiation skills and the effect they have on output, you will also grow a greater awareness of your own "development opportunities." The following model relates to four psychological states involved in progressing from incompetence to competence in a skill. The key to becoming more effective as a negotiator is to become a "conscious competent," by being able to consciously and competently to perform a skill or ability (see Figure 8.1).

The advanced state of "unconscious competence" has its own handicap in that you tend to assume too much based on previous experience. So remaining in the "conscious competent" state for the purpose of negotiating is highly appropriate. Never assume anything in negotiation.

The Unconscious Incompetent Negotiator When you are unaware of what and how you need to perform so are vulnerable.	**The Conscious Incompetent Negotiator** When you are aware of what you could or might be doing but still have yet to perform to your potential.
The Conscious Competent Negotiator When you perform in your negotiations with absolute focus and without taking anything for granted.	**The Unconscious Competent Negotiator** When you perform in your negotiation but can be prone to being too familiar resulting in allowing too many assumptions.

Figure 8.1 The four stages of competence.

BROKEN RECORD

The entrepreneur we were talking to leaned across the table with his advisors by his side and said once more "the price for the business is $200,000,000." It was the fourth time in 15 minutes the price was iterated, which was consistent with the pre-negotiation communication that had taken place. Our agenda included phasing, performance triggers, warranties, and the realization of the existing product pipeline. The technology on offer was worth it but we needed more certainty around the "total opportunity." I said, "OK, its $200,000,000 now let's discuss the terms as we have outlined associated with this number." My client could afford it and would have paid considerably more but I concluded that the sellers had a number in their head, were sticking to it like a broken record, and if we wanted to progress we had to park the price issue. The number was staying and the more it was stated the more credible it became. Once more the number was stated, this time as the minimum acceptable. We offered $100,000,000 in cash, $50,000,000 in shares in the larger buying company, and £50,000,000 on delivery of the new product pipeline due within six months. There were about 20 other smaller details involved at this stage, but we were trying to say yes to the number whilst managing some of the risk. Three days later we reconvened. The broken record returned, this time with $200,000,000 in cash. He then agreed that he would continue to work in the business until the new product pipeline was released. The broken record had taken hold. During the three days the buyers concentrated on raising the funds fearing that the deal was slipping away. Eventually $160,000,000 was paid with an exit payment of $40,000,000 on delivery of the new products. The entrepreneur had secured his number, helped partly by the broken record. Like most tactics used in negotiation, they are not right or wrong and may suit some relationships and not others. The choice, circumstances, and consequences remain for you to judge.

BECOMING A CONSCIOUSLY COMPETENT NEGOTIATOR THROUGH UNDERSTANDING TA

Back in the 1950s, Dr. Eric Berne defined the ego states known to us today as transactional analysis (TA). In the book *I'm OK, You're OK*, the author Thomas Harris analyzed Berne's work, which was made up of definitions of ego states and how they affect the way we communicate with each other. These are defined as the roles of:

- parent (critical and nurturing)
- adult
- child (free and adaptive)

These are communication styles that we all use subconsciously whilst communicating with others. Within negotiation, these ego states resonate in the language and behavior used, which can directly impact expectations, respect, irrationality, arrogance, and other attitudes exercised during discussions.

The "parent" ego state

The "parent" ego state is made up of two ego states: the "critical parent" and the "nurturing parent."

The language of the critical parent's ego state is "black and white" or "right and wrong" with very few shades of grey, suggesting that they are in a position to make the rules, judge, and criticize others. However, what is important in your negotiations is that you do not allow such communication to affect the way you read the situation.

In negotiation, some people have been known to use this stance to take control. It can be a difficult force to reason with when they remain inflexible and stubborn, especially when they are negotiating from a position of power. They will know it and will use it, sometimes naturally and sometimes orchestrated, but always aimed at controlling your aspirations.

The "nurturing parent," on the other hand, wants to advise and guide. They want respect and want to be needed. They want to protect, so any "child" showing respect and asking for help is likely to attract a positive response from a nurturing parent. However, they are also at risk of becoming manipulated by those communicating as a "child."

The "child" ego state

The "child" ego state is also made up of two ego states: the "free child" and the "adapted child."

The "free child" is spontaneous, creative, fun-loving in their attitude and communication, whereas the "adapted child" is rebellious, non-compliant, and manipulative ("It's not fair." "See what you've made me do.").

The "child" commonly shirks responsibility, is sometimes manipulative, sometimes subservient, but is always a product of those around them. These behaviors, thoughts, and feelings are replayed from our own childhood and, depending on our circumstances, will feature in how we communicate throughout our lives. This can result in our feeling victimized by the rules that others lay down or underpin our desire to challenge authority.

Responses to ego states

In negotiation, behaving in the "parent" ego state can result in others adopting the behavioral response of a "child" ego state. Where you find yourself negotiating with a "critical parent" character, you may choose instead to appeal to their nurturing parent instinct. Two "parents" clashing is simply two egos

(*Continued*)

vying for control and domination, which will frequently lead to impasse, and the breakdown of the relationship and any pending negotiations.

If you adopt the "child" ego state, you are, of course, effectively manipulating their ego by asking them how they might be able to help you, given your weaker position. There are risks to this, in that they may choose to manipulate the situation even further. However, once the "parent" recognizes that there is no fight to be had, and that you are asking for help, their nurturing ego is triggered and they generally become far more accommodating.

The "adult" ego state

When in our "adult" ego state, we are more able to see people and situations as they are, rather than being intimidated or manipulative. We are more likely to make decisions based on a pragmatic, objective analysis of any given situation, rather than be swayed by the emotional ego that exists in the "child" or "parent" states. If there was a preferred default position from which to negotiate, it would be the "adult" ego state.

Listen and watch out for the behavior of the "black and white," "right and wrong" dominant "parent."

Listen and watch out for the positioning of the "child," who seeks to seduce you, or makes irrational demands, in that they need your help and appeal to your sense of parenting.

The "adult," on the other hand, is objective in thought, can accommodate many shades of grey, can recognize irrational behavior, and sees most types of behavior and language for what they are. They generally operate as conscious competent negotiators.

Clearly, though, this is only an ego state and even "adults" can still be quickly influenced into moving to other ego states during negotiations. Imagine you were challenged on your opening position by a "parent," who tells you how ridiculous you are being, and not to come back until you are prepared to be sensible. The decision here is whether to respond as a "critical parent" and challenge them – with the risk of intensifying the conflict – or adopt the ego state of the "free child" and ask them for help. If you are not sure, you may choose to maintain your composure as an "adult," dismiss their behavior, and wait patiently for them to calm down before continuing. As always, it depends on the circumstances. What is important is that we recognize these states in others as well as ourselves and that we adapt accordingly, rather than continue, oblivious to the emotion influencing the dynamics of the relationship and communication.

The "E" factor can make or break a deal, or the longer-term prospects of a relationship. This makes self-awareness an important part of the Complete Skilled Negotiator's make-up. Those who are successful at negotiating in the long term are more likely to have "adult-to-adult" relationships, although in the real world irrational behavior is in no short supply.

YOUR VALUES

Your personal values and your business values are often remarkably similar. They can be based on such qualities as integrity, honesty, reliability, and others. They provide you with the parameters to judge what you believe is fair, what behavior you find acceptable, and the degree to which you are prepared to allow others to use the power they have during your dealings.

Your values may well provide you with a balance in how you lead your life, how you make decisions, interpret right from wrong, and so on. However, in negotiation, they can often serve to distort your thinking (see behavior 1, Chapter 5). Whether the behavior of the other party is ethical, "fair," or "right" is of little consequence in negotiation. If they have the power and decide to be irrational with it, it is your job to manage the situation as you find it. It is not the time to start making value judgments. Cling to your ideals, and you will become emotionally challenged and compromised.

EMOTIONAL INTELLIGENCE

If there is one critical competency central to effective negotiation, I would suggest it is emotional intelligence. It underpins the balance of communication between you and those you negotiate with and promotes the concept of negotiating from inside their head.

In his 1995 book, *Emotional Intelligence,* Daniel Goleman describes how emotional intelligence is made up of two parts. He claims that to be effective in business, you need to have a high level of self-awareness and self-control around your emotions and those of the other party:

- first, by understanding yourself, your intentions, your responses, and your own behavior;
- second, by understanding others and their feelings.

This is critical in negotiations because you are responsible for the feelings of those you negotiate with. Antagonize the other party and watch any hope of cooperation dissolve. Goleman goes on to describe the five "domains" of emotional intelligence:

1. Knowing your emotions.
2. Managing your own emotions.
3. Motivating yourself.
4. Recognizing and understanding other people's emotions.
5. Managing relationships and the emotions of others.

Extroverts, who tend to be more communicative, tend to be more openly emotional people. They are more inclined to share and articulate their views, likes, and dislikes. However, extroverts are faced with a greater challenge because the control required during a negotiation involves a greater level of self-discipline than it does with introverts, who are naturally more considered in their responses.

Introverts are more inclined to reflect, weigh, and consider before responding.

Imagine watching a film that involves two parties negotiating. The actors are engaged in a negotiation, and one of them is performing so poorly that it starts to make you cringe. "Why did they say that?" "You've just given away your position by saying that." "I would never have responded in that way," you think to yourself.

During negotiation workshops at The Gap Partnership, we often provide challenging case study exercises for individuals and groups to negotiate with each other. The negotiations are recorded on video to help the attendees observe and learn about the appropriateness of their behavior given their objectives. We help them to analyze their planning, behavior, self-control, and performance. Today we work with hundreds of case studies from our library, which are each designed to focus on different learning outcomes in different industries, working with different groups of negotiating variables. There are some multi-issue case studies that so accurately lead to predictable behavior that I have used them time after time. You could predict, minutes before an attendee negotiating did something, what they were going to do. The coaching that follows is based around the appropriateness of their motives, emotions, and decision making, which provides a powerful lesson in self-awareness every time.

But what was it that made their actions so predictable? Competitiveness? Pride? The need to perform? A desire to use the skills we had already covered to positive effect? It was their ego and the competitive situation that led to a narrowing of their capacity to think, weigh, and consider. It becomes personal, despite the considerable commercial experience and background of those I have worked with. It has driven individuals (thousands over the years) to justify their often short-term irrational behavior because of the pressure they felt resulting from the circumstances they had been placed in. They were willing, under certain circumstances, to compete, even though their brief was to focus on the total value opportunity.

Negotiating agreements successfully in business can be particularly challenging in that commercial pressures combined with an obligation to deliver will naturally stimulate competitiveness. Business is all about "winning" and outperforming your competitors. However, your competitor is not the person you are negotiating with. From the many organizations where I have spent time facilitating negotiations, I have concluded that the bigger the desire to "win," the greater the chance of distorted thinking during negotiations and the less emotional intelligence used. Resist the temptation to allow your ego to color your judgment.

Winning in negotiation means building successful agreements that the other party will deliver against. It is about building value and enhancing the bottom line. In some cases it might be about gaining a commitment to change that minimizes disruption, or simply reducing the risks associated with an existing arrangement. What it is not about is you, or whether you have won. If you allow this thought or feeling to dominate your motivation your performance will most likely be compromised.

THE ART OF LOSING

Negotiation is about the art of losing, or the art of letting others have *your* way. With your ego out of the way, and your attitude firmly focused on the outcome of the agreement, you are free to behave in any way you believe to be appropriate to your interests. Being what you need to be and doing what you need to do includes allowing the other party to enjoy the "symbols of success" whilst you focus on the total value of the agreement. This means understanding others and their needs and then trading off no more than you need to in order to optimize your net position. It means letting them win on items of less significance whilst you focus on the more significant, value-adding variables. You could argue that you cannot afford to set precedents by allowing them to win the psychological battle even on some issues (depending on whether or not there is an ongoing trading relationship), or that if you concede on certain issues they will expect this in the future. However, your job as a negotiator is also to help the other party to feel as though they have won.

In situations like this when you feel as though you are losing control of the relationship, emotions can take over and your decision-making capacity can become compromised. Your position and scope to negotiate also become compromised by circumstances and the proactivity being employed by your prospective customer. Your immediate reaction may be, "this is not fair, not right, and I'm not even sure I want to work with them anymore," which runs counter to your business interests. Despite your reactive stance, now is the time to consider your response and advise them of your position. Develop your strategy and do not react emotionally. There are two options for preventing this type of situation *before you even start to negotiate:*

1. Always establish whether there is a buying process involved that you should be aware of.
2. Always identify the decision maker(s) and any other stakeholders who are involved in the sign-off of agreements.

MANAGING THE EMOTIONAL NEED FOR SATISFACTION

We touched briefly on the need for satisfaction in Chapter 1. The need that individuals have for "satisfaction" – meaning getting a better deal than what was originally available – can be so strong that many negotiators use relative positioning and inflexibility at the start of a negotiation with the aim of letting the other party achieve what they thought at the beginning of discussions to be difficult if not impossible. Open your tough negotiations at a position you know they will reject and it is the start of the process of "give and take," which will allow you to start managing the other party's need for satisfaction. Many inexperienced negotiators start with a figure that they know the other party can accept because of the fear of hearing the word "no."

Get used to the word "no." When you open with a position that is extreme and yet realistic, you are going to hear it a lot. It is part of the process, and you should expect it. Keep the dialogue open and they are less likely to walk away. If they tell you they can't or won't agree to your opening offer, invite them to tell you how close they can get to your offer. It keeps the dialog going and it gets them to talk about your position. Rather than allowing them to get emotional, ask them what they would agree to rather than what they will not agree to. Then stop and consider your next move.

One of the benefits of opening first in negotiation is that you create an anchor, a position to move from and a position for them to attack. This should be on the right side of where you expect to finish up, rather than reacting to their position and playing in their "ballpark." Be proactive and open first. Take the rejection and then move forward. You are managing their satisfaction and at the same time you are involved in the process of securing the best possible deal. It provides you with the opportunity to maximize the deal whilst still allowing them to take emotional satisfaction even though they may be finishing on their own break point.

THE NEED TO MANAGE SATISFACTION

Ivan Chen is the general manager at the Hong Kong-based paint company White and White, who specialize in eco-friendly lime wash paints with an "unmatched color range." Following an article in a *Condé Nast* magazine, White and White benefited from a fourfold surge in overseas orders, which was sustained for six consecutive months. Following this unsolicited success, White and White decided to engage in an advertising campaign via the Condé Nast group.

Six full pages, one each month for six months, was the plan. Their rate card price per page advert was $35,000 for global coverage (31 publications) plus charges for an online presence, called the dual package.

Following several calls and emails with their VP of advertising, Ivan offered $154,000 for the six slots. He responded with a copy of the rate card stating that the fee was $270,000 for the dual package, minus a 15 percent discount for six slots. The price at the bottom of the email was a daunting $229,500 but Ivan ignored "the power of the written word." He agreed to meet a week later offering them time to think about it. He was authorized to go up to $200,000 for the six slots.

In the second meeting, he felt he was not making progress so he adjourned and arranged a third meeting with the VP and also Gary Chow, the President of Marketing, at their offices in Causeway Bay. During this final two-hour meeting, Gary offered additional extras including digital advertising footage, and enhanced in-magazine positioning, in an attempt to close the deal. Ivan increased his offer to $174,000, subject to artwork support for the adverts and additional mentions in the opening address from the Editor.

At 6.30 p.m. and with pressure mounting, Gary introduced the idea of an additional advertorial at no extra cost – a half-page article presented by W&W independently and yet favorably. Ivan made his final move. "If you agree to $188,500 per six-slot campaign, I will agree to run two campaigns over 24 months at one slot every other month. That's 12 slots in total subject to us maintaining our current enquiry levels, otherwise, I can execute an opt-out clause after the first six slots." Ivan had increased volume, managed risk, and provided price satisfaction in his move. Gary took the deal.

Ivan might have offered the full $200,000 but understood that this was a limit and not a target. He was satisfied that the extra

(*Continued*)

(Continued)

concessions agreed were good value and had been authorized to increase the scope of the offer to 12 slots. The satisfaction of both parties and the commitment to the deal came from the many hours it took to finally agree. It felt worth having. The harder you work on a deal, the more challenging it is to complete, and so commitments are more likely to be honored. Conversely, if it's too good to be true, and the deal is wrapped up too quickly, it shouldn't surprise you how many of these agreements fall apart as quickly as they come together.

Banks and real-estate agents are known for trying to manage satisfaction, but often the individuals responsible for the negotiations simply don't have the nerve to carry through the transaction in a controlled manner. The estate agent who tells you: "Our fee is 1.75 percent of the selling price, but we know it's a competitive market . . . so we are prepared to do it for 1.5 percent." Did I get any satisfaction from this move? No. It was quick, unconditional, and transparent. They didn't even wait for a response find out whether I had already been offered 1.5 percent elsewhere or establish that I wanted to work with them anyway because of their great service levels, for example. The bank manager who states: "We are currently offering our business clients an overdraft facility of base plus 6 percent. However, in your case we are prepared to offer base plus 5.5 percent."

Why? So that I feel better? I did not have to work for it or even meet a condition. It wasn't even a deciding factor at the time, so why offer it? Satisfaction comes from having to work for it. Even those in the crowds at the sales have to hunt down the deals in the high street, investing hours of time to get the 25 percent off deal. They may not have negotiated, but they have invested their time and effort. To those involved in the process, they will feel satisfied with their bargain.

If someone agrees too easily, you have a decision and commitment that can just as easily be reversed. Psychologically, things that are hard to attain carry a greater value. Deals that have been hard fought for are more likely to be honored. Regard the process of working toward agreement as an investment in the agreement's sustainability or the likelihood of it being honored.

Remember that you can get a great price but a lousy deal if the other party does not deliver on their commitments as has been agreed. For example, if it does not arrive on time, or if it doesn't do the job you need it for – the price makes up only one part of the overall equation.

Working within fixed budgets can mean that your budget is finite. When restricted in this way, it is important to understand the effect this may have on what you agree regarding specification. Will the product or service be de-specified to allow for the price? Is this clear upfront or is it likely to come to light only once the agreement has been made? Maintaining focus and discipline throughout your negotiation means ensuring you are thorough when it comes to covering all the issues, risks, specification, timing, and any other factors that could result in you receiving less than what you believe you had agreed to. Unfortunately, those who remain in denial use budget constraints as an excuse for poor deals that often fail to deliver.

TRUST, TACTICS, AND EMOTIONS

The trust and respect that you build in your relationships allow for discussion and the opportunity to build agreements. Your energy can then be spent on the deal rather than on positioning and managing the emotional needs of those involved. Between 9 o'clock and 12 o'clock this relationship state provides the ideal place to maximize value. Some negotiators say they want to work in a partnership and yet behave tactically back around at 6 o'clock. They may even start to introduce demands that they don't even want. Why? Because they are still attempting to provide you with the satisfaction of negotiating their demands off the table.

Like most tactics, this can be transparent and can prove detrimental to your interests, especially if you need to maintain trust and integrity for the relationship to work. It can also result in the discussions being emotionally charged and most likely result in transactional agreements yielding less value.

TRUST IS VALUABLE AND YET FRAGILE

One of many solar companies to launch in Egypt in 2020 was Schmid Solar whose main shareholders were German energy companies.

Decentralized off-grid solar was deemed to be their solution to numerous power issues experienced across Africa. The solar solution rather than hydroelectric, geothermal, and wind power was regarded as cost effective and flexible compared with other renewables. It's relatively cheap and can be installed just about anywhere, which can help farmers who are not connected to the central power grid.

Having gained a power producer license from the Egyptian energy authority, Schmid Solar was negotiating a contract with Egyptian agricultural developer Omar to construct 25 small electricity stations for its farm cooperative. The power purchase agreement (PPA) model was the central issue on the negotiation agenda, which were the terms that Omar (via its own clients), would have to satisfy for the facility. The agreement was to be based on a 30-year payback period by way of an "adapted electricity tariff." Essentially, through the costs they would be charged for the electricity.

This was to be a long-term contract requiring a collaborative relationship. The two key negotiators were Bernd Gaullet representing Schmid Solar and Akiiki Beah representing Omar. It was their fourth meeting, the previous three via online conferencing, which had gone well as they worked through an agenda and consulted with their legal teams. It was agreed that if discussions went well, installations could begin within eight weeks.

An hour into the face-to-face meeting Akiiki turned to Bernd and made a surprising proposal. "If you reduced your tariff demand by a further 18 percent, we would introduce you to a further 40 sites that you can service." This was not on the agenda, would take months to conduct diligence on, and almost impossible to calculate and therefore respond to. Bernd referenced the agenda they were working on and politely suggested that further opportunities would be dealt with under a separate agreement. Akiiki then implied that unless the further 40 sites could be included it was going to be difficult to sign any agreement off> Stop He added that he had lined up a competitor to discuss the overall opportunity who were ready to engage in case progress could not be made. Bernd could feel the collaborative atmosphere cooling and called for a time out to consider their next move. A further session lasting an hour followed during which Bernd sensed that Akiiki had judged that the new offer to be positive news and the threat would get an agreement across the line. In fact, if anything, Bernd and his legal representatives were becoming more cautious and removed than before. Trust in the process and therefore the relationship had been challenged. Fearing what else Akiiki might now present, they adjourned for the evening committing to reconvene at 10 a.m. the next morning. Bernd and his team worked through the night constructing a "bolt on contract" that he could, with numerous terms and conditions, accept the additional 40 sites in a second phase roll out. The overall tariff adjustment was 3 percent but only if phase two was deemed viable. Both parties struggled through the day

(*Continued*)

(Continued)

focusing on the legal terms and less on the warm relationship that had helped facilitate events thus far. People tend not to like late surprises and although a new opportunity, it had resulted in guarded positions being taken up. This was after all supposed to be a joint partnership. Akiiki quickly understood that the lawyers were prepared as several new clauses had been introduced to ensure there was no room for misinterpretation and liabilities had been strengthened to protect any future surprises from surfacing. By the end of the day papers were signed. The atmosphere was "business-like" but there was a bruising that implied that from now on the relationship would be managed on a formal "arms length" basis.

VISIBLE EMOTION

Visible emotion is also used tactically in negotiation. One such tactic known as the "professional flinch" (see Chapters 5 and 8) involves one party making their opening proposal and the other responding with an exaggerated emotional reaction, implying that the offer is ridiculous. The emotion, orchestrated, is designed to provide a far more powerful form of rejection than a simple "no." As a negotiator you need to read the situation and be confident of your actions. There is no place for uncontrolled emotion in negotiation. As a Complete Skilled Negotiator, you need to be in control of your thinking, reactions, what you say, and what you decide not to say.

Another way of deliberately controlling visible emotions is when negotiators make power statements during the opening exchanges of a discussion as part of anchoring the aspirations of the other party. As they do so, they are consciously waiting for the reactions to gauge how far they might push a particular issue. For example: "We're pleased we've been able to get together to discuss some of the issues around our compensation claim today," or "Clearly you recognize that this is most unusual and that any settlement is likely to take months if not years to conclude given the complexity of the issue." The anchor statement may have no substance at all. The person making the statement is watching and listening for the emotional signals that suggest rejection or acceptance of the statement. The Complete Skilled Negotiator would counter with an alternative statement. This effectively reverses the power statement back to the other party.

Emotion, pressure, and stress are commonplace in negotiation. With the implications of deadlock, the responsibility to deliver, and the frustration that can come with working through agreements, self-control often gives way to our subconscious. You start to do things you are not even aware of. Most people I have worked with do not believe this until they see it for themselves on video, but non-verbal communication becomes exaggerated during stressful times, especially when statements or threats are being made.

Telling the other party what you *will* do at any given point in your discussions (even if it's not the best offer you could make) is a useful discipline for getting them to focus on your position. You have to accommodate the silence, patience, and frustration whilst they think. Sometimes the other party themselves may start to show signs of emotion or stress. Usually this is most evident when responding to or making a proposal.

Imagine you know that you can agree at $1,000 but have opened your position at $600. They ask you, "Is that your best price?", to which you reply, "That's the price I am prepared to pay." They then make you an offer of $1,100. You say, "I can move to $725 but that will need to include the service agreement and delivery by Monday." All the time you are seeking to trade price against other value items but, in the back of your mind, you know that you can go further and would be prepared to do so if the alternative was to lose the deal, which even at $1,000 is as good as your best alternative. They pause, having heard you say $725, and there is a moment of silence. Are they thinking about it, preparing to walk away, or considering their next move? The 20 seconds that have passed feel like five minutes.

Their silence may be suggesting to you that your offer is ridiculous and that they have no interest in further conversations. The fact that they are still in discussions is a non-verbal suggestion that there is still some level of interest. The Complete Skilled Negotiator understands that nothing happens by accident in negotiation. Everything, every movement, statement, response, and moment of silence happens for a reason, so they maintain composure, will watch, and will listen.

Your job as a negotiator is to read and interpret the correlation between what is being *said* and *how* the other party is *behaving*.

During the thousands of experiential negotiation workshops I have facilitated, attendees have the opportunity to negotiate agreements whilst being recorded on video, allowing for detailed analysis of everything that takes place. It allows negotiators to see for themselves the degree to which their actions and emotions are visible. Most people completely deny that they would give any type of signal away until they see themselves on camera. Once they have and accept this, it results in a significant leap in consciously controlled performances. Listen to what they say, watch what they do, and then calculate your response.

Conscious negotiators are capable of active listening. This involves intentionally demonstrating to others that you are listening, engaged, and open-minded, if that's what you want them to think. In other words, they are skilled at providing the signals through their own body language that they want the other party to receive. Part of getting into the other party's head is getting them to think what you *want* them to think.

Emotional ego

How many times have you seen emotion or ego-fueled behavior at charity auctions, let alone business auctions? The entire event is geared to provide maximum personal exposure in the room. The compère walks around calling the bidders by their name, "Now that's $5,000 for the football shirt, has Mr. McCarthy the nerve to increase his bid?" As he turns to Mr. McCarthy, so does the attention of the audience.

Of course Mr. McCarthy has the nerve, and he doesn't want to lose face. These businessmen at the auctions who are clearly successful, and who have probably worked extremely hard for such sums, regard this as a fun process. They are seduced by the immediate public recognition for their generosity and dismiss the very judgment they usually exercise that probably helped them make the money in the first place. It's for charity. It is their money (although not always) so I can understand their "fun." However, on many occasions similar actions have been witnessed in the business world where the egos of those involved use "company money," fueled by the need to win, and exercise disregard for the very shareholders they are working on behalf of.

Emotion distorts objectivity. If your spouse was being held captive and a ransom was being demanded for their release, the last person who should negotiate the agreement is you. You are emotionally involved and therefore immediately compromised. You would probably give everything you own for their release, probably in your first offer, assuming the kidnappers had not already stated their demand. You should, of course, delegate the role of negotiating to another person. They may be no more competent than you at negotiating, but they will be without the emotional attachment that you have to the outcome.

Careful planning ahead of your negotiation may help your confidence and provide you with considered options. However, emotional control and recognizing the actions of the other party, together with circumstantial changes, require nerve, self-awareness, and self-control, otherwise your composure and performance will be compromised.

NOW DO THIS!

- Understand yourself, your intentions, your responses, your emotions, and your own behavior.
- Understand how important the deal is **from inside the other party's head,** their priorities, interests, pressures, and the emotions they are feeling.

- Listen, understand, calculate, think, and **slow down.** It will increase your mental capacity and will make a real difference to your performance.
- When unclear, feeling under pressure, or without the clarity you need, **take time out.**
- Don't be seduced by large concessions. Their extreme opening position may well have been designed to shock and then satisfy you.
- Never assume how others will behave. Human beings under pressure can and do become irrational in their thinking and in their behavior.

CHAPTER 9

Authority and Empowerment

"No one should be without accountability. It is a dangerous and lonely place to be."

— Unknown

UNDERSTANDING EMPOWERMENT

Your negotiations can only progress if communication flows and those who are involved are allowed to make decisions. Therefore, understanding the role of empowerment in your negotiation is fundamental to managing the relationships and communications that stand between you and progress.

However, with empowerment comes exposure and this brings with it risk. It is this risk that organizations seek to control by empowering individuals with limits, or caps, beyond which they must escalate to higher authority. Too much empowerment and any individual can become dangerous or vulnerable and therefore so can the organization they work for.

The Complete Skilled Negotiator will understand empowerment in terms of:

- how it can be used to protect you;
- how it affects your ability to be creative;
- how it affects your ability to build value;
- how it affects the other party's thinking and behavior.

Essentially, it is the degree to which you can negotiate and make decisions without having to refer or escalate them to a higher authority. In other words, empowerment relates to the scope and range of variables and the authority within which you have to negotiate or operate. If you regard empowerment as simply a gauge to broaden or narrow your trading opportunities, or to provide "stop limits" up to which you can negotiate, you can start to get a feel for how empowerment can work for you, as well as against you.

To negotiate collaboratively on the left-hand side of the clock face (6–12 o'clock) requires the scope or empowerment to work with many variables and possibilities. Limiting this, as many organizations do, can help you to protect yourself from the escalation and disempowerment tactics used by others. So getting this right is fundamental to where you will finish up on the clock face. As with any balancing act, the setting of appropriate limits helps to maximize opportunity, but without overexposure.

Great negotiators tend to be unsung heroes. Great deals become so over time as the contract delivers the value it was intended to offer, rather than necessarily at the time when the deal was completed. Negotiators often work as part of a team, which can involve specialist lawyers, finance directors, and others. Because the last person to become involved in the negotiation dealings is the boss, the act of negotiation is usually and appropriately delegated further down the line, further diluting the transparency of who is actually controlling events. And when the deal is done, the need for confidentiality as well as the need to protect the operations of those companies involved means that the actual facts and figures agreed are rarely publicized to the degree to which you can measure the relative performance of the negotiators involved.

Most high-profile negotiators tend to be political figures or union leaders because they use PR as part of posturing during or leading up to discussions. However, these individuals neither work by themselves nor are they fully empowered to negotiate on all issues. Using the press and media is part of how they frame, anchor, and publicize their position and progress to those they represent, the parties they are negotiating with, and any other third parties.

One of my personal experiences as a negotiator involved facilitating a highly charged negotiation between a Japanese electronics company and a trade union in the UK. The level of trust between the parties involved, together with the climate of the meeting and the relationship, was poor, hence the need to bring in a neutral to facilitate events. On advice to my client, I was provided with no scope with which to negotiate, which allowed me to focus on the process and not be drawn into specific proposals. My role included helping the parties with establishing solutions, starting with why they thought they could not agree to the terms that had already been tabled.

How empowered are they?

Rushing into negotiations without qualifying whether the other party is empowered to negotiate is a mistake many eager and ultimately frustrated account managers have made. The need to question, qualify, and explore requires patience. It is during this phase of initial discussions that the issue of empowerment should be qualified by simply asking, "Are you in a position to sign off the agreement?" or "Who else would you need to consult with as part of signing off this agreement?" or even "What limits are there that might prevent you from signing off the agreement?" All of these questions will help you to decide whether you are dealing with the right person or people.

Being disempowered

We are socially conditioned to conform and most of us lead our lives respecting the laws of where we live and others around us. In some instances, laws provide freedom of movement, for example, effectively empowering us to travel and choose how and where we travel. Laws can also disempower us, in that we may not travel faster than a given speed or, when driving, having drunk alcohol, and so on.

The written word carries an assumed authority in that it has been published. It is designed to be legitimate. In your negotiation the other party may present you with, say, a price list. Rather than accepting this as it is, you should regard it as their opening position. Different situations require different considerations, yet many will wrongly assume that not only is the printed price fixed but the person issuing it is disempowered to negotiate.

The more empowered you are, however, the more exposed you become. You may carry more risk to your business and therefore be accountable for the total impact of your actions. Organizations have a tough challenge in providing a level of empowerment to their employees, which helps the business conduct "good business" but not with such risks that the "good business" will or could be concluded with unintended risks or unforeseen costs.

Many organizations actively promote business values such as creativity, entrepreneurship, and even empowerment. Yet when negotiating with suppliers and customers they recognize that there have to be limits within which individuals are empowered to operate, otherwise the business will lose total control of its operation. They operate a disempowered structure to protect their own business operation.

For example, as suggested earlier, they might use a price list, which serves to disempower the salesperson, as does the accompanying printed discount structure. Under these circumstances, the salesperson is disempowered to the point where they are little more than an order taker.

If the customer demands better terms, they have to speak to the boss. The boss, a supervisor, is also disempowered. They have a boss and if you can get to them, because they are usually "out of town," you may just be able to negotiate a better deal.

Tactically, empowerment allows you to use a third party, citing your lack of authority to move further, which serves to deflect the pressure away from you. If not used carefully though, it can backfire. (See Figure 9.1.)

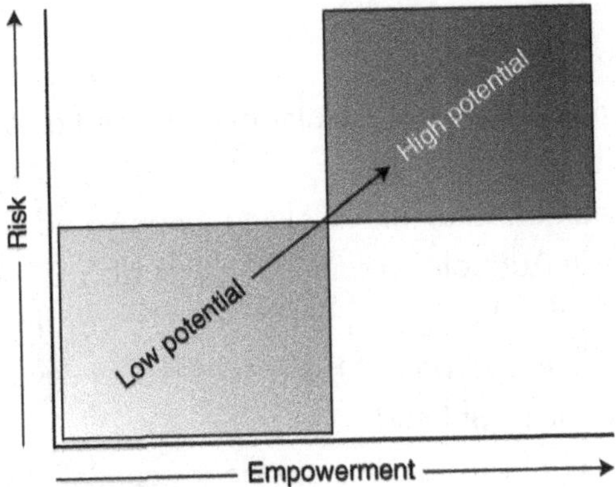

Figure 9.1 Empowerment.

Fully empowered individuals can become particularly dangerous

Rogue traders acting beyond their company's agreed levels of empowerment provide us with ample evidence of just how badly things can go wrong if scope, when provided, goes unchecked.

HISTORY'S LESSONS FROM THOSE WHO WERE "EMPOWERED"

In 2022, Goldman Sachs were fined $3 billion when banker Roger Ng was found guilty in an embezzlement scandal that involved looting a Malaysian investment fund. His boss, Tim Leissner was also found guilty of lying, bribing officials with more than $1 billion so that it could win contracts worth $6 billion. Ng is looking at a 30-year sentence.

The biggest fraud in history was carried out by Jerome Kerviel of Société Générale, who had taken up hedging positions that cost his business €4.9 billion. At one point, he ran up about €38 billion in unauthorized trades, which when discovered had to be

(*Continued*)

(Continued)

carefully unwound. The bank almost collapsed as a result of the losses discovered in 2008.

Another notable example involving empowered City traders is that of Kweku Adoboli, who in 2011 lost UBS £1.4 billion. He was described as being "a gamble or two away from destroying Switzerland's largest bank." He was jailed for seven years after being found guilty of fraud.

At the center of the subprime mortgage scandal at Credit Suisse in London, David Higgs was found guilty of falsifying accounts in a New York court. As Managing Director of Credit Suisse in London in 2007 and 2008 he had inflated the value of mortgage securities in the bank's portfolio. The overstatement forced Credit Suisse to announce a $2.85 billion (£1.8 billion) write down.

These are just a few of the more well-publicized examples of what can happen when those who have been partially empowered operate outside the limits set, and without the necessary transparency and checks to protect everyone concerned.

Being partially empowered

Every industry uses empowerment limits to protect their business. Call centers use this to make it almost impossible for customers to negotiate with their representatives, who stick rigidly to their scripts. Any demand proposal made by the customer that sits outside the script has to be escalated to their supervisor – a classic avoidance strategy where the customer has to escalate or, if not, give up and concede. However where the discussion does deadlock and the customer cancels the order, supply, or subscription you have to ask is it not better to provide the call center operator with some tools and skills to work with. Other examples include: the insurance industry with the salesperson who can only refer to the underwriter for a decision; the shop assistant who has to refer to their manager when challenged by a customer; and the hotel receptionist who has to check with their manager before agreeing to that special rate. Even the empowered negotiator may sometimes use the tactic of suggesting that their boss would not agree and therefore cannot agree to the offer on the table.

In life we are surrounded by limits and rules, for the most part set in place to protect us from ourselves. For instance, a police officer can stop you, arrest you, or take you into custody, but is not empowered to sentence you. That is the role of a judge, who in turn is governed by the rule of law, the jury, and the evidence. This process serves to prevent corruption and protects the system, whichever side of it you may be on. Within the context of a job, in the case of the police, they have the authority, responsibility, and ultimately have been empowered to go only so far in the apprehension process. What they can and can't do as part of apprehending a suspect has been clearly defined in law and in their training. It provides them with the confidence to escalate issues that are outside of their remit in the same way that you should operate with pre-agreed parameters within which you have been authorized.

YOUR BOSS CAN BE YOUR WORST ENEMY

The most dangerous person in any organization is the person with the most authority – usually the boss. The person who can say "yes" and knows that they are able to do so is more likely to do so, and under pressure they often do. If you have ever attended a meeting alongside your boss you may well have experienced the following typical and yet frustrating scenario. It is *your* client relationship but your boss wants to sit in for whatever reason. The meeting begins, and you set out to discuss some of the challenging issues with your client, and then your boss starts to take over the conversation. In no time at all, your client and boss are fully engaged in the discussion; they start exploring solutions and ultimately start trading concessions that you would not have been empowered to offer yourself. Your boss still thinks that they are doing the right thing and a great job at that.

What has happened, though, is that your boss is as keen as you are to resolve the issue. They are, however, more empowered (which, as we know, makes them more dangerous). Before long, your boss has concluded the meeting having built an agreement. Your boss has probably involved you along the way yet may still have undermined your relationship and credibility with your client. Guess who the client asks to see at the next meeting?

Your boss may be highly skilled, have tremendous nerve, and be very capable of managing relationships. However, they have a greater responsibility and accountability than you and therefore will be more exposed and will have more to lose if the deal deadlocks. As they are most empowered, they hold the weakest negotiating position of anyone in your organization. Imagine your king in a game of chess. The king is not as mobile as the other pieces. If your king is in check, you will always be vulnerable no matter how many pieces you have on the board. Therefore, your job is to protect your king, to ensure that the other party does not gain access to them. In negotiation, your king is your boss, and it is not in your interest to expose your boss directly to the other party, otherwise you could find yourself in a compromised position. There is a famous mantra preached by buyers: "Another level, another percent." The buyer will negotiate hard with their counterpart and then try to escalate to the next level to get that extra percent concession, and then escalate again for another percent, and so on.

Who is in the background?

So if you are ultimately accountable it is in your interests to disempower yourself as this will protect you. Better to manage in the background and let the discussions unfold, than to be the focus of attention. Make it known that others will be making the decisions and that you will back whatever decisions are made.

In any negotiation, never assume that you are dealing with the ultimate decision maker. You may find yourself being enlightened at the end of your discussions, i.e., they have to refer the final decision to someone else. The person you thought you were negotiating with was, in fact, not empowered to make the final decision. They may have also made offers that their business will not carry out. You may have even offered concessions in return for discount levels that the other person is ultimately not authorized to agree. Therefore it's imperative always to qualify the degree to which the other person is empowered:

- establish who the decision maker is; and
- establish who else will need to agree.

Do this before the negotiation begins. If not, you will leave yourself wide open to tactics, stalling, escalation or, worse still, agree to a contract that will not be delivered on, because the terms agreed were not viable to start with (see Figure 9.2).

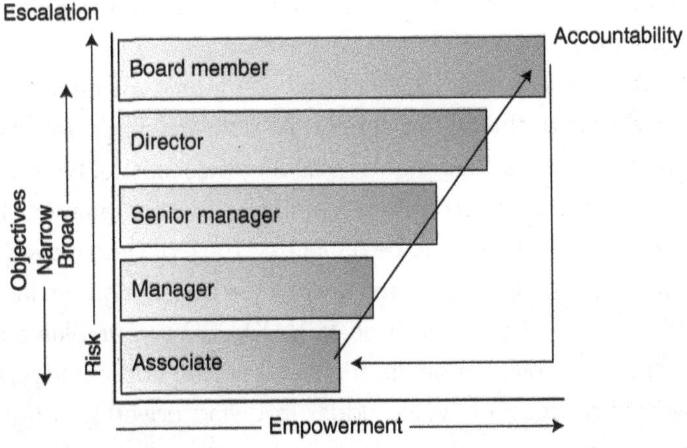

Figure 9.2 Escalation.

Gaining "in principle" agreements

Another way of using the boss to help negotiations flow where there is likely to be a high level of resistance is in arranging top-to-top meetings between senior management. These meetings are used to outline ideas and for gaining "in-principle" agreements, allowing for follow-up on details of the negotiations. This is used in both political and business environments as a means of protecting the boss from specific exposure, whilst allowing for trust and an understanding to be built between the two parties at a senior level.

MAKING USE OF HIGHER AUTHORITY

Basketball has been part of the Summer Olympic program since 1936 and remains very competitive. NBA teams in the US have keenly adopted AI technology to track and learn about every player they have. The pursuit of sporting glory is about fine margins.

In data analysis, correlations between activity and performance are analyzed, training schedules are optimized according to the progress of each player, and statistics are compared with productivity. It can even be linked to diets, recovery periods, and player strengths, which offers coaches clear actions to optimize performance.

In 2018, Ron Jordon COO of an NBA team was responsible for renewing a contract to supply 'AI data insights'; with their technology partner Blue Sight. Following a successful three-year run, the contract had six months left and was up for renewal. The partnership was deemed to be a success. The team had moved up the rankings and Ron was keen to continue benefiting from the AI insights. The contract was worth $2,500,000 a year. Blue Sight was keen to capitalize on the success that they had contributed, so set out a range of "value adds" involving advertising rights, marketing exposure, corporate activities, as well as a five-year term with a 5 percent price hike. Ron delegated the negotiating to Karen, a junior in the team, who was given specific boundaries beyond which she could not agree without escalation that at first felt frustrating for Blue Sight. Further, he introduced a second layer between himself and Karen to ensure that he would only be available at the end of negotiation to sign the deal off and could be used as the "higher authority" during discussions. Meanwhile, Ron managed to attract some media coverage of himself dining out with the CEO of a competitor of Blue Sight. Eight weeks later, Karen returned with a deal that was agreeable. No price hike, some marketing exposure, and a two-year break claûse. Ron was delighted but rejected it. He then instructed Karen's boss, Emma to speak directly to the Blue Sight CEO to explain that she could only sign the deal off if they received full exclusivity for 12 months over all new Blue Sight innovations. "It's the only way I am going to get the deal past Ron, and you know he has been talking to the market." They agreed. By keeping higher authority at arm's length and escalating at the end, directly contributed to the additional value that was secured.

STARTING WITH TOP-TO-TOP AGREEMENTS

Top-to-top meetings serve to set the tone, promote, and reinforce trust, as well as setting parameters of pending negotiations. They also provide the opportunity to pre-condition the other party by setting out expectations without getting drawn into the finite details.

Would you trade in Crypto currency? I mean at a business level? This is high-tech, high-volatility currency, held via a Stable coin yet paid at the agreed Bitcoin rate, which is updated every 15 seconds! Even Warren Buffett once said: "Bitcoin is a gambling device,

(Continued)

(Continued)

a pyramid scheme and Rat poison." Well, that's exactly what Temp agency HR Jacobson did. In 2020 they believed it was the future and were keen to trial the concept. Thirty-day terms payable on the supply of temporary staff for warehouse duties to Priton.

Priton, a local food wholesaler was experiencing 50 percent of their team reporting off work with Covid. They were struggling to keep up during the pandemic and the customer demand driven by eating at home.

Temp agency, HR Jacobson offered Priton, warehouse operatives a $25 an hour rate, meaning that a monthly wage for 12 operatives would equate to $48,000.

Before discussions with the HR team even started the founder of HR at Jacobson, Mike Cleary, asked for a meeting with the MD of Priton, Lucy Gray to discuss an innovative means of payment. A top-to-top meeting. Fortunately for Mike, Lucy was not only a personal follower of Crypto but held three bitcoins herself, which had increased in value five-fold since she purchased them. Even so, this was gambling, surely, and you can't do that, especially if you think the price will continue to rise. Or can you? Why not pay the dollar, budget for what you can afford and be accountable for the impact? The answer as it turned out was that Lucy, the owner of Priton, was intrigued by the idea. She agreed that subject to other terms to be agreed with HR that she would pay four bitcoins per month. They needed 12 temps. The bitcoin rate in June 2020 was trading at $9,300 meaning that the cost would be $37,200 divided by 12 temps, divided by 4 x 40 hour shifts equated to $19.37 an hour. Less than the $25 an hour rate usually charged but with 30-day exposure. Lucy then handed over to her HR team with the headline rate agreed. By July, the rate had risen to $10,000 not as high as Mike had hoped. The four-week deal, which left the HR team perplexed was concluded. The experiment would never have been possible without the top-to-top meeting with two empowered individuals to start with.

EMPOWERMENT WITHIN TEAM ROLES

When negotiating in teams, it is important to be organized in such a way that you perform well as a unit. Understanding who is empowered to do what and who will take the final decisions is also key to the workings of any team in pressured situations. Negotiating in teams can only be effective when everyone understands and keeps to their role and is able to contribute toward the team's efforts. There are four distinct team roles that are typically adopted:

- the spokesperson;
- the figures person;
- the observer; and
- the leader.

Each is designed to help your team perform to the best of its varied abilities.

The spokesperson

The spokesperson is empowered. Their role is to:

- conduct most of the dialog;
- table proposals within agreed parameters with the leader in the negotiation team; and
- trade variables on behalf of the team while still needing to refer to their leader to get final agreement.

That is not to say that others should not or cannot talk but they should do so through invitation from the spokesperson. The team is there to support the spokesperson.

The figures person

The figures person should not typically be involved in the dialog unless invited to do so. They:

- understand the implications of movement on each of the variables;
- advise on possibilities, calculate movements, possibilities, and proposals;
- understand the total value of the agreement at any given point in time; and
- advise the leader as the negotiation proceeds.

The observer

The observer is also disempowered. Their role is to:

- watch and monitor the other party;
- hear the things that others may be too preoccupied to hear;
- understand the motives, interests, and priorities of the other party; and
- read the size, timing, and nature of the moves that are taking place.

The purpose of the role is to help you to understand what is driving the other party. The observer is your eyes and ears in the room. They generally work out what's happening in the room when others are too preoccupied.

The leader

The leader is usually the person with the greatest level of authority. They are the person who speaks least but speaks loudest. Their role is to:

- set out the agenda and form the climate for the meeting;
- allow the spokesperson to manage the trading on behalf of the team; and
- summarize from time to time where clarity is required and make the final decision.

However, the leader is not the negotiator. This task is delegated to the spokesperson, who is the voice of the team.

More than four

Often the team is larger than four members. More frequently, you will have to play all four roles yourself, at the same time. This makes your task of negotiating more demanding because there are many things to think about, consider, and respond to. This is one of the reasons why preparation is so important for you. You should never think on your feet, never seek to rush the deal, and always understand the pace at which you can operate and then manage your meetings accordingly.

For some, disempowerment feels like a straitjacket – for others, a suit of armor. It works both ways and is used by companies to expand or narrow the scope and risk. It is used as a tactic to protect or deflect conflict, as well as a negotiating lever.

Even a pilot landing their aircraft will take instructions from air traffic control regarding flight path, timings, and other relevant instructions during descent. They are part of a team and different members of the team will carry different forms of responsibility and will be empowered to make certain decisions. Fortunately, everything the pilot does can be seen by everyone who has an interest in their activity.

GETTING EMPOWERED BEFORE YOU START

Often before negotiations start, you may find yourself involved in internal negotiations to agree your parameters and how far you are authorized to go, or whether you will entertain discussions on particular variables as part of concluding an agreement. This is an important part of the planning process. Without these parameters, you could in theory become dangerous because you could agree to anything. So, degrees of empowerment are usually put in place to protect you (providing you with a basis for trading), and to protect your businesses.

Equally, the other party will have parameters within which they can operate. It is quite common for some people to open a negotiation discussion outlining the areas that are non-negotiable "deal breakers" and the areas that are available for discussion. The likelihood is that they are either not empowered to negotiate over certain areas because of the parameters that have been set, or they have decided for now to introduce such parameters, allowing them to broaden the agenda during later discussions.

DEFENCE IN DEPTH

The seller says: "If you can agree to a price of $19 a unit on 30 days delivery, we will agree to payment terms of 30 days." The buyer says: "I am able to agree to that, but I just need to run that past my boss as it is above my authorization level, I'll call you this afternoon." That afternoon, the buyer calls the salesman: "Good news, my boss says that if you can agree to $18 a unit he will sign it off." The salesman sees this as a tactic they have come across before, called "defence in depth." However, he needs the deal, so yields to the offer: "OK, but I need a confirmation in writing back by the morning." "That's great," says the buyer, "We can now put the agreement before the head of buying for the final sign-off and I'll have it back to you by the morning." The following morning arrives and the buyer calls the seller. "The head of buying says that if the deal meets our standard payment terms of 45 days, he will sign the agreement. Of course I would have signed it off, but it's out of my hands now." The seller is so close and because he is empowered to authorize the 45 days, he agrees: "Just sign it and get it back to me."

The pressure the salesman is under to get the agreement signed, and the fact that he works for an "empowering" sales organization, has resulted in the salesman's position being compromised. Had he been disempowered to move beyond certain predefined limits, the buyer may well have had to review their approach or renegotiated on other variables. This higher authority tactic is used frequently where one party does not qualify the decision-making process beyond the person they are dealing with, leaving themselves exposed to further negotiations.

DECISION-MAKING AUTHORITY

Linking empowerment to accountability

ENSURING THE NEGOTIATOR IS ACCOUNTABLE FOR THE "TOTAL VALUE"

The cost? 150,000 euros! For what? Fabio was the business manager for Efficienza, a Milan based 3D printing company who made and serviced mobile robots better known as drones. As a business they had evolved from a software business into AI technology, which was used to support 3D printing using fused filament fabrication technology. They had good long-term contracts agreed with various departments within the Italian government ranging from the police, sea and mountain rescue, and the armed forces. Their USP was that they could 3D print and supply any part for a drone within 24 hours saving time and cost ensuring that all of their drone models remained operational once in service. Drones were prone to operator "accidents" so the parts side of the business flourished and also reinforced Efficienza's USP of speed and cost. In March 2022, Fabio received notification of a 40 percent price increase in Thermoplastic printing polymers used for printing 80 percent of the parts they supplied from their main supplier, Chem Plus. Price rises were common in 2022 with inflationary pressures; however, the five-year contracts that Efficienza's had secured had no scope to pass on the cost. Following several conversations with their supplier, Chem Plus, Fabio explained that he was authorized to go to 7.5 percent but no more. He explained that beyond this point his superiors would put the contract back out to tender. Fabio was keen to save the relationship. Efficienza could source from elsewhere, however, price rises were happening across the industry and the volume/discount level they had in place with their primary supplier was worth hanging on to. A counteroffer was received from Chem Plus accepting the 7.5

(Continued)

(Continued)

percent price increase in return for a new thermoplastic material they would provide. With all other terms and conditions unchanged Fabio signed the deal off and reported back the good news. Six weeks later, issues began to appear with the clogging of nozzles in the printing process. Output slowed, and at one point stopped completely. An internal investigation revealed that the specification of the new thermoplastic was incompatible with their print machine nozzles and changing them would not be straightforward. The issue of Fabio agreeing to and authorized to agree to a price resulted in Efficienza's operation coming to a near standstill for two weeks while they negotiated terms with a new supplier. The cost? 150,000 euros!

Any individual who is empowered to negotiate the best deal must also be made accountable for the broader implications of their agreements; otherwise what looks like a great deal could turn out to be a disaster for the organization. The challenge for the empowered negotiator is therefore to understand and negotiate/mitigate for the risks and, when in doubt, escalate.

EMPOWERMENT AND SCOPE TO CREATE VALUE

So, responsibility and accountability go hand in hand. Some businesses want their managers to be entrepreneurial. They want to empower them to make decisions, to be creative, to build agreements, and to maximize value within the agreements they are involved in.

In fact, high-potential deals come from creative thinking (trait 9, Chapter 4). Creative thinking comes from those who are empowered and therefore encouraged to think more broadly. If you disempower someone by providing them with limited scope to operate, it will limit their thinking and attract responses such as: "I didn't even consider the prospect of a joint venture; it's not part of my remit."

If you want to negotiate incremental value in your agreements you need to be empowered with as much scope as possible.

The importance of defining value

Having greater scope with moderate forms of empowerment offers a balance that many organizations adopt. However, scope and creativity must also be linked to accountability. You might ask someone to build creative deals that maximize value. However, unless you define *how* value will be measured, they may overlook the risks they have accepted in their quest to extract value. If the personal benefits associated with highly profitable agreements are exceedingly high, limits of authority may be worth building into the negotiator's brief. As we witnessed in the global banking industry in the lead-up to the credit crunch during 2007/2008, individuals will entertain risk in the quest for personal gain, especially when they are authorized to do so.

Empowerment works just like authority. The more empowered you are, the more scope you have to negotiate with. The positives are that with greater scope you can be more creative by working with a broader agenda and more variables. The negatives are that you can become exposed to pressure because you are empowered to say yes. In other words, it is often those with the authority who need protecting, which is why the act of negotiation is often delegated to others.

NOW DO THIS!

- Seek a higher authority and disempower yourself where appropriate.
- Agree to whom and when you should escalate discussions or decision making before you start negotiating.
- Agree (and negotiate if necessary) the scope and parameters of your empowerment before you start.
- Qualify the level of empowerment of those you are dealing with.
- When they say *they* are unable to agree, escalate the matter to someone who can.

CHAPTER 10

Tactics and Values

"Experience is not what happens to you; it's what you do with what happens to you."

— Aldous Huxley

The decisions you take and the way you behave during your negotiations will be influenced by how much power you think you have and by the way your own values or ethics influence your behavior.

The tactics you employ will be limited by both how much power you have and whether you have a short- or long-term relationship to consider, which may influence how ethical you choose to be during your negotiations.

The dilemma of where the value of fairness fits into negotiation has challenged many organizations. For instance, some organizations that hold strong views on being fair and reasonable may take exception when faced with a trading partner who behaves in a manipulative or irrational manner. On principle, they will not tolerate the behavior and will exit the relationship.

Recognizing the process and the gamesmanship in play

Because of the way the balance of power is split, and how it shifts with time and circumstance, you cannot expect agreements to always be, or appear to be, balanced, fair, or even consistent. You can, however, work towards getting the best possible deal given the circumstances you face. Some, faced with such situations, turn to tactics and some become victims of the tactics in play. The Complete Skilled Negotiator recognizes the tactics in play for what they are and where necessary uses counter tactics to neutralize their effects.

I am not implying here what is right or wrong. You will conduct business based on values that are probably different from those of others. This does not make yours right or wrong; it does not make the other party's values right or wrong. It simply means that your interpretation, understanding, and use of tactics will differ from others as the implications of making use of them will differ based on your circumstances and your view of what comprises acceptable behavior.

As a general rule, negotiations that focus on short-term agreements with parties with whom we have no ongoing relationship, or prospect of one in the future, are more inclined to gravitate towards value distribution (1–6 o'clock) negotiations. Tactics tend to be more readily used in these styles of negotiations as the relationships involved tend not to be long-term.

A QUESTION OF CHOICES AND PERSONAL STYLE

The concept of "fairness" is exploited by some negotiators through the use of tactics. Western democratic societies are designed to offer freedom and choice. This serves to remove the notion of being controlled, and, as long as we have choices, many perceive this as freedom and fairness. So choices are designed to signal fairness. However, if like governments you are *controlling* the options or choices, then you have the power to influence the outcome.

However, if you are overtly unfair in the choices you provide others, trust will be difficult to build and, with no trust, it is difficult to negotiate collaboratively (7–12 o'clock on the clock face).

Social laws, or the ever-changing and unwritten laws of society, influence our view of what is fair and reasonable under whatever circumstances. Trust is vital in business partnerships to maintain productive relationships and jointly solve problems by working together to create incremental value.

Business partnerships, where there is a need to maintain productive relationships and the need to jointly problem-solve or develop incremental value by working together, require at least some level of trust.

In order to be perceived as fair in business, you need to offer choices: choices that are not so one-sided that they quickly become regarded as transparent and unfair.

Personal attributes

Your personal values and how they influence your behavior will have a powerful bearing on where you and the other party gravitate to on the clock face. They can, if not managed, directly influence whether you build relationships or whether you enter into combat each time you seek to agree terms. Below are some of the personal attributes to consider and the influences they will exert during your negotiations.

Trust in business has to be earned and is easily broken. It implies that you are good for your word. If you say something will happen, it happens, consistently. You approach the conversation from their perspective, sharing their concerns and working on the problems that together, you both identify. It does not mean that you have to pay by conceding on terms, by offering personal favors, or by being more transparent with your interests.

Respect comes from being firm, consistent, and reliable. If you are too flexible or concede too easily, the other party will regard you as being weak. In negotiation you should ensure that everything is possible, but difficult. The fact that it is difficult ensures that the work you put into the deal, engineering the terms, and moving reluctantly, attracts respect for you, your position, and your credibility.

Integrity comes from consistency. This can present issues for negotiators who are too focused on not being unpredictable. Maintaining confidentiality and being reliable, in that you follow through with your commitments, also help promote integrity, which in some relationships or even industries is critical if business is to take place at all.

Honesty. You never need to lie in negotiation. You don't even have to tell them what you won't do. Focus on what you will do. Think "how" or "on what basis could we/they?" By telling them you are prepared to pay $100 when you know that you could pay $150 is not lying. You are simply telling them what you are prepared to pay. Don't confuse the process of negotiation with lying and telling the truth. If you lie in negotiation, you could be taking unnecessary risks, and in some cases completely compromising relationships; however, don't expect everyone to adhere to this discipline.

Consideration of the needs of the other party. If you don't understand these you are not ready to negotiate. Your planning, preparation, research, and exploration meetings are all there to help you to establish their position, motives, priorities, and interests. To place a value on these you have to understand the deal the way they do from inside their head. Considering the facts will allow you to remain sensitive to the issues and respectful where necessary.

Empathy is about understanding and appreciating the challenges from their perspective, but never compromising because of your understanding.

Responsibility. It is you who will conduct your negotiations and you who will make the decisions with the authority limits available to you. The more trust that genuinely exists within your relationships, the more scope you have to open up the agenda and work together creatively. This will only come about if you cultivate the necessary climate in discussions.

Risky attributes

Openness. This can be dangerous in negotiation. Information is power and the more you share with the other party, the more you will expose yourself. Be open but stay within the parameters that you set yourself. If you don't understand this from the outset, you will place yourself in an extremely vulnerable position.

Compassion. In the tough world of business your job is to maximize opportunity. You will most likely achieve this with those you can work with and depend on. Compassion, like generosity, has to take a back seat once a negotiation commences unless, of course, you have a longer-term plan in mind.

WHAT ARE TACTICS?

When do tactics usually come into play?

Tactics tend to be used more frequently when one party has more power than the other and tries to take advantage of it. Tactics are also more frequently used where the nature of the negotiation is based on value distribution and the focus is on taking as much value off the table as possible.

Dealing with tactics and when to use them

There are dozens of books written on negotiation that present tactics as the basis of negotiation. They are given names that serve to explain the approach: "The Russian front," "The Trojan horse," and so on. The most important thing about tactics is to recognize them for what they are.

- They are neither clever nor sophisticated.
- They are designed to apply pressure and usually by those who can because they have enough power or think they have enough power to do so, or those who think they are clever enough to do so without any consequences.

However, they are used with such regularity that one has to recognize and understand them, adapt to them and, where necessary and appropriate, even use them. To help with this I have categorized a range of tactics (see Figure 10.1) using a simple scale of 1–10 (1 is low and 10 is high) against two factors:

- **Power required:** the amount of power you will need to have or be perceived to have relative to the other party for this tactic to work.

- **Relationship erosion:** the degree to which your relationship or any trust that may exist within it will be eroded, if the tactic once used becomes obvious or transparent to the other party.

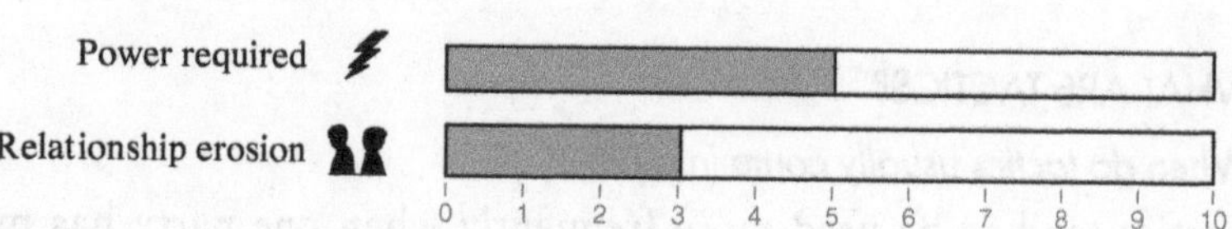

Figure 10.1 Tactics scale.

For the purpose of outlining some of the more widely used tactics, I have placed them into one of seven categories. These are:

	Tactics
1. Information	- "The hypothetical question" - "Off the record" - Full disclosure and openness - Why?
2. Time and momentum	- Deadlines - "And just one more thing" - Denied access - Time constraint - The auction - Time out
3. Fear or guilt	- Physically disturbing them - Good guy, bad guy - The Russian front - Personal favor - Guilty party - The social smell - Silence
4. Anchoring	- Sow the seed early - The power statement - The mock shock - The professional flinch - The broken record

	Tactics
5. Empowerment	- Higher authority - Defense in depth - Use of official authority - "It's all I can afford" - Onus transfer - Off-limits - New faces
6. Moving the costs around	- The building block technique - Wipe the proposal off the table without saying no - Linking the issues - Side issue or red herring - The slice
7. Deceit	- Trojan horse - The incorrect summary - Deliberate misunderstanding - The dumb foreigner - The loss leader

1. Information

Information is power. The more information you have about the options, circumstances, and priorities of the other party, the more powerful you will become.

"The hypothetical question"

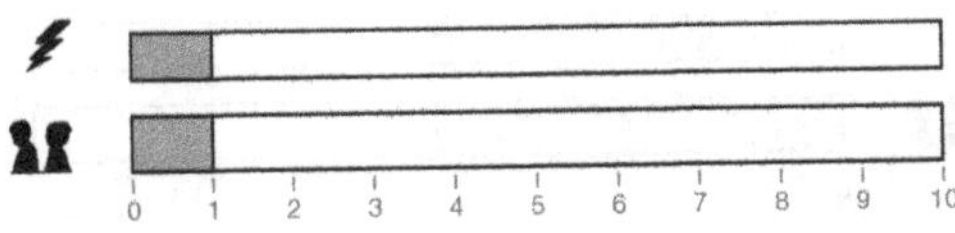

"What if" and "Suppose that" questions used during the exploratory and closing stages can help you to work out the degree of flexibility the other party is prepared to offer, or the relative value of the issues being discussed.

For example, "What if we were to 'hypothetically' increase the order after three months, how might that change the fee structure?" There may be no intention of doing so, but the idea is to test assumptions, gain insights, and ultimately trade more effectively later on during your negotiation. It can be used to explore possibilities, especially where deadlock is looming.

"Off the record"

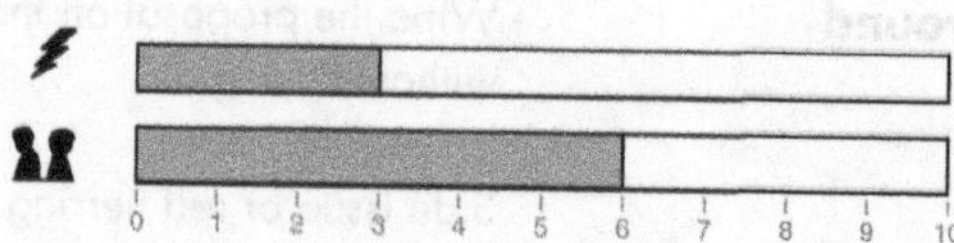

This is where one party asks the other for a view, a comment, or to simply share an insight, in the name of helping both parties make progress. Their intentions may be genuine, but the information is sought for one reason only: to get inside your head. You may choose to use it yourself for the same reason. However, when asked for an "off the record" meeting, always remember the real risks you carry. Any indications, signals, comments or even attitudes you imply will be read into. There is no such thing as an "off the record" meeting. Anything you tell them or their business will quickly make its way to the decision maker and is likely to influence the outcome. By all means make use of "off the record," but do not get used by it.

Full disclosure and openness

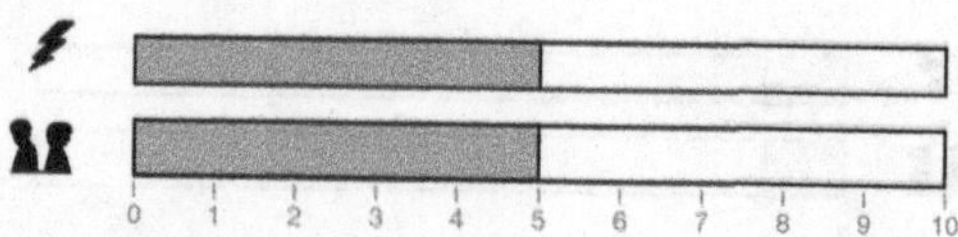

When a request for full disclosure is made before or during a meeting, there needs to be a reasonable degree of trust or mutual dependency before parties tend to agree. Even then it tends to come with conditions or limits: "We will share our data with you on the current site but feel that extending this to our overall operation to be unnecessary," is the type of response you will get. Some will say: "I'm going to be really open with you," which usually means they are not. This is also the case when people use such words as "really," "actually," "genuinely," "seriously," "sincerely" and, most common of all, "honestly." Whenever I have heard these words in negotiation where people are under pressure, I have concluded that the truth has not been in play. Listen out for them and remain mindful of the longer-term implications of full disclosure.

In reality, you can assume that something will usually be held back. The process of due diligence is used for particularly good reasons: to ensure the integrity of information provided is true and complete.

Why?

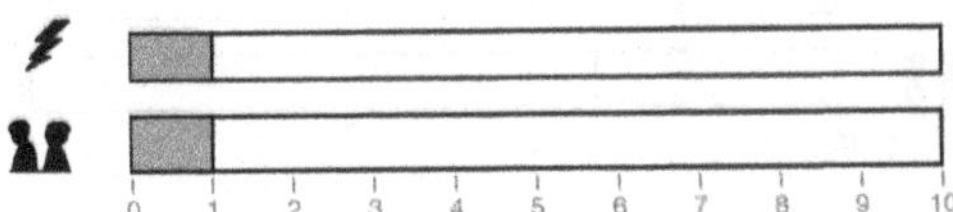

This simple question can be used to challenge everything from interests, priorities, agenda items, or even new proposals. It has been used as an effective way of establishing the thinking and importance of any issue or statement. Anyone can ask "why?", which is why curious children ask it time after time in their quest for knowledge. The information you receive will always provide an insight, even if it's something like: "We are not prepared to go into detail on that issue." During exploration discussions, it's worth asking why the other party is asking the very question that they are; and what insight this gives you into their thinking.

2. Time and momentum

Time is the most powerful lever available to any negotiator. Time and circumstances affect the value of just about every product or service bought and sold around the world. If I was going to provide you with a full advertising plan to support your June election campaign, but could not actually start until June, my services would be deemed useless and without value. However, if the service could commence in March and run for three months peaking with tailored activity throughout June, the service could attract a premium. It's the same service with a different time slot, which makes all the difference. So, understanding the time pressures of the other party is vital to you being able to optimize the leverage during your negotiations. How you communicate your own time pressures or use the other party's time pressures to gain movement or agreement can be directly influenced by the tactics you use.

Deadlines

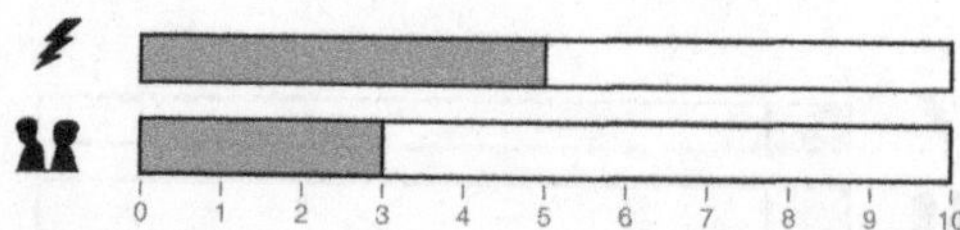

"If you do not agree by Friday we will not be able to start the project in the timescales you have stipulated."

"We are closing the book on this one so we will need to know by this afternoon if you want to take part."

"If we can agree in principle today, I will ensure you get the business, subject to us 'ironing out' the terms."

The pressure that deadlines can exert means that some may not only use this tactic as a closing device, but also to provide you with the feeling of having "won." Deadlines are used in many other ways, for example: "Because of changes in our business, after today's deadline, any agreement will have to be signed off by my boss." On some occasions, once the other party has established your deadlines they will employ this need as a trading variable. They will imply that the timing issue is not so critical to them. Be careful when providing total transparency relating to the implications of deadlines; it can be a highly effective and manipulative tool.

"And just one more thing"

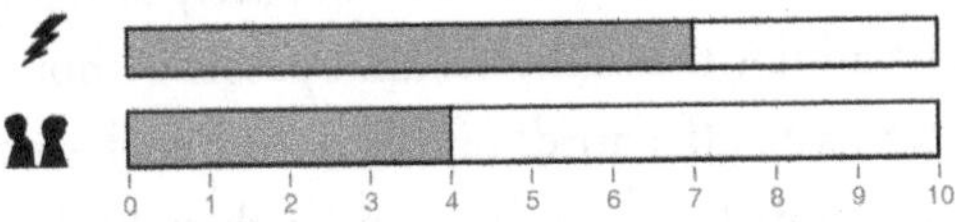

This is often used at the end of the negotiation when the deal is regarded as all but done. One party turns to the other just as you are about to shake hands and says: "Just one more thing, you will of course be including the flexible payment scheduling we discussed earlier?" They pause and wait with their hand held out. You think, I'm there, deal done, finished, closed. Do I now open the discussion again, or worse still, compromise the agreement by saying "No, but I didn't think that flexible payment scheduling was ever part of the terms we had agreed."

As you can see, this tactic has a higher relationship erosion factor. If the other party has either power or enough nerve, they will and should challenge the assumption by attaching a condition to the flexible payment scheduling in the same way they would have if it had been raised earlier during the formal discussions.

Denied access

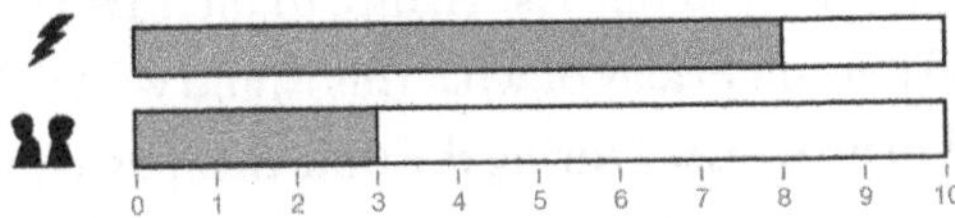

When you need to move discussions along, perhaps due to time pressure or the implications of deadlines, some will use denied access as a tactic. They simply ensure they are not available. They tell their colleagues and assistants to pass on the message they are in back-to-back meetings, out of town, away, or anything that ensures that you, the other party, cannot make progress until they are ready.

One way of dealing with this situation when you are confident that denied access is in play is to leave a message for the other party, bringing your deadline artificially forward, adding that if the deadline passes without agreement, the deal is off or the terms on offer are diminished. Although risky, this buys you a window of opportunity between the deadline they think you are working towards and the one actually in play. Another is to introduce a credible option, perhaps another party or option that you plan to take up and you need to let them know within certain timescales. If you don't hear back, you will place the order, reluctantly, elsewhere. Of course these options carry risks but often work as a way of unlocking the denied access tactic.

Time constraint

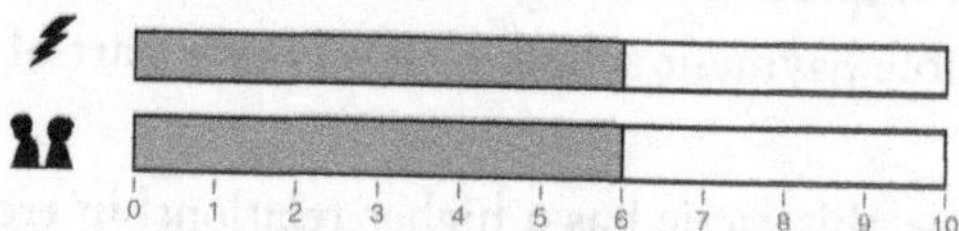

This is used where the other party introduces artificial timelines or deadlines, stating that their offer expires on a certain date. Further demands are then introduced as a consequence of the deadline not being met as "compensation" against the implications.

Time constraints are also used where one party is near agreement on most of the terms, but the other decides to hold out for a better fee rate. They say: "We will give you one last chance to increase your offer. Please advise us by 5:30 p.m. on Friday of what this is, and we will let you know if we are prepared to progress." During the time that passes, which is aimed at fuelling uncertainty and doubt, the other party is often pressured into improving their final offer.

The auction

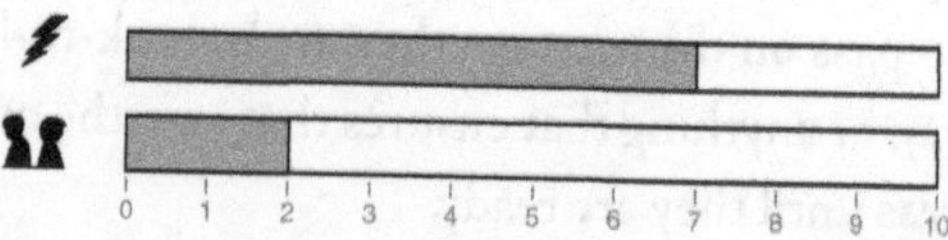

The bidding process is designed to create competition. The process is engineered and controlled by the organizers. As the bids increase, rational judgment is tested and for those with high egos, winning has been known to take over as the predominant driver of behavior. Time and momentum work against those willing to continue bidding, so a clear and absolute break point must feature as part of your planning if you are to enter such a process.

Time out

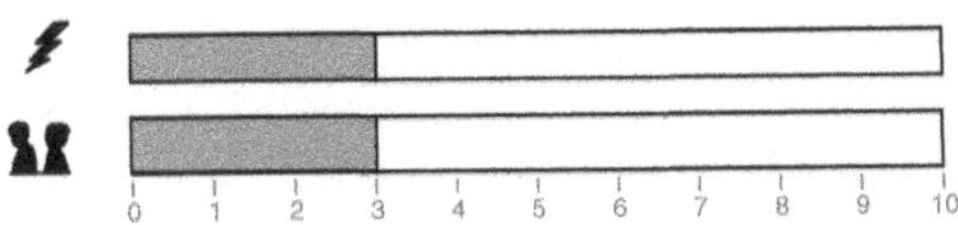

When in doubt, for whatever reason, adjourn the meeting and take a time out to regroup. You need to understand the implications, risks, or finances if you are to maintain clarity and be able to work out how you are going to move forward. It is often used when new information comes to the fore, or if deadlock is looming and a need for a "fresh look" at the deal is needed. It's also used when time is running out and one party chooses to put the other under pressure by removing themselves from the room until time pressures become critical.

3. Fear or guilt

This next category raises the stakes in the relationship and heightens the risk. With high levels of power, threats are used in subtle ways to create movement. It is the fear of these threats or the fear of losing the deal that is played upon by those seeking to manipulate the power they have.

Physically disturbing them

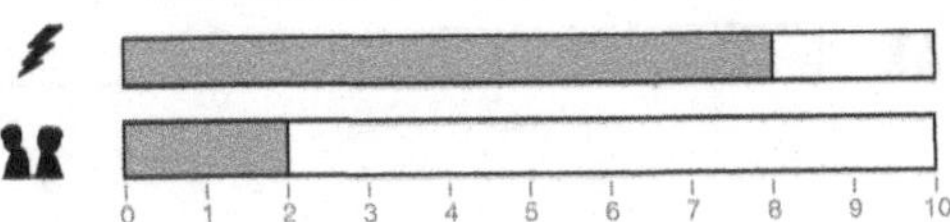

This is made up of a variety of non-violent yet physical gestures, which are introduced to unsettle and distract you. This can include leaning across the table to invade your personal space, sitting too close to you, or changing the seating pattern, so they are sat next to you. Seating positioned to face the sunlight or groups crammed into very small rooms are all part of the environment used to intimidate. Remember, you are in charge and that includes your environment, so if it does not feel right, challenge it, question it, and change it. You'll attract respect for doing so and set the scene for equal respect in the meeting.

Good guy, bad guy

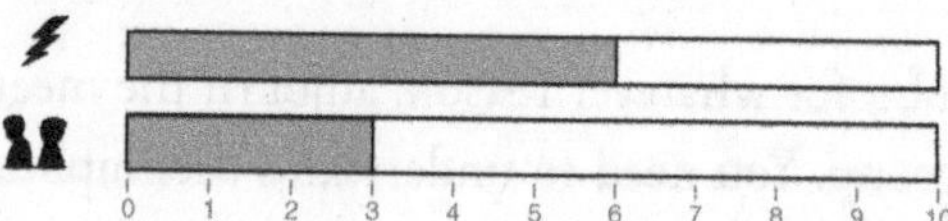

Typically used in team negotiations where one member of the team makes exceedingly high or irrational demands, and the other offers a more reasonable approach, or one is challenging and dismissive whilst their colleague presents themselves as far more understanding. The approach is designed to make the "good guys" appear reasonable, rational, and understanding, and therefore all the more agreeable. Essentially it's using the law of relativity to attract cooperation. It's transparent enough and certainly erodes any potential for trust, so ensure next time you are exposed to it that you see it for what it is.

The Russian front

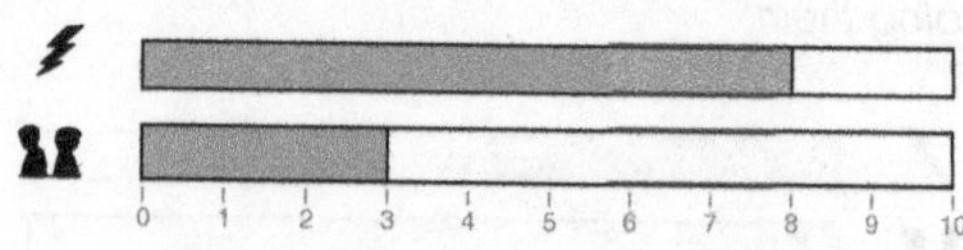

As described by Gavin Kennedy in his book *Everything is Negotiable*, this tactic is taken from the Second World War where a Russian lieutenant was told by his colonel that he would be sent to the Russian front unless he did as asked. The colonel had the power, the lieutenant believed it was for real, and the result was predictable. He would do whatever was asked willingly, rather than be sent to the Russian front. In negotiation, it is referred to when providing two options. One you know will prove challenging and the other an outright disaster. If the whole concept is not rejected, the chances are you will be seduced into agreeing to the challenging lesser of the two evils. A more recent example is when Acer, the computer manufacturer was a casualty of an earlier attack on Microsoft Exchange in which hackers used a vulnerability in Microsoft's Proxy-Logon to target Acer. Acer's identity and corporate data were posted on a data leakage site "Happy Blog" on March 18, and the attackers gave the company 10 days to pay the ransom of $50 million. If the ransom was not paid by the stipulated date, it would double to $100 million. It was to date, the largest cyber-attack pay out in history.

Personal favor

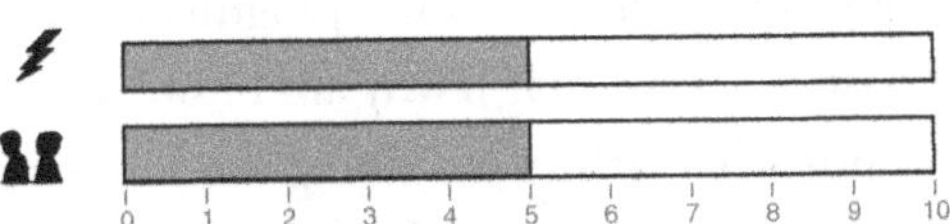

This tactic attempts to make the position or request "personal" and works most effectively in familiar relationships: "You can do this for old times' sake," or "If you do this for me I will ensure your proposal is accepted," or "You scratch my back and I'll scratch yours." It leans on a sense of obligation to the point where it's aimed at leaving you feeling embarrassed if you do not yield. You must remain firm, point out the compromising position this would leave you in and explain that it's not personal, just business.

Guilty party

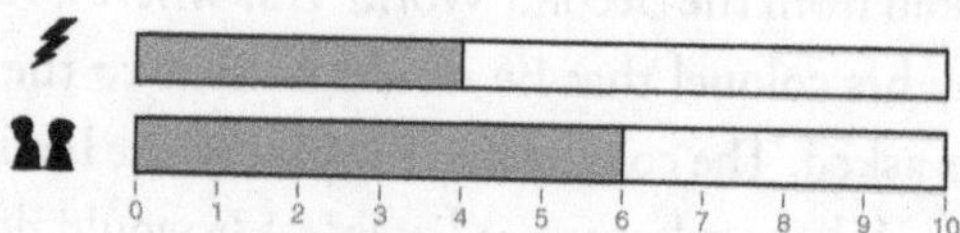

This involves suggesting that the other party is breaking some code or agreement, or that they are going against the industry norm, or that a commitment has not been met or a performance not as it should be. This tactic is used to full effect where one party is negotiating compensation to include inconvenience, loss of face, indirect loss of earnings, even future risk; this results in a demand far beyond the normal financial obligations.

The social smell

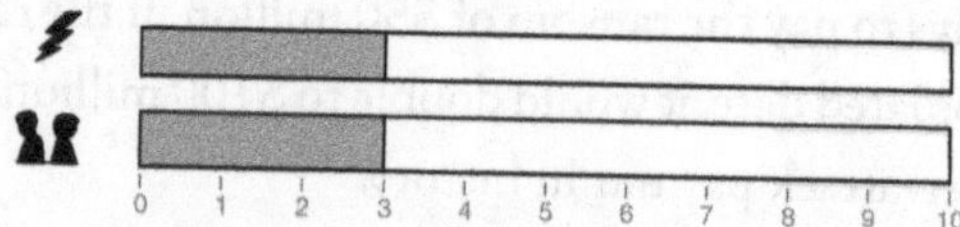

The social smell is used to imply that you are the odd one out. It's designed to make you question your own judgment: "If everyone else is behaving in a certain way (agreeing), why am I not?" It comes in the form of a statement about what "others are doing" and importantly what you are not. It implies that you are out of sync, the odd one out, and that you are missing out or even being irrational. "Everyone else has committed . . . you'll be the only one not included so you are likely to miss out whilst your competitors have all agreed." The idea is that it helps apply pressure to conform, highlights isolation, and promotes self-doubt.

Silence

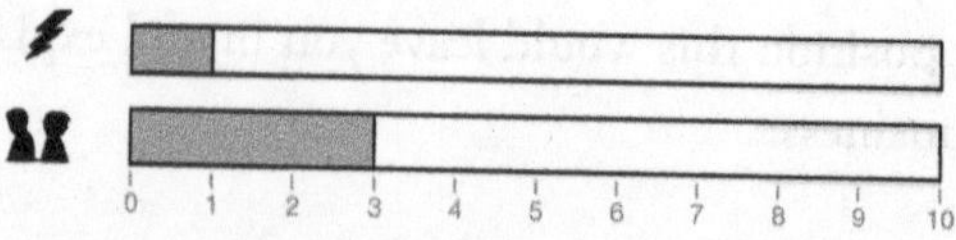

As a powerful tactic, silence is used to unnerve the other party. It can result in a waiting game because the first to talk is likely to be the first to concede. For many, the discomfort alone of continued silence can result in a concession or offer of further flexibility. And yet for the experienced negotiator, it may be that they simply need time to think through their next move. Silence is best used directly after you have stated your proposal or after they have stated theirs. Just wait. Even if they respond, wait further. The pressure builds and often leads to more concessions.

4. Anchoring

This is where one party sets out to form an anchor (an opening position taken up by one party from which they will move but such movement will come at a price). The aim of anchoring is to adjust the expectations of the other party by providing an extreme and yet realistic opening position. Movement becomes relative to the anchor. If you open with your position first and are able to get the other party talking about it, even if this means them rejecting it, it is your position that has becomes anchored in their mind. Unless they make a counteroffer. Often they become so preoccupied with attacking your position, they forget all about their own position.

Sow the seed early

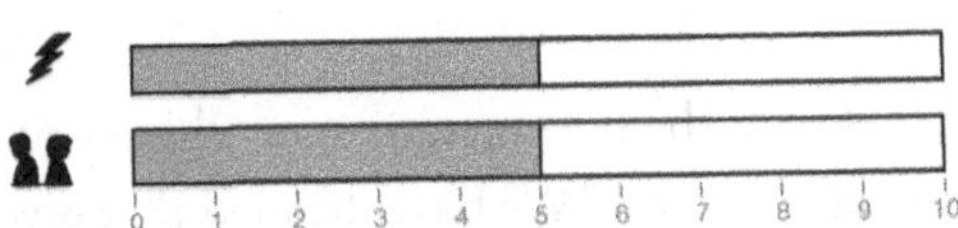

This can take the form of the advance telephone call, which is designed to introduce an idea or a position, allowing for any emotional reaction to take place prior to the meeting. Or ideas that are introduced and parked in earlier meetings in the knowledge that they will need to be addressed in subsequent meetings. Sowing the seed early is based on getting inside their heads and adjusting their expectations.

The power statement

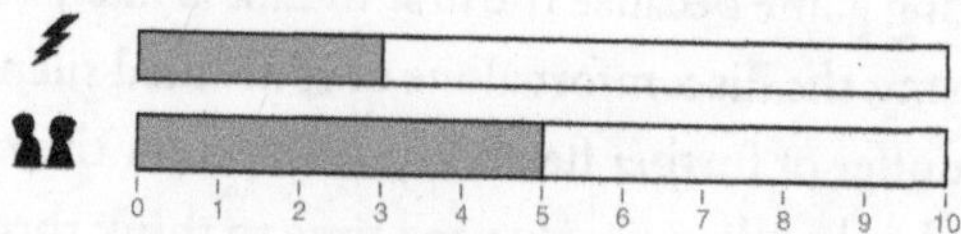

Opening power statements are designed to manage the aspirations of the other party. They are usually used as a statement in the form of an assumed fact. The idea is to test an assumed position of power by effectively telling them that, whilst you are in a position of "indifference," they are under pressure to conclude the deal with you: "I understand that you need an agreement in place by the end of the day," or "Mr Walker, I want to make it clear that todays discussions are to ensure that we have given you every opportunity to close the deal at £4m subject to our terms." The language is that used by a "critical parent" by implying assumed authority designed to get the other party talking and thinking about how they are going to move towards you.

The mock shock

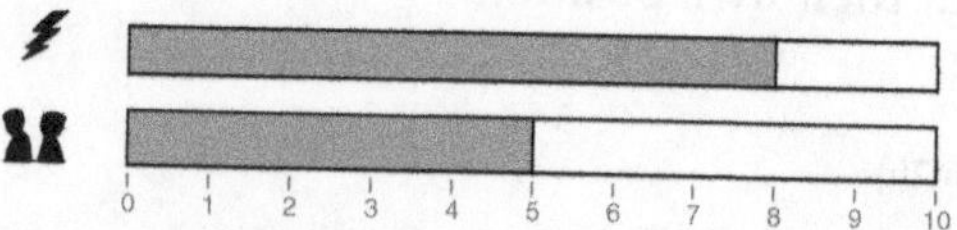

This is an extension to the power statement where you start the meeting by implying that all is lost: "We have decided that given your current performance levels and clearly no desire to offer compensation, terminating the contract is the only option for us." Or, "This may only be a small order, but failure to agree could affect all of your business with us." The devastating consequences of non-cooperation can shock the other party into reconsidering their position or backtracking from the outset, where saving the relationship becomes their primary objective.

The professional flinch

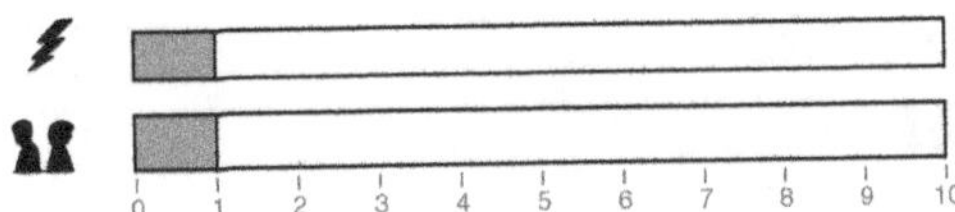

This is a shock reaction to their opening position. Both physically whether by extreme facial reaction and/or verbally, you are demonstrating your shock and surprise at their position. Used regardless of their opening offer and designed to lower their aspirations, the professional flinch has the effect of undermining their confidence in their position and expectations.

The broken record

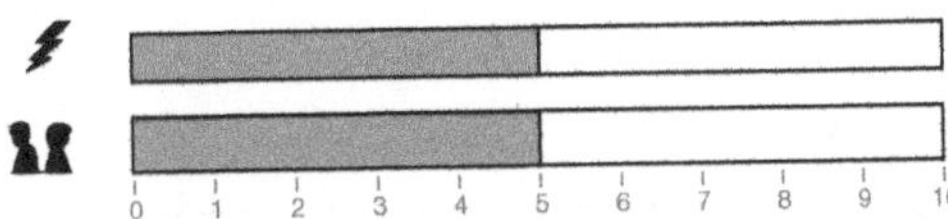

One party repeats their position. The more they repeat it, the more credible it becomes. The more their position is discussed, the more likely the discussion will revolve around their position. They start to sound like a broken record but the message gets through. Of course this can be interpreted as intransigence and can result in you losing patience and concluding the meeting. They will require a moderate amount of power of around 4/10 to be able to carry it off.

5. Empowerment

This involves the degree to which you are authorized to trade (see also Chapter 9) and the extent to which others need to be involved in the decision-making process.

Higher authority

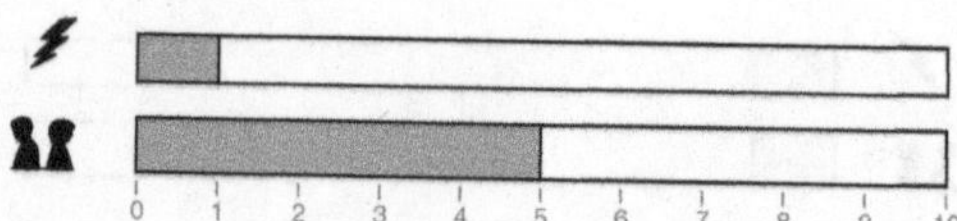

The use of the boss or a mysterious and distant overseeing body required to sign off anything beyond those limits that you are allowed to trade. The idea is to convince the other party to agree within the level you are authorized to go to, so that they can complete the deal today, rather than risk the deal being jeopardized, or so as not to allow your boss to see the other concessions that you have already offered. It's also used to disassociate yourself from not being able to accept a proposal: "That's out of my control, and I will need to come back to you on that one."

Defense in depth

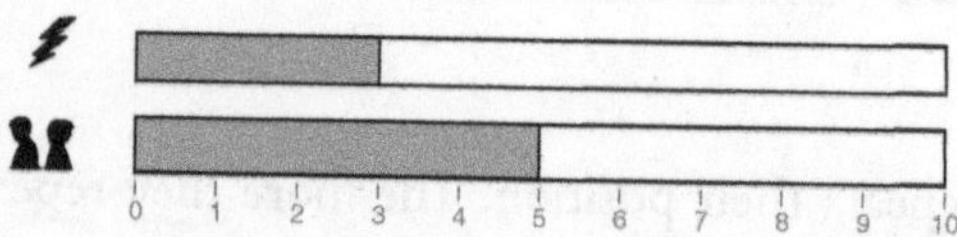

This is where several layers of decision-making authority allow for further conditions to be applied each time the agreement is referred. Typically it's where your supplier or customer states that they will take the deal for sign-off to their boss. A day later, the call comes that, subject to one final concession, the deal will be agreed. You reluctantly agree. A day later, they call and state that their boss has signed it off and it's now been sent for approval to the board and that if you could just agree to the 30-day payment terms it will gain agreement. Reluctantly you agree and ask if they will let you know when it has been approved. The next day, they call to again advise you that the board has now signed it off and they have now handed it over to Health and Safety for final approval and then advise you of yet another small concession that will be necessary if "final" sign-off is to be achieved. You should always understand the decision-making levels and process, otherwise you leave yourself exposed to defense in depth.

Use of official authority

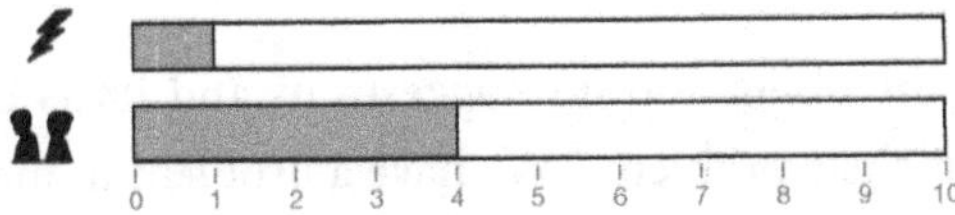

This is used where one party disempowers themselves, saying that they cannot or are not allowed to change the terms. They refer to their own company policy, legal requirements, association requirements, or even historical precedents and, although sometimes true, it's often a tactic in play used to legitimize their position. "Our company policy is 60 days payment on all transactions, and there is nothing we can do about that." It's frequently used to provide rationale in an attempt to bolster the credibility of their proposal. Ensure you insist that such constraints are their problem and that you welcome suggestions on how they plan to work around them in order to avoid you having to escalate the issue.

"It's all I can afford"

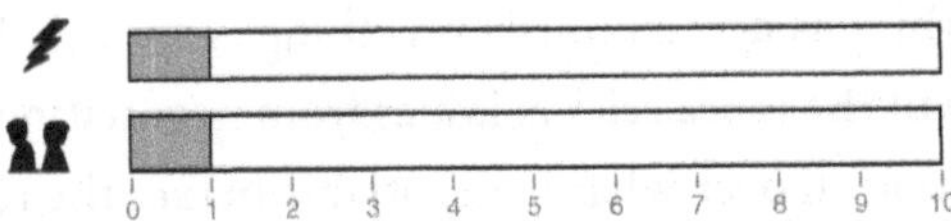

This is used to suggest that budgets are finite, the specification is fixed, and that it's all that is available: "I have no other funds available so take it or leave it." It's designed to place the onus of obligation on the other party, implying that they need to work within that which you can afford. In contrast, when faced with such tactics the receiving party can change the specification, the volume, the timing or any variable that helps to Neutralize the implications of the fixed fee.

Onus transfer

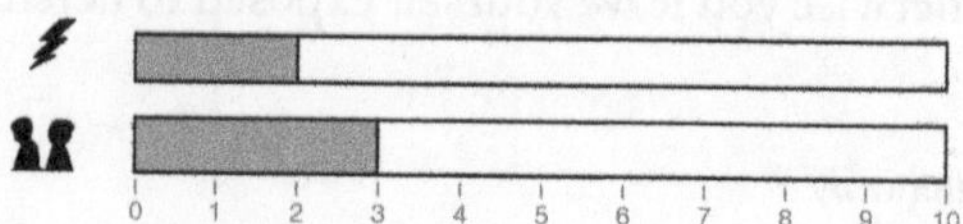

Transferring the obligation for suggestions and ideas onto the other party, to make it their problem. "We have a problem in making our payment on time this month. We can make the transfer but it is going to be five days late, how do you want to deal with this?" Once they have been advised, the problem becomes a shared one. The implications may still sit squarely with you but you have transferred the onus onto the other party.

Off-limits

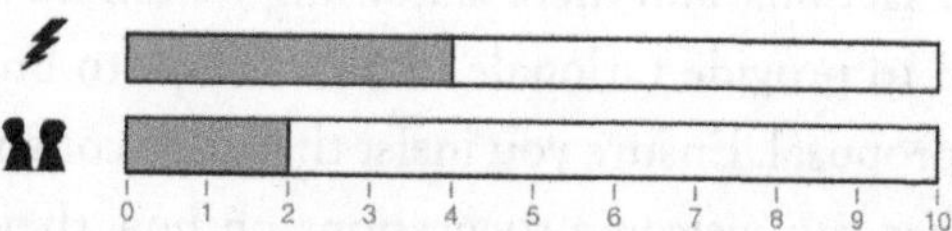

Where issues are positioned as off-limits (non-negotiable or "off the agenda" for the purpose of these discussions), they are often described as "things I can't agree, so let's focus on the terms we can agree today." Remember, nothing is agreed until everything is agreed. Their motive is to protect some of the more critical issues from negotiation. This can also result in a negotiation over what is negotiable before the real negotiation even begins. This tactic is commonly used in political negotiations but regularly features in all types of commercial settlement negotiations too.

New faces

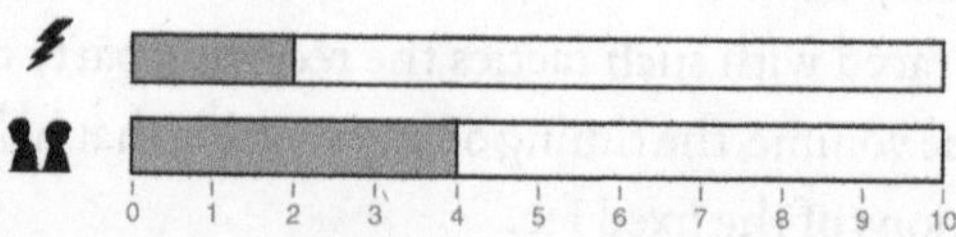

When a new person takes over the relationship or a new account manager is introduced, both past precedents and history carry far less relevance. New faces need not be tied to or constrained by what has happened in the past. They can sometimes offer a solution to deadlock where personalities stand in the way of progress. They can provide for a fresh examination of affairs or can even be used to intimidate the other party where the seniority of the new negotiator carries certain gravitas. Retailers are renowned for changing their buyers systematically and periodically so that new faces remove the familiarity of an existing trading relationship. This keeps the focus on terms fresh and removes any scope for complacency.

6. Moving the costs around

This category comes from reconfiguring the package or specification or manipulating the terms in order to provide a different complexion to the deal. The relationship between specification and price is used by many tactical negotiators as a means of manipulating the cost of supply, whilst attracting the best possible price.

The building block technique

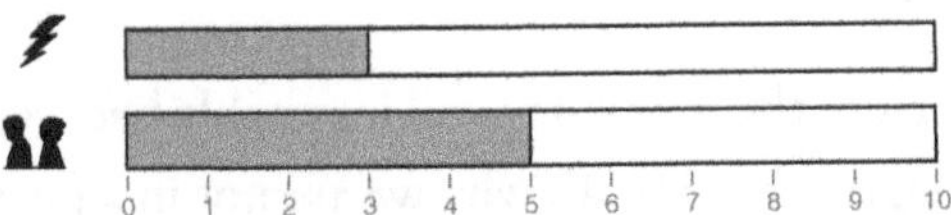

This is where one party requests a price but only for part of their actual requirements. You then request prices for various quantity arrangements, ranging up to and including your actual needs. The idea is to manage expectations in the first instance and understand the relative cost/price differences and implications across the different arrangements. This can reveal much about their cost base and margin structure. You then negotiate for a one-year agreement, for example, in the knowledge that you can raise this to a three-year agreement. You then seek incentives from the other party in the event that you could extend the agreement to two years, and then negotiate incremental terms for this "doubling" of the contract. Finally, you broaden the discussion to a three-year partnership. Of course, to agree to such a deal, you will require more preferential terms.

The building block technique involves planning out your stages, which can apply to any variable and provides time for the other party to adjust to concessions that would otherwise be difficult to extract.

Wipe the proposal off the table without saying no

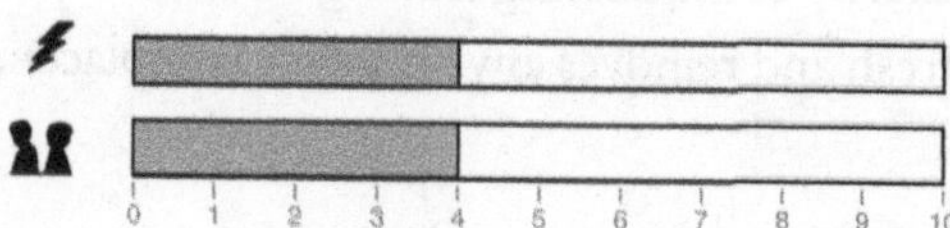

Each time they make a proposal, you say: "Yes, subject to our terms."

Your terms turn out to be either equally as outrageous or are financially designed to offset the implications of agreeing to them. One party says: "Your discount levels based on last year's performance are being adjusted from 10% to 7.5% for the year ahead." And the other party responds: "Subject to you improving your promotional funding from $100,000 to $250,000 for the year, we will accept the reduction in discount."

The response from the first party will inevitably be: "We can't do that" to which you suggest: "And that's why we are not in a position to accept your position." You rarely need say no in a negotiation. Just find a way, a basis, a set of conditions upon which the consequences, be they financial, risk, or third-party implications, are neutralized by the terms you attach to it.

Linking the issues

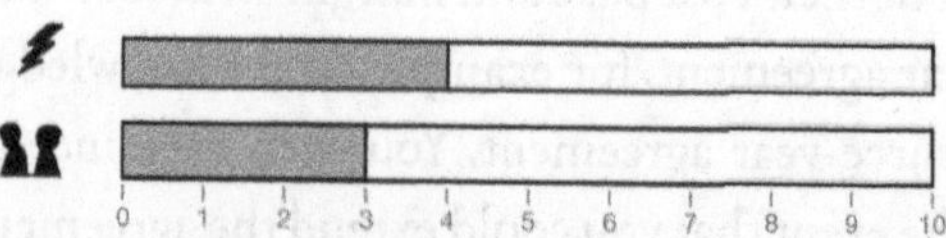

Everything is conditional and therefore linked to other conditions. Linking the relative values and importance of issues is key to ensuring that linked issues gain the attention you require. This is sometimes used to protect certain terms. For example, if the contract length was very important to one party and they knew that a high-value variable to the other party was attracting a 10,000-volume order, the two could be linked to ensure that the contract length issues could not be easily dismissed.

Side issue or red herring

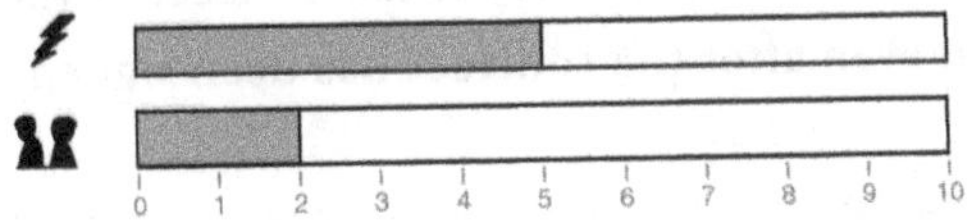

This is where some issues are introduced onto the agenda that have been positioned to lose or trade off against. Later during the negotiation, value is traded as each of the "red herrings" is conceded, having played their part in attracting improved terms elsewhere. For example, you need to attract shorter lead times and improved discounts. Both items are on the agenda as is a new termination clause, allowing you to terminate the contract with short notice and lower volume discount thresholds. The last two are effectively red herrings, which you expect to concede on. However, in doing so you are able to trade for better terms on lead times and discounts.

The slice

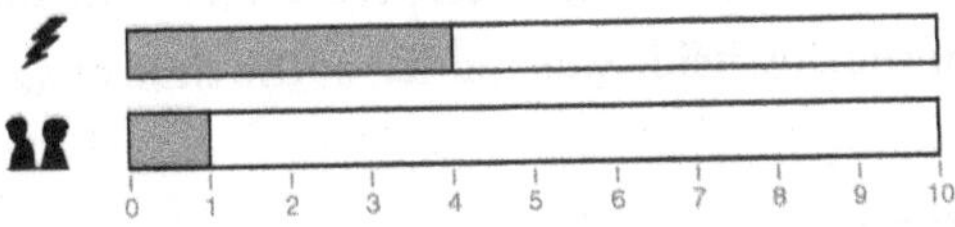

This is where you believe that the issue is of high value to the other party and trade against the issue in "slices." For example, you know that volume is critical to them. You are currently at 50,000 units and know that your requirement is for an order of 150,000 units. Rather than trade up to 150,000 units, you trade to 80,000 in return for a concession. Later you trade to 100,000 for a further concession, then to 115,000, and so on. Each move is conditional on a concession, ensuring that the value of your total move is maximized.

7. Deceit

There is no other way to describe this final category: Deceit. If reputation or relationships hold any value to you or your business, think twice before using the following. More importantly, be wary of those who carry a different view and choose to use deceit – they may choose to use it on you even after the contract has been signed.

Trojan horse

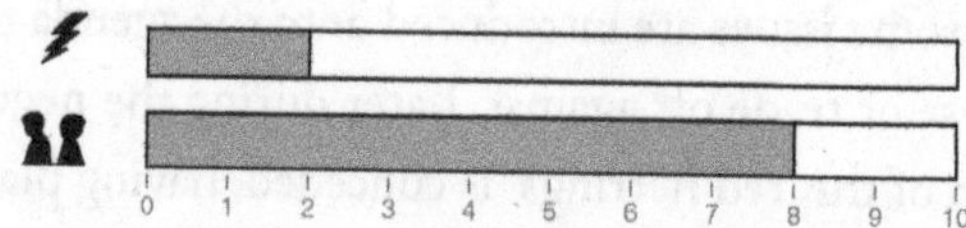

This is named after a tactic used during the ancient war on Troy, which led to the saying: "Beware of Greeks bearing gifts." The Greeks left a gift in the form of a wooden horse outside Troy. The Trojans accepted the gift and brought it inside the city only to find that the horse was full of soldiers ready to invade. Beware if the deal is too good to be true. This relates to the hidden small print, and the conditions and issues that can literally come out of the woodwork after the deal has been completed. The Trojan horse represents a package created to entice you. Once accepted, it has some surprises in store because much of the downside was hidden at the time of agreement.

The incorrect summary

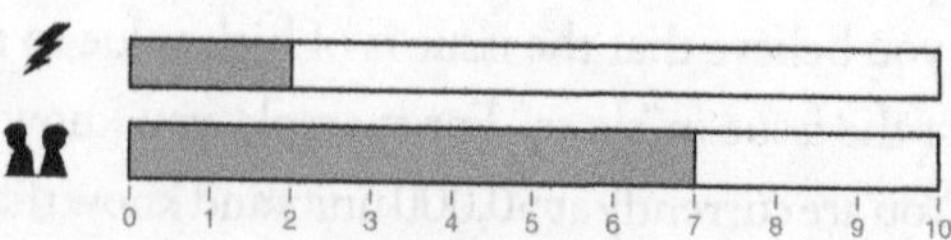

This is where one party summarizes from their perspective, leaving out or even adjusting some of the terms discussed earlier. The idea is that you won't notice or won't challenge through fear of jeopardizing progress. Try to ensure that you summarize progress throughout the meeting and that you do so from your perspective. Also, ensure that you summarize in writing after the meeting. If you don't agree on what you believe you have agreed, then you're unlikely to have an agreement that is going to stand the test of time.

Deliberate misunderstanding

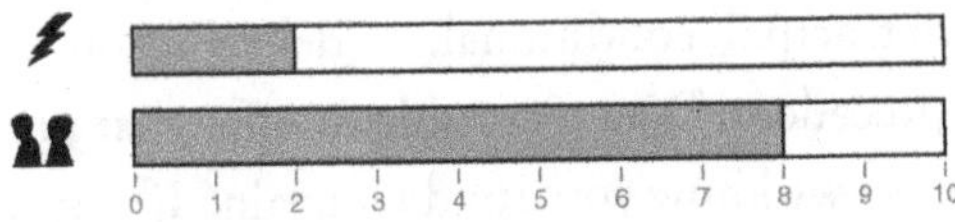

So as to open up areas that have already been regarded as concluded, one party introduces a condition that they know to be unacceptable. After you have responded with confusion or start to demand clarity they adopt an "innocent misunderstanding" stance. Their motives could be varied, but it is usually related to stalling progress or allowing them to try and renegotiate terms that have otherwise been regarded as closed.

The dumb foreigner

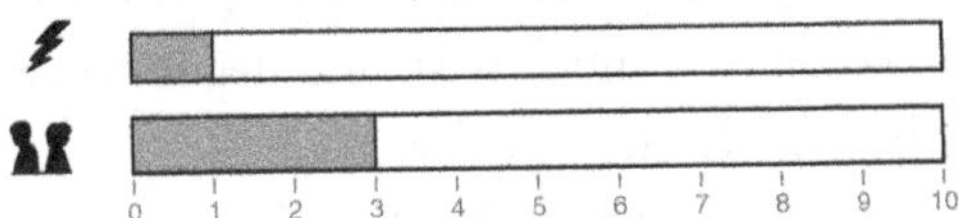

They choose not to understand you at a given time during the negotiation due to language difficulty. This is especially used once the subject of price is introduced. As they seek to take up a firm position, they appear increasingly confused by what you have to say as you attempt to explain your position. When faced with such behavior, patience, restating your position, and maybe even a "time out" is needed to dampen their confidence.

The loss leader

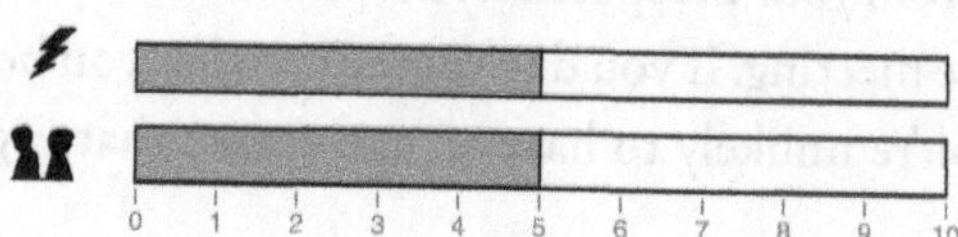

This involves one party convincing the other to agree to a deal at highly preferential rates, which will lead to benefits in the future. These "benefits" are often not contractual, conditional, or delivered on. In fact they are often used as a precedent: "You were able to offer that price last time we worked with you so we know you can do it again." If you are to enter into such agreements always ensure that it is in writing and the conditions are clearly stated in the contract.

Influential tactics in negotiation have been used for thousands of years as a means of gaining leverage and advantage. They can be as subtle as providing misleading information or as blatant as an outright lie. As you never need to lie in negotiation, many tactics are regarded as a fast route to destroying trust.

NOW DO THIS!

- Qualify and challenge tactics or where appropriate just ignore them.
- Use tactics based on how much trust and dependency you require in the relationship once the deal is done.
- Judge the risk/benefit of using tactics based on your own circumstances, risks, objectives, motivation, and values.
- Watch out for more than one tactic being used at once designed to increase pressure as others will seek to manipulate your actions.
- Perform as a conscious competent negotiator with increased awareness of the tactics in play.

CHAPTER 11

Planning and Preparation That Helps You to Build Value

"There is only one good, knowledge, and one evil, ignorance."

—Socrates

Planning and preparation is the most fundamental element of negotiating and it is only when the deal is done that the value of this can be fully appreciated. In simple terms, the more reactive you are, the more likely you will negotiate tactically. The more proactive you are, the more choices you will create, more opportunity for collaboration and in turn scope for value. In all my experience I have concluded that there is a direct correlation between how well you have planned and the outcome of your negotiations. Timing is everything. If time is against you, you have already lost power. Uncertainty is the seed of stress so ensuring that "Time" is on your side through planning will not only provide you with power and options it will reduce the temptation to become unnecessarily reactive, weak, and compromising.

To start with it is important not to get confused between knowledge and action. What you understand will help you to perform but this knowledge counts for nothing if you don't possess the motivation to *do* and that requires being available to plan and prepare. Ignore or avoid this reality at your peril. There will be many reasons, excuses, and time distractions that will impact on your performance as a negotiator. However, if you are disciplined enough to plan and prepare, if you regard the time as more important than the negotiation itself, you will create value and achieve results that would simply not be possible. So, regard planning not as pre-negotiation but part of which without, you are accepting a suboptimal starting position.

Planning creative trade-offs which realize additional value

If you have ever played the game *Tetris* you will know there is a skill involved in getting the right shapes in the right places and in the right order to maximize your score. If you do not adjust the pieces or move the shapes as they become visible they will simply stack up on each other, leaving you with lots of gaps and a low score.

Similarly, in negotiation and working with variables, there is a skill in agreeing to the way and order in which you position the variables. Your motivation, mindset, and flexibility in moving variables around, resulting from your planning, provide endless possibilities to maximize the value. In the negotiation, the value you create can depend on the degree to which you can shape each variable to minimize any gaps between you and the other party.

As a Complete Skilled Negotiator the number of negotiation variables, the possibilities and scope to negotiate will be more easily identified during your planning and preparation than during the negotiation itself although they are not exclusive. A proactive and open-minded approach provides a fundamental advantage in working out what each aspect of the deal means to you and to the other party. You would not try to build a house without having completed the drawings, worked through your calculations, and estimated your costs. You would know instinctively that the project would most likely fail without a plan. Negotiation is no different because, once you have started, you should seek to maintain dialog and a proactive position so as to remain in control. Without a plan, you are more likely to be in a reactive position, exposing yourself to circumstances and a position that could easily spiral out of your control.

EACH AND EVERY DEAL IS UNIQUE

Every negotiation you enter will have a set of circumstances surrounding it that effectively make it unique, even those that exist in familiar relationships. Your relationship, timings, market changes, the options you may have, how important the agreement is, and the issues to be agreed will all contribute to the dynamics that create each unique set of circumstances. Working out exactly what is unique to each negotiation will also enable you to be creative in your planning. Recognizing this also helps you to get "inside the other person's head," work with a more complex mix of variables with clear financial values, and tackle the more ambiguous or intangible variables, which can often hold the key to additional value.

Even when you have invested time preparing it's important to realize that, once discussions get under way, you should expect the unexpected. New ideas, consequences, and issues will surface during meetings. These may come in the form of a proposal or a demand you may not have considered before. You will then need to be available to think through the possible implications and, of course, your response. However, just because an idea is new, don't reject it because you have yet to consider the implications or cannot calculate the risks immediately. Often there's a signal within the proposal that relates to what's important to the other party. New ideas can also help you to work out what is going on in the other party's head.

UNDERSTANDING VALUE

There are six things that can happen to value in negotiation. You can:

1. Give it
2. Create it
3. Share it
4. Protect it
5. Take it
6. Dissolve it

As part of your tactical planning you will have considered the clock face and decided on your strategy. If you are planning to increase prices and there are no trade-offs involved, they may regard the negotiation as you simply looking to "take" value. However, before you can impose such a price increase you need to consider the balance of power. For example, the fact that you can tell your kids what to do doesn't mean that it will always be the best thing to do, as you consider the longer-term implications for your relationship. In other words, the more powerful you are, the more options you have, but you need to remain mindful of the longer-term dependency in play.

The three dynamics of value

In negotiation, as in business, the general offer is that you can have "it" quick, good, or cheap. Now pick any two.

In other words, if you are offered all three, you are likely to be getting something that is too good to be true. "Quick" usually means now but for most suppliers it means additional cost. "Good" can mean high quality but will usually come at greater cost. "Cheap" may be possible but the quality may suffer and the speed may not be as quick as you need.

There are many things in life you can obtain quick and cheap. Take the hamburger: the quality is not going to be that of a prime steak, despite what the marketing might suggest. You can get a great first-class airline seat immediately (good and quick) but it will cost you more. You can get a great app to manage your finances that's instant and cheap, but you can't customize it to your precise needs so it's only partially useful and then it will ask you to upgrade to premium at a price! You can have a beautiful garden if you plant and tend it yourself at a reasonable price, but it might take a year or two for the benefits to arrive. These three dynamics of value fit together in the same way as risk and benefit go hand in hand in that one will nearly always affect the other. For instance, if you want low risk you expect the cost to rise because low risk comes at a price. Similarly, if you are prepared to take greater risks you will probably be offered better returns.

What do we mean by total value?

In most negotiations there is a central issue. This might relate to the price of an office lease, a trade union challenging changes to working practices, or an internal negotiation over who gets what percentage of the marketing budget. Whatever the issue, this provides you with an opportunity to better negotiate around it by introducing and trading it against other related variables, considerations, and implications, all of which will have some bearing on the total value.

A GREAT PRICE OFTEN LEADS TO A LOUSY DEAL

Anyone who drives price as the only consideration is likely to end up with regrets if you accept the mantra "you get what you pay for." Effective negotiators will use power derived from time and circumstance, the power resulting from supply and demand and from the available options that one party or the other has. How much you understand these and how much you decide to use them will be down to your judgment. Where there is some level of dependency in play once the deal is done (as in most B2B situations), then total value carries a greater consequence than simply price. If you feel comfortable booking laser eye surgery or a vasectomy at the lowest price then you have to come to terms with the risk you take at a very personal level. Would you hire the cheapest lawyer to manage your divorce or send your kids to the cheapest dentist because of price? Probably not. There will be many other variables in play and you will probably place a value on each of them.

Try to remove *price* as the main issue of contention. It is the most transparent and contentious of issues ("what you get, I lose and what I get, you lose"), especially when dealt with in isolation. Even if you negotiate creatively around a range of variables but leave price until the end, you are likely to finish up back at 4 o'clock – hard bargaining. With nowhere to go you are just as likely to deadlock over price at the end as if this had been the only issue under consideration. By introducing it early instead, you can always revisit it as part of changing other terms during the negotiation. Keep it in the mix, and conditional.

Total value comes not only from the basic terms agreed, but also from certainty or whether the deal will actually deliver the value intended over the lifetime of the agreement.

Where you are reliant on the other party's motivation to deliver over the lifetime of the agreement, to perform or comply, and in the event that their performance falters, you, or your business will be exposed to the implications of such shortfalls. So part of your consideration needs to focus on the period of time known as "follow through." This means setting out terms to protect and ensure adequate compensation in the case of lack of compliance or performance. These terms should also ensure that the consequences to you are addressed and compensated for, removing the need for further negotiations. Essentially you are "future proofing" the agreement.

THE SEVEN PRIMARY VARIABLES

There are seven primary variables that tend to feature across any type of deal from business to politics. This helps to capture all the issues that are likely to affect the total value of your agreements. Once defined, you can use them to broaden out the scope of the agreement and to consider the consequences of performance around each of these variables. During your planning this also provides you with the opportunity to introduce a range of conditions linked to each variable.

1. **Price, fee, or margin** (how much will be paid).
2. **Volume** (how many, how much, or what types).
3. **Delivery** (when, where, response times).
4. **Contract period** (when it will start, how long it will run for, under what circumstances it will or can be terminated, when it will be reviewed, etc.).

5. **Payment terms** (when, how, currency, etc.).
6. **Specification** (what the product, service, or agreement will include, the quality or how it will be supported).
7. **Risk** (who is accountable for what and how will deviations be remedied).

1. Price, fee, or margin

You can build agreements that feature differing pricing structures. These can be linked to issues such as:

- the purpose for which the product or service is to be used;
- geography (regional pricing to be used and by whom); and
- relationship loyalty.

They should also be linked directly to the other six primary variables. If this is not done, then the transparency involving "what I get, you lose and what you get, I lose" will usually result in tough positional bargaining. So try wherever possible to link price with other issues.

2. Volume

There are few cases where volume does not feature in negotiations and in most cases there is a direct relationship between price and volume unless you are buying a one-off event or specific tangible item. The economies of scale usually provide for this, so much so that some businesses will present price/volume relationships on a published discount tariff. As an extension to the price list, this is also designed in an attempt to preempt further negotiation. Volume thresholds can sometimes be linked to retrospective discounts (a discount you receive on the whole order, but only when a certain volume order has been achieved) or can provide increased discount levels, depending on volume levels to promote loyalty and volume orders.

3. Delivery

This refers to where, by when and how, the physical product or services are to be delivered or completed.

Where delivery is stipulated to be by the end of the month, for example, further variables can be introduced to stipulate the consequences of not meeting these delivery commitments. This can take the form of a penalty clause, or other forms of compensation linked to protecting against implications in the event that commitments are not met.

The construction industry uses this approach where contractors have to finish within certain timelines to enable others to start work. If they do not, there are financial implications for both the main contractor and other sub-contractors. So the risk and consequences are negotiated into the agreement so that responsibility and implications around timescales sit with the sub-contractor. They in turn may choose to negotiate terms that accommodate shared risk, recognizing circumstances beyond their control like weather:

"If it rains for more than 50 percent of the days we have to complete the job, we will be allowed a further ten days to complete without penalty."

4. Contract period

Think of the contract duration. The start, stop, pause, cancel, recommence terms, each with different circumstances attached, and you can start to imagine just how many variables could be included when you consider contract period. For those involved in negotiating lease contracts, this is one of the most valuable variables, in that to attract a five-year agreement rather than a one-year agreement buys so much more security and certainty.

Even if it is a rolling contract (ongoing) there will still be circumstances upon which an opt-out clause can be contractually exercised. Another variable designed to protect contract period commitments is termination, where you stipulate where one party can terminate the contract with or without reason or consequence as well as defining when the option to renew becomes available.

5. Payment terms

There are so many ways of constructing payment terms to reflect the risk to those involved, the commitment to see the work through, or simply to increase the value of the deal. They can be broken down to include:

- when and how payment will be made;
- advanced deposits;
- phased payments;
- even circumstances where delayed payment may be acceptable; and
- late payment penalties.

Proposals that include payment terms can be triggered based on performance, can be held on account, paid retrospectively, be refundable, or with a defined number of days credit.

Sometimes payment terms reflect cash flow requirements, the risks associated with the creditworthiness or history of the other party or simply a reflection of the standard terms of the dominant party in the negotiation.

Whichever one of these features, payment terms have a financial implication for both parties and will feature as a primary variable.

6. Specification

Specification relates to almost anything that affects the quality of the product or service being offered. As a simple illustration, the materials specification of a garment in addition to design can relate to size, fabric, wash type, buttons, zips, lining, finishing, presentation, and packaging, and each of these will have a multitude of options each impacting on the cost or value of the finished product. Imagine the number of variables involved for a company sourcing aircraft from one of the main manufacturers with literally thousands of specifications, which all affect the total outcome of the agreement. The complexity of the product or service, where it is being sourced from, the financing arrangements, and the relationships involved will all have some impact on the level of detail and the number of variables that will relate to specification.

7 Risks

Often found in standard terms and conditions is what happens in the event that one party deviates from the agreement or who is responsible for what. When you understand the other's perception of risk or ability to negotiate it you have a variable that is not only valued differently but provides you with a way of de-risking an agreement or obtaining better terms especially when it clearly important to the other party. Presenting these risks as part of your standard terms and conditions suggests that the terms are "off the table" yet understanding the terms from the other parties perspective can often create more flexibility around issues that would otherwise be difficult to move.

Risk clauses are often attached to performance or compliance issues and represent a powerful negotiating variable when different parties have a different perception of the risks in play.

WORKING WITH VARIABLES

Whenever the focus and pressure is on price, there is a tendency to renegotiate other variables as part of offsetting any implications on price movement. This usually involves introducing other variables as part of compensation for or adjusting the price point. This enables the Complete Skilled Negotiator to maintain the total value on offer despite price pressures. In other words, this is about moving the package around to reduce risk and to grow the total value. Everything is conditional – which allows you to protect the value – so if one variable needs adjusting down others can be moved to offset the implications.

NEGOTIATING FOR WHAT'S IMPORTANT TO YOU. . .AND THEM

Makers of the finance app Dymest, a Polish tech start up team had successfully launched their app designed to create a personalized

P&L directly from your bank statement allowing everyone "transparency and clarity around their finances." The 15 Euros a month subscription, following a free one-month trial appeared to be working as their social media had promoted 10,000 subscribers in its first three months of operating, well in excess of their expected forecast.

With three employees in the business and an external platform provider Luna, known for their reliability, the business was already working on its first upgrade as well as dealing with minor user experience issues. On day 81 of operation the system crashed and the guaranteed backup failed to trigger. All data was saved but had to be transferred across to a mirrored version manually which took two days. The result was 2,300 subscription cancellations and three media articles warning of the risks of managing personal finance via "simple apps."

This major setback had short-term revenue implications. It also had brand damaging implications and confidence broken because assurances of a triggered backup did not happen and therefore how could it be trusted that it would not happen again?

A Zoom meeting was called to discuss the issues and implications. Dymest had invested too much to walk away from the Luna platform and start again. Luna recognized that they had obligations that would need to be addressed. Luna opened the meeting with an explanation of how it happened and why it could not happen again, their view of their accountability, and then outlined a three-year heavily discounted scheme as a compensation package. Apart from being severely financially compromised in their first year of trading, Dymest had a genuine brand issue that was certain to damage their performance, even their viability as a first-year startup. The founder of Dymest outlined their actual losses (assuming a three-year subscription by 2,300 users), he

(*Continued*)

(Continued)

doubled it to accommodate the users they would probably not get in the short-term and said: "Before we talk about brand reputation and how you can help with this and what future service guarantees you are offering and how you plan to make these work there is a sum of 828,000 euros immediate loss to our business." With that he shared a document breaking down the figure. The account manager for Luna flinched and indicated that he would need to escalate to his boss before discussing any direct compensation. A week later, the two companies met at Dymest's small office in Warsaw. The Account manager for Luna, Country manager and company lawyer all attended the meeting. They opened the meeting with a compensation offer of 1.2m euros. The Dymest team again reiterated the issue of brand damage and the loss of confidence in Luna's ability to guarantee service levels. The meeting lasted three hours but the issues were never fully addressed. Dymest finally agreed to a figure of 1.5 million euros, concluded the meeting. Within a week they set about sourcing a new platform provider who were prepared to invest the funds in the migration project that would follow. Had Luna provided PR support and a second and third layer system integrity support, the compensation could probably have been less and they would have saved a client. Luna simply refused to listen, acknowledge what was being said, or address the real concerns. They focused on a financial solution. It cost 1.5 million euros which was not even conditional on any future commitment. However, it did offer them a non-disclosure agreement and brand protection of their own. Had Dymest understood the importance of the NDA Luna's lawyer had tabled, Dymest may have negotiated and held out even longer.

KNOWING WHAT VARIABLES YOU HAVE TO WORK WITH

Your planning and preparation should help you to create more value from your agreement, starting with expanding the issues and variables available.

It's easier to visualize the need to plan when negotiating over something with a physical form, such as an aircraft, compared with planning simply to build a service agreement. You can more easily imagine the design and planning needed when creating a new aircraft, critical to it ever coming together, let alone flying, in the first place. The creativity employed by an artist, starting with a blank canvas and with all the work to do ahead of them, requires flexibility and a mental picture for what will be. In both cases, options and creativity play a significant part in ensuring a successful outcome, as well as necessity for some visionary thought.

During the planning phase, scoping and taking the opportunity to create value starts with understanding the options and bringing together component parts or variables that will make the deal both possible and ultimately more valuable (see Figure 11.1).

Moving conditional proposals or variables around, changing who takes responsibility for what, and shifting performance triggers, discount thresholds, performance conditions, and contract terms in your negotia-

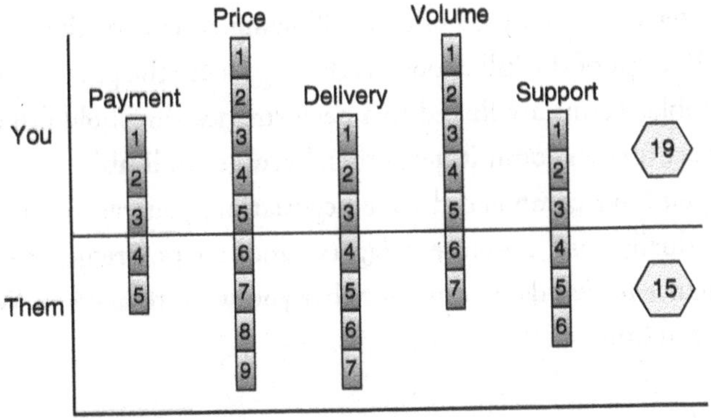

Figure 11.1 Trading off variables.

tions is essentially about you establishing the point where both parties will and can agree.

Attaching triggers to variables

Most variables can be used on a sliding scale. For example, if you are discussing volume, the order could be anything from one to one million, which would in turn affect other variables.

However, volume can be linked to a trigger that sets off other terms you agree. For example, once you have ordered 1,000 the 5 percent discount commences, or if you are able to place an order for 10,000 in any given month the delivery becomes free or, by agreeing to the total order now, we will allow you to draw off stock as you require it over the next six months. Each condition serves as a trigger that, if met, provides for the benefit offered.

Triggers can be applied to any variable and serve to motivate the behaviors of the other party as well as to protect your interests. Variables can also have triggers attached to them that relate to a particular performance, beyond or up to which another condition is met. For example, a discount that kicks in after the order for the first 200 has been received. The 200th order represents the trigger for the discount to become applicable. The payment terms can only be offered following receipt of the 20 percent deposit. Receipt of the full deposit is the trigger for the payment terms to be applicable. Terms are linked to a performance threshold (an order of 200), where further commitments then become applicable.

Once you have commenced your negotiation, you can trade-off variables gradually, use absolute triggers, and adapt trigger thresholds (performance levels) depending on what you want to achieve. With any variable, you can:

- adjust it;
- link it;
- place a trigger on it; or
- even move it bit by bit.

This is commonly known as **the "salami" tactic.** As an example of trading off a variable gradually, you could link a quicker guaranteed response on the service provided conditional of a reduction in payment terms from 45 days to 40 days. You may trade a commitment to flexible delivery timings in return for a further move of payment terms to 36 days. Perhaps you have the knowledge that they are really keen to get their 30 days payment agreed, which is their "symbol of success." So you go back and finally offer them the 30 days in return for a shorter termination notice period. Each time, you are attracting more value (or less risk by your calculation) than the very 15 days payment terms that you expected to move to in the first place. By this time, you may have calculated that, although the 15 days have cost you the equivalent of 0.5 percent on the deal, the concessions you have attracted are worth 1.1 percent.

The "salami" tactic
Negotiating each variable slice by slice and each time attracting a benefit in return.

RISK AS A NEGOTIABLE

As Anja Shortland highlights in her excellent book *Kidnap*, inside the ransom business, managing risk is the key to unlocking opportunities. A philosophy that equally applies to buying ice cream applies to negotiating the freedom of a hostage.

Even if you have business partnership relationship, based on an aligned strategy, how do you reasonably ensure that you remain continuously aligned as both your companies continue to reassess their strategies?

In other words, when considering the future and the contract you are about to sign, never assume a constant state. Things will always change over time. Performance, reliability, the market, and demand can and usually do change, and should challenge your assumptions about how profitable the deal is, will be, or has been. It is these very issues driven by change that you need to factor into your planning. The value to you of a guarantee that protects you against change, and the value of accountability and responsibility are often different from the cost of accepting them.

For example, the price or value of a flexible airline ticket will mean different things to you and the airline in the transaction; for example, the convenience of being able to switch and change can provide tremendous value to you. Imagine if you are having difficulty getting home from a business meeting late on a Friday night following a flight cancellation. Yet the absolute cost to the airline of offering a flexible service in many cases is negligible. So how much is this protection against change or the cost of inconvenience following change worth to you? Again, that depends on your circumstances. Creative negotiators understand how to use convenience and flexibility and choose to build even greater levels of "total value" into their agreements starting from inside the head of the other party.

Where it is difficult to estimate or agree on risk, insurance also plays its part as a variable in negotiation. By insuring yourself or the other party against certain risks or insisting that they take out policies to protect against risks, you can overcome some of the more challenging aspects of uncertainty.

You may not think twice about insuring your own contents in your home because of the known risks or insuring your home from damage as for many it is their greatest asset. Equally, many people insure their health, their car (because the law says they have to), even their washing machine, just in case it stops working. Insuring against the possible and in some cases probable is a further variable that can be used for accounting for risks. This same thought process is used as part of a negotiator's thinking as they identify ways of agreeing to terms whilst balancing the risks involved.

"In the event that you fail to meet the payment schedule, we reserve the right to reclaim the stock, or we will insure you against non-payment." The premium will be built into the overall pricing structure. Either way you mitigate against the risk which is agreed as part of the negotiation based on the level of risk you see in play.

Protecting the value

This involves protecting the value you think you have created in your agreement. What if delivery, specification, or payment terms are not adhered to? What are the implications to you and how do you protect against them within the terms agreed? Negotiating risk first involves identifying the risks which could prevent the contract delivering what it's supposed to and ensuring that the terms of the agreement reflect those risks to both parties.

Risks come in many forms and are often overlooked, as they do not necessarily reflect immediately on the profit and loss sheet. Ask any bank selling mortgages between 2004 and 2009. Ignore risk at your peril. Better still, trade it creatively against each of the primary variables. Insurance companies treat risk as a defined tangible issue and so should those of us buying or selling tangible products or services.

Accountability

Once risks are identified, you can focus on who will take, insure, mitigate against, or accept liability for the risks. Your next step involves building into your proposals a basis upon which the risks will be accommodated or compensated for. One challenge or opportunity – depending on how you see it – comes from understanding both parties' attitude to risk. If you have had a particularly bad experience in the past and the cost of putting it right still resonates, your attitude towards protecting against it and the value you associate with such cover may be greater than the cost implications for the other party providing it.

The guarantees provided with a second-hand car bought from a main dealer will have some value for which we accept that there will be a premium built into the price compared with buying privately. Many will regard this premium as a price worth paying. They are buying out the risk, buying confidence in that what they are paying is the maximum total price following any issues they may have with the car over the guaranteed period. They are buying certainty and for that they are prepared to pay. The way each party interprets the level of risk, or even the severity of that risk, often varies based on their own circumstances and those individuals involved in the decision making on their behalf.

Risk is different for different people

In the same way that supply and demand, and time and circumstances serve to set the balance of power in negotiations, risk and reward provide us with the basis for weighing up investment opportunities. Different industries have different tools for assessing risk and placing a premium on it, to hedge against it or to insure against it. In some cases where the deal is of strategic importance they may even be prepared to accept some degree of uncertainty. Dealing with uncertainty over the long term may represent a good bet given the potential value at stake. Risk as a variable is not bad or to be avoided, it just needs to be recognized, understood, and managed. Whether you are a private equity firm buying into a business, negotiating for mining rights, or buying computer chips from Korea, risk will feature in your considerations and the terms you agree.

In the field of litigation, for example, how do you place a cost or value on the risk or benefit of negotiating an out-of-court settlement? How does any company view the implications of risk associated with bad PR exposure and the degree to which this could affect their reputation, versus the legal costs of defending one's reputation? It is probably too late to insure against such risks, so you need to remain as objective as possible, set your break points, and get inside the other party's head. Each case will be unique and can only be assessed by those facing the consequences.

Managing compliance and performance

If you missed your mortgage payment this month, your lender would want the outstanding payment at the earliest moment. They would also insist on charging further interest on the late payment. This same philosophy or consideration should exist with any agreement where risks are to be addressed. Without this consideration you may well find yourself involved with relationship issues through a lack of clarity around obligations where commitments are not met.

A useful way of exploring risk is to ask the question "What would happen if . . .?"

- they do not meet their deadlines?
- the specification falls short?
- they want to terminate early?

- their circumstances change?
- our circumstances change, and we need more flexibility?
- exchange rates fluctuate wildly?
- their key personnel leave?

And so on. There are so many possibilities relating to the potential for change, which many businesses are renowned for building into their "standard terms" in the small print. The reality is that these risks are two-way and wherever possible you should include them as part of your negotiation agenda.

PREPARING TO MANAGE COMPLEXITY

The shape of most deals, where a range of issues are involved, changes each time a new proposal is tabled. Changes in terms of total value happen throughout the negotiation until both parties agree to settle with a particular set of terms and conditions. The process provides a fluid situation, like watching Shifting sands. The shape may get bigger or smaller, longer or shorter, fatter or thinner. This can make tracking the deal and the implications of changes difficult.

Building an agreement that entails a process involving many proposals is challenging because of the need to trade around specific variables whilst remaining mindful of the overall picture and total value implications.

For example, whilst negotiating an agreement that involves agreeing to guarantee that a job will be finished by the end of the month you may want to consider the things that you cannot control, such as circumstances that might make the commitment difficult to meet. These could be categorized by both parties as valid reasons for the job being delayed.

Exploring all possibilities

Other issues that will need resolving during your negotiations could also come at a price, so the concept of "nothing is agreed until everything is agreed" allows you to carefully explore all possibilities and agree in principle to ideas subject to all other conditions being agreeable. If necessary you can take proposals back off the table in the event that conditions discussed latterly are not agreed or the overall deal becomes unacceptable. One danger to watch for as you explore possibilities is sending the other party signals regarding which issues you are prepared to agree to, or those that are of particular importance to you. It's okay to say yes to proposals in principle providing the other party is aware that any one proposal is subject to all other conditions being acceptable. With some trust, and the appropriate climate, the shape of the deal should be allowed to change and evolve. Most of the issues will be in some way inter-related because most will impact on the total cost or value.

I have heard of more challenging negotiations being compared with the building of a 10,000-piece jigsaw. First you group pieces together, perhaps edges, then you gather the pieces into color zones. Then you start to piece together sections of the picture, leaving some pieces not fitting, so you go off in search of the right piece so that you can continue. You need patience, persistence, and an eye for how the picture is coming together. You know you have enough pieces, it's just a matter of the sequence and matching what's needed. With a jigsaw you have a picture forming, providing instant feedback on your progress. In negotiation you only have the response of the other party to rely on, but the way you approach the task has many similarities. With a jigsaw, however, the next piece may or may not fit. In negotiation a proposal that was rejected earlier may be accepted later under different circumstances. With a jigsaw you know it's possible from the outset as you have the right number of pieces at the start to finish the task. In negotiation there is no such certainty, whereas with a jigsaw there is one outcome that is as predictable as the picture is on the box. In negotiation, the shape of the deal can and usually does vary depending on how the negotiators have responded to each other's ideas and positions.

Taking your time and being patient

Working on the deal does not mean that each proposal should be met with approval, rejection, or even a counterproposal. Some ideas need more work and time to consider before you can even respond to them. Be prepared to park issues that you can come back to later.

Where the number of variables makes the negotiation complex, you should (subject to time constraints) take the time to adjourn and consider the possibilities. When you are in need of further authorization or stakeholder buy-in, take the time to consult before responding. This is especially the case if your ideas are new or include fewer tangible issues such as flexibility, convenience, or risk.

Being open to new ideas

Flexibility not only increases the chances of your performance being more productive but will also throw up new ideas for consideration that you might otherwise have filtered out very early on through being too single-minded or focused.

- If sustainable profit growth is the endgame, then allow yourself to explore how this can come about and make the time to do this.
- If you are involved in a conflict resolution negotiation, there may be a range of options available to you that achieve the same end, each with its own merits.
- If agreement to a "change in working practices" with the trade unions is what you are faced with, there will be a range of options available, each of which may facilitate an acceptance of change.

There is often more than one way to achieve your end result so try to remain focused on building solutions even where there is ambiguity or irrational behaviors in play. The next time you feel the need for a quick resolution and find yourself considering compromises, ask yourself: "Am I buying myself certainty in obtaining an early commitment and effectively buying myself some 'comfort,' or should I make more time and be patient with the process?"

Agreeing in principle

Throughout your discussions you've agreed to nothing until the end. Of course, this could result in you sending the wrong messages and signals if you appear too open to ideas that are clearly not acceptable. Your attitude and responses should remain balanced and, where necessary, point out how challenging some areas will be to entertain. Slow down and provide yourself time to think things through. Examine the "what ifs" and adopt a mindset of "how" and "under what circumstances," rather than "no," "can't," or "won't," which are so easy to adopt when you can't see the total picture.

Changing the shape of the deal – repackaging

Creative negotiators avoid deadlock by identifying ways of changing the shape of the deal, which allows the other party to move. They do this whilst at the same time moving the value of the deal forward for themselves. The more you understand about the other party's position and points of interest, the more obvious this becomes.

Try to focus on what you can do, move your instinctive attitude from "blame" or "defend" to "qualify," and then build solution-based proposals. Problem-solving is far more rewarding and sustainable than seeking simply to drive down their terms.

FOCUS ON THE PROBLEM, NOT ON THE PEOPLE

Focus on the problem, not the people

Chicago metal supply company IQM Trading had agreements to supply five car makers with various metals not least of all Nickel, used to create lithium-ion cells used in electrical vehicles. Nickel is regarded as one of the biggest challenges facing car manufacturers as they scale up their production and for IQM this was proving a genuine challenge as new market competition was emerging.

Furthermore, as part of their agreements, they also agreed to commit to de-risk and diversify their sources from China, which processed 80 percent of the world's nickel to Brazil and Canada. They did this in order to reduce the risk of dependency, as demand was set to result in prices forecast to increase by 10-fold over the following 10 years. The surge in demand for electric vehicle batteries had already resulted in the price of nickel increasing by 50 percent in 2022 alone not helped by the war in Ukraine.

They had a volume, price, and sustainable supply issue and were offering contracts to producers capable of mining nickel efficiently and in an environmentally sensitive way.

Canada mining firm Brankshaw produced 76,000 tonnes of nickel in 2021. Their CEO was keen to improve performance and transform their business into a "Partnership based Supplier," recognizing that car makers needed more nickel as the electric car momentum continued. The prices nickel was attracting was also a big draw relative to their copper and iron ore margins.

Following serval meetings and presentations, IQM set out a phased quality and quantity schedule. All other issues appeared to have been resolved including the securing of price guarantees. The quantity schedule, set to increase dramatically meant that Brankshaw had to invest heavily in new mining equipment even after reallocating that which could be used from their copper operation. The short-term capital challenge resulted in tough negotiations with a real risk of deadlock. The significant benefits for both businesses (a five-year deal worth £125 million) was worth

(*Continued*)

(Continued)

fighting for but Brankshaw had to raise £25 million to be able to scale up its operation. They were already highly leveraged, and the risk/benefit was dividing the board and their own backers as to how flexible to be. Brankshaw tabled a proposal, which offered a slower delivery on lower volumes than those requested but speeding up in year three. This did not work for IQM based on the terms and volume guarantees already offered. Following three months of meetings, IQM came back to the table. They had finally worked out what the real issue was: financing. Not a fact that had been openly shared by the Brankshaw team as they had focused on what they could do and not why this was the case. IQM made an offer to co-invest £20 million in return for an adjustment to terms, in fact over 11 different terms were introduced, which ultimately turned out to be agreeable. I am simplifying the issues here to make the point that once the real challenge had been identified, both teams were able to work on the problem and finally agree to a workable partnership agreement.

PLANNING FROM A PRACTICAL PERSPECTIVE

I have saved what is probably the most important element of negotiation until the end. It is then both easy to find as a reference and to share with others. If preparation is critical to negotiation then preparing in a team, as a team, using the same thinking, language, and approach is just as important as the act itself (see Chapter 9, under "Empowerment within team roles").

This approach, consisting of a number of tools, provides a standard for preparation that is easy to utilize and delivers consistency, confidence, and certainty. It also ensures that you are thinking from inside the head of the other party in the way that you evaluate the importance and value of variables, and build an agenda aimed at maximizing value. The beauty of the planning process is that you can start with your primary variables of price, volume, timescales, contract length, specification, and payment terms. Your planning can then move on to examining the hidden costs.

Your first challenge is the discipline required to make the time and use it productively to plan through your negotiation. Some lack the belief that preparation will really pay off. Another challenge could be that in the past there has been a lack of a clear or respected process that has proved to deliver results, which can also dampen motivation. There are always other things you could be doing with your time but rarely one that will provide you with such certainty, alignment, and confidence for your negotiation as a well-thought-through plan.

Planning is by its nature proactive and where you make the time to work through the possibilities you have already gained an advantage before entering the negotiating room.

The process

To help simplify the scoping and planning process, we have created a number of basic pro formas, which fit together logically and have been used by hundreds of businesses globally for their negotiation planning.

The aim of the negotiation planning tools is to help you scope the potential of your deal, work out the relative values, plan out your initial proposals, and then monitor the value of your agreement as discussions unfold (see Figure 11.2).

Trade-storming

The first step in the planning process is commonly known as brainstorming; we call it trade-storming. It is the starting point from which you may want to involve other stakeholders to pool ideas or to challenge any assumptions.

This tool is represented by a simple honeycomb model. It invites you to list each of the issues that you believe will feature as part of your pending negotiation, and then start to identify potential connections or

Tool	Purpose
Trade-storming (honeycomb) ↓	Helps you to brainstorm potential issues
Trade surveyor ↓	Helps you to prioritize low-cost/high-value trades
Issue map ↓	Helps you to link and group relationships between tradable issues
Agenda* ↓	Helps you to structure and gain clarity before and during the negotiation
Move planner* ↓	Helps you to define initial specific conditional details
Record of offers*	Helps you to record and track proposals throughout the negotiation process

*Operational tools used during the negotiation

Figure 11.2 Planning tools.

relationships between them. These are not always obvious to start with, which is why this tool is useful in helping you to visualize as you think through and expand on the more obvious variables. The Complete Skilled Negotiator will develop several variables using the trade-storming tool as they consider how each variable can become linked or grouped by association with other variables. Delivery may be one variable but, when you start to consider the issues that sit around delivery and are worthy of negotiation, you could list timing, venues, response times, accuracy, regularity, and so on. All will have some bearing on the value or cost associated with this element of the agreement (see Figure 11.3).

Trade surveyor

Ultimately, you will need to form some initial conditional proposals for your meeting. Having worked through the variables most likely to feature on your agenda, your next job is then to work out the relative values involved for you and the other party.

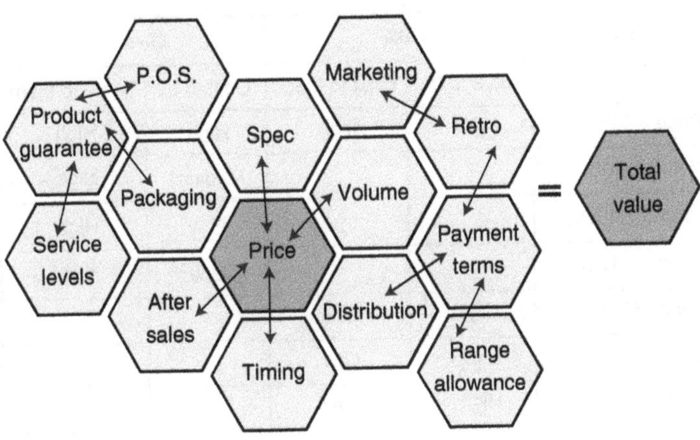

Figure 11.3 Trade-storming.

This means categorizing each variable according to the interests, priorities, and values the other party places on them. It is an opportunity to compare the relative cost and benefit values involved from both parties' perspectives. For this we use a pro forma known as a trade surveyor. It's useful to use this as part of your exploration meetings with the other party. During the discussions, you can qualify any assumptions that you may have on the value that they place on each issue (see Figure 11.4).

Building value in negotiation relies partly on trading low-cost variables in return for high-value variables. The trade surveyor helps you identify the variables that provide you (or both parties) with an incremental gain. This approach provides a useful way of understanding the most likely value relationships in play and should help inform you when developing conditional proposals prior to your meeting. Because of a lack of transparency, win–win usually means that one party wins (gains more value), but that the other party wins more. In other words, it's not about the fair, equitable 50–50 sharing of value as the term win–win might suggest. It is simply a process that attracts the interests of both parties because of the potential benefits available, however this might be split; and conditional trading is central to this.

Issues	Take		Give	
	Value to us	Cost to them	Cost to us	Value to them
Price	High	High	High	High
Volume discount			Medium	High
Promotion fees			Low	High
Payment terms			Low	High
Distribution	High	Low		
Volumes	High	Low		
Promotions	High	Low		
Exclusivity			Low	High

Rate: High/Medium/Low   For the purpose of examining possibilities

Figure 11.4 Trade surveyor.

Issue map

We use the issue map to visually work through the relative low-cost, high-value relationships and examine the different ways in which any one variable can be coupled with others, as part of building initial, conditional proposals.

Depending on the relative values you place on each variable, you can use the issue map to explore possible linkages. You may link price to volume or payment terms to delivery scheduling, and so on. This is only a basic way of playing with possibilities, but it allows you to consider different options before constructing specific proposals (see Figure 11.5).

On your issue map you may, for example:

- draw a line for your own reference to indicate a potential coupling between price and volume; or
- draw a line to couple price and specification as you weigh up the best way of linking issues.

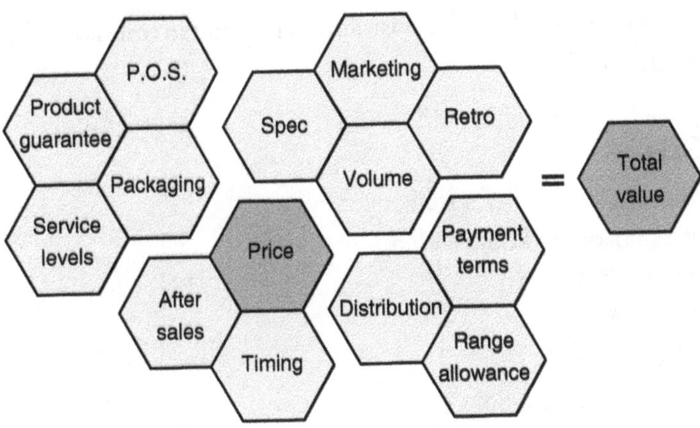

Figure 11.5 Issue map.

Using your trade surveyor, you can start to draw potential links between each of the variables. You can start to visualize how they may be coupled for the purpose of constructing proposals.

Agenda

Having qualified the variables, it's time to pull together and communicate an agenda – preferably one that you can both agree on and that will provide the basis and parameters for discussions.

The one benefit of a qualified agenda is that you know what has been tabled and what is outstanding. Say you have worked through the timescales, costings, and quality but know from the agenda that contract length and payment terms are outstanding issues. You would still have plenty of scope to negotiate even if that means bringing timescales back on to the table by linking them to contract length. You can address unacceptable terms by linking them to proposals that are yet to be tabled. It can feel very open-ended at first, but by leaving flexibility around some of the issues as discussions evolve, you can discuss more openly and, depending on the level of trust, explore different options. Of course, there will be tension and positions in play that you will need to manage, so just remember to ensure that your position at any point in time is conditional and clearly linked.

AGENDA

1. Service and quality specification
2. Information and data sharing
3. Volume ordering
4. Fee structure
5. Discount levels
6. Commencement date
7. Contract period
8. Payment terms
9. Confidentiality

A mutually agreed agenda to work from can help you to manage some initial ambiguity and will help build trust. A comprehensive agenda provides a list of those issues that need to be agreed, giving everyone involved transparency. The idea of agreeing to one issue without everything else being lined up can feel exposing and is the one area of ambiguity that you will have to accommodate.

The move planner

The move planner is used to detail the specific conditional terms against each of the trade-offs you plan to make, providing you with a list of well-thought-through proposals.

Move Planner

If you. . .	**Then we. . .**
Distribution 500	Price £14.90
Volume 1m	Volume discount 1.5%
Volume 1.3m Promotions 6	Marketing investment £80k

Figure 11.6 Sample agenda.

Each proposal needs to be specific, allowing the other party the chance to calculate, weigh, consider, and respond. It is no help to simply ask for improved payment terms in return for a higher-volume order. You have to be more specific. If not, you can't reasonably expect them to take the offer seriously or be able to respond to it. If it's 60 days for a 10 percent increase, say so. Detail it on your move planner. It is the one place to record your proposals in advance of discussions. They are the conditions that you have thought through, calculated, and considered objectively in the cold light of day (see Figure 11.7).

Before you start to make any proposals, qualify their priorities one last time. It is amazing how these can change over relatively short time periods.

"Last week you told me that delivery by week 12 would work for you, now you are saying week 8. Just how important is week 8?"

Understanding how they value things right now is critical. Don't assume! I have seen people in negotiations trying to negotiate for what they think they want, rather than for what they actually need. Your questioning should be aimed at qualifying what they *need*.

Imagine a construction manager who insists on the scaffolding being removed from the construction site with one day's notice. He regards it as critical. The hire company is able to accommodate the request but will charge a premium for a quick response. When the builder is questioned, it becomes known that his construction contract states that he has seven days to clear the site. Seven days' notice will save him a 5 percent premium

Move Planner

If you...	Then we...
Distribution 500	Price £14.90
Volume 1m	Volume discount 1.5%
Volume 1.3m Promotions 6	Marketing investment £80k

Figure 11.7 Move planner.

on the scaffold rental. It's not dissimilar to price. Most people think they want a better price but often it's a better deal or enhanced value that they really seek.

When tabling a conditional proposal, at first try to avoid introducing more than three items at once. It can prove difficult for the other party to calculate or respond to the proposal in any meaningful way. It also slows down any momentum created. If you table every conditional proposal you have prepared all at once, you are more likely to draw a blank or a delayed response from the other party for the following three reasons:

1. They will find it incredibly difficult under pressure to calculate what it all means. Therefore, they are likely to only pick off the terms they do like, whilst ignoring the conditions attached to them.
2. They are left with the task of working out links or relationships between each conditional proposal, which will potentially confuse them further still.
3. They will have some ideas that you might want to weigh up before tabling your entire position.

This approach of gradually tabling your proposals and allowing the deal to build requires patience and a certain degree of comfort with early ambiguity.

To start with, neither party will be able to see the whole deal and yet may be asked to respond to part of it. Remember, where there is complexity, you may need to park elements and come back to them later, having examined some of the other agenda points first.

The record of offers

This is especially important when you are dealing with many variables and you need to maintain a clear record of progress. Negotiators are often found scribbling notes in no particular order as the deal unfolds. Before long, you can barely make sense of the notes, or what the other party has suggested, let alone the last full position tabled. The "record of offers" table

Issue	Yours	Theirs	Yours	Theirs	Yours	Theirs
Price/case	£14.90	£12.20	£14.50	£13.00		£13.60
Volume discount	1.5%	2.0%	1.75%	2.0%		
Marketing investment	£80,000	£150,000		£100,000		
Payment terms	30	60	60			
Distribution	500	400		500		
Volumes/pa	1,000,000	1,000,000	1,300,000	1,500,000		
Promotions	6	8	10	10		
Exclusivity	12 months	12 months				

Figure 11.8 Record of offers.

allows you to record all positions and movement, enabling you to keep track of where you are up to now and how you got there (see Figure 11.8).

As you move across the page tracking your position with theirs, it allows you to summarize accurately and ensure that your facts are clear when you come to write up the agreement. Over time the record of offers allows you to:

- monitor the size of the moves they have made and on which variables; and
- summarize across the variables with your running total of your last position.

If you don't confirm what you have agreed to, how do you know what decisions were actually made? In many cases, this can lead to yet another negotiation later on.

Now you are ready to negotiate. The planning is done, the tactics understood, the behaviors tuned, and the thinking from inside their head in motion allowing you to see the deal opportunities as the other party sees them.

The Complete Skilled Negotiator is only as complete as their planning, and never so complete that they can take anything for granted. Never assuming, always enquiring. Never rushed, always **considered and respectful.** It's a tough balance requiring nerve, confidence, and tenacity, and it is for this reason that you can never afford to be complacent.

NOW DO THIS!

- Plan to plan. Without preparation before you enter the "negotiation arena," all the theory in the world (and indeed in this book!) will add up to nothing.
- Map out all the possible variables and value each from inside the other party's head.
- Focus on the potential **total value** of your agreement.
- Stay versatile: Identify ways you can change the shape of the deal, which allows the other party to move.
- Use negotiation planning tools to scope the potential of your deal.

Final Thoughts

Your ability to build agreements, dissolve deadlock situations, precondition expectations, and close sustainable deals requires all of the skills, attributes, knowledge, and self-awareness we have covered in *The Negotiation Book*.

For many, the challenges presented by negotiation do not come naturally and, as with any performance coupled with your own motivation to continuously improve, you have one of the most rewarding personal development opportunities available.

Negotiating effectively is first about accepting that it is only you who can influence the situations you are faced with. You can blame the market, personalities, timing, your options, the power balance, or any circumstance that you may think happens to be working against you. But ultimately, it is you who can turn around situations (including deadlock situations) into workable and profitable deals.

It is time to stay calm, see the tactics for what they are, be proactive, and exercise nerve and patience. Power, real or perceived, however generated, will play its part in your negotiations. No matter how good you are as a negotiator, where the balance of power is against you or your circumstances, you will no doubt experience the frustration of feeling compromised. Trust your instincts, exercise composure. It will make the difference between the agreements where you create value and the ones where you simply distribute it.

If you have to take a time-out, adjourn the meeting, or go back and revisit the options, the fact that you recognize this and are prepared to take the necessary time is an indication that you are now behaving in an appropriate and conscious manner.

Know what you are trying to achieve and always try to work out what others are trying to achieve. This requires clarity in purpose and an acceptance, for those who are competitive in nature, that negotiation is not about winning, it is about optimizing value. To do this you must see the deal as they do.

Taking control of any situation requires planning and never is this as true as in negotiation. Negotiators who find themselves reacting to their environment and situations tend to place themselves in weaker than necessary positions. Always be as proactive and prepared as possible. It is the one thing you can do to enhance your prospects.

Self-awareness is another dimension that differentiates the performance of the Complete Skilled Negotiator from others. They are not driven by fairness or consumed by their own ego. They and you should do that which is appropriate after having weighed and considered each set of circumstances you are faced with.

To listen, think, reflect, and to understand those around you and then consciously apply those skills you have learned is hopefully what I have promoted and explained in *The Negotiation Book*.

Negotiation is like no other skill. From my experience, I know, as well as that of my team, my clients, and my family, and friends that negotiation offers huge and well-earned rewards for anyone ready to become the Complete Skilled Negotiator.

About The Gap Partnership

The Gap Partnership is a global management consultancy specializing in negotiation. Their expert consultants work with some of the world's biggest companies, helping them to achieve their commercial objectives through enhanced negotiation performance. They offer innovative solutions that blend strategic consulting with capability development, to embed a high-performing negotiation culture within their clients' organizations. To find out more about what they do, visit www.thegappartnership.com

The Gap Partnership also offers a range of digital negotiation resources to support commercial negotiators in their continuing professional development. These include bite-sized negotiation films, thought leadership across a wide range of topics, online negotiation courses, and a global online negotiation competition. Learn more at www.thenegotiationsociety.com

Index